The Birder's Guide
to MONTANA

by
Terry McEneaney

Illustrations by
Karen L. McEneaney

FALCON
PRESS®

Helena, Montana

Dedication

To the great state of Montana—its beautiful mountains, widespread prairies, crystal clear lakes, meandering rivers, spacious skies, changing weather conditions, unique smells, interesting sounds, colorful plants, and sensational wildlife. And to the many friendships and acquaintances I have made in Montana. But most importantly to Montana birds.

Copyright ©1993 by Falcon Press Publishing Co., Inc.

Printed in the United States of America

Falcon Press Publishing Co., Inc.
P.O. Box 1718, Helena, MT 59624

Edited by Will Harmon
Front cover photo: Great Gray Owl by Diana Stratton
Back cover photo: Harlequin Ducks by Terry McEneaney
Illustrations by Karen L. McEneaney
♻ Text pages printed on recyled paper.

Library of Congress Cataloging-in-Publication Data

McEneaney, Terry
  Birder's guide to Montana / Terry McEneaney.
     p.   cm.
  Includes bibliographical references and index.
  ISBN 1-56044-189-5
  1. Bird watching—Montana—Guidebooks.   I. Title.
QL684.M9M34   1993
598'.07234786—dc20   92-55084
                                                      CIP

CONTENTS

"East or west there is a profound quietness lying just beneath the surface of the small sounds the earth makes. And within 20 minutes of slow driving from any city in Montana, you are suddenly in it—and alone. It has always been there—and you feel it, that old, that primitive affinity for where you came from some limitless time ago."

K. Ross Toole

ACKNOWLEDGMENTS

No one is an expert on Montana birds. The state is just too large and diverse for one person to proclaim to be the state-wide expert. Producing this guide required a team effort incorporating the knowledge and experience of many birders. The following people spent a tremendous amount of time in the field, and I feel fortunate that they have shared their knowledge with me. The list is a who's who of birders in Montana: Margaret Adams (Great Falls), Mark Andreasen (Libby Dam), Dale Becker (Ekalaka-Long Pines, Ninepipe NWR, Pablo NWR, Polson), Marcy Bishop (Nat'l Bison Range, Ninepipe NWR, Pablo NWR, Swan River NWR), Lou Bruno (Glacier Nat'l Park, Blackfeet Indian Reservation), Chuck Carlson (C. M. Russell NWR, Fort Peck), Helen Carlson (Billings), Dan Casey (Kalispell), John Foster (C. M. Russell NWR), Steve Gniadek (Glacier Nat'l Park), Bill Haglan (C. M. Russell NWR), Dale Hanson (Miles City), John Hartman (Butte, Anaconda, Deer Lodge), Paul Hedren (Fort Union), Denver Holt (Missoula, Lee Metcalf NWR, Ninepipe NWR, Pablo NWR, Polson), George Holton (Helena), Jack Kirkley (Dillon), Harriet Marble (Havre, Chester), Steve Martin (Benton Lake NWR, Great Falls, Medicine Lake NWR), Terry Peters (Bighorn Canyon), Bill Pryor (Billings), Fritz Prellwitz (Bowdoin NWR), Sue Reel (Missoula, Seeley Lake), Bill Roney (Billings), Everett Russell (C. M. Russell NWR), Gene Sipes (Bowdoin NWR), Don Skaar (Fortine-Eureka, Bull River, Libby), Jim Sparks (Bozeman), Don Stoecker (Butte, Anaconda), Andy Stolzenburg (Livingston), Dan Sullivan (Helena), Mike Switters (Freezout Lake), Bob Twist (Lee Metcalf NWR), Richard Wernham (Libby Dam), and the late Winton Weydemeyer (Fortine-Eureka).

Another group of people that deserve recognition are friends and fellow members of the Montana Bird Records Committee who have been more than generous in supporting the concept of this book. They are Chuck Carlson (Fort Peck), Helen Carlson (Billings), Dan Casey (Kalispell), Dr. Bob Eng (Bozeman), Bebe Fitzgerald (Billings), Harriet Marble (Chester), Fritz Prelwitz (Malta), and Dr. Phil Wright (Missoula).

Much of the historical information found in this book has been taken from two valuable sources that need to be recognized: *Names on the Face of Montana—The Story of Montana's Place Names* by Roberta C. Chaney, and *Fielding's Lewis and Clark Trail* by Gerald W. Olmsted. This information adds a nice touch to our understanding of Montana as we are birding.

There are a number of people who have had a profound influence on my life, an inspiration you might say, either in the form of wildlife biology, birding, mountaineering, or plain outdoor fun, who deserve to be recognized. They are Al Brown, Chuck Carlson, Frank Craighead Jr., John Craighead, Al Day, Bob Eng, Steve Gilbert, Dick Hutto, Bart O'Gara, Dave Skaar, Gray Thompson, Larry Thompson, Bob Twist, Bill Weiland, and Phil Wright.

Chris Cauble, Randall Green, Will Harmon, and Bill Schneider of Falcon

Press were a joy to work with. I am particularly delighted they contacted me to do this project. And to my good birding friend Paul Baicich, who managed to find the time to provide constructive criticism of the manuscript.

Everyone can use a word of encouragement. Janet Ellis, George Holton, Bill Pryor, and Dan Sullivan provided information and encouragement that turned out to be extremely helpful. I am deeply indebted to my friends Sandy and Len Sargent of the Cinnabar Foundation for believing in the project and providing financial support. Without their assistance, this guide would not have been possible.

Naturally, it goes almost without saying that this guide would not have been possible had it not been for the grand illustrations, ideas, organization, and loving support of my wife Karen. Not to mention the thousands of miles of travel, hundreds of campsites, great birds, nasty weather, wild goose chases, and fun times while discovering the Big Sky country.

If I've forgotten to mention someone, please pardon the oversight. Believe me, it was not intentional. It will probably come to me after the fact. Every effort has been made to eliminate mistakes in *The Birder's Guide To Montana*. Should mistakes be noticed, they are my fault and mine only. If you find something wrong, confusing, incomplete, or misleading, please let me know. If both myself and Falcon Press feel changes are warranted, we will make a concerted effort to make corrections in the next printing of this guide. Please send your comments to Terry McEneaney, c/o Falcon Press, P.O. Box 1718, Helena, MT 59624.

Great Gray Owl. Phantom of the forest. Best identified by the whitish or whitish yellow beak, part down the middle of the skull, and a white bow tie.

PREFACE

"Somebody should write a birder's guide to Montana." This wish was often repeated by birders in Montana. But who could do it? Who could find the time? Who knew the state well enough, besides knowing the birds and the birders? Of course, no one person could hope to be an expert on all the birds of Montana. The state is much too large and diverse for anyone to master all of it. However, what is unique about this book is the spirit of cooperation expressed by birders from all over the state. Nobody knows an area better than a local qualified birder, and a special feature of this book was the way birders shared their friendship, time, expertise and experience with me. Without the assistance of these local birders, this book would not have become reality.

For me, it all started with a telephone call from Bill Schneider of Falcon Press in Helena, Montana. Bill knew me from social gatherings at the Windbag Saloon in Helena, from competitive sports events, and through my interest and excitement about Montana and its birdlife. When he asked whether I would be interested in writing a birder's guide to Montana, I was delighted with the offer, thought it over, and shortly accepted this exciting challenge, with a book outline set in the back of my mind.

Writing *The Birder's Guide To Montana* was an honor. I took on the project, not to see what I could get from it, but rather with the hope that I could give back something to a place that means so much to me. *The Birder's Guide To Montana* is my humble contribution to the great state of Montana. This Big Sky palace has brought me nothing but happiness and joy and is truly a paradise for those who enjoy the outdoors. I still vividly remember: standing on the awesome summit of Mount St. Nicholas in Glacier National Park as Rosy Finches flew by; or the White-tailed Ptarmigan that I nearly stepped on while rappelling down the face of Mount Wilbur; the American Pipits near our base camp on the Beartooth Plateau overlooking Granite Peak; the Harlequin Ducks on the Clark Fork River right in the middle of Missoula; the Trumpeter Swans, Tundra Swans, Whooping Cranes, and Peregrine Falcons repeatedly seen from our living room window at Red Rocks; the countless Snow Geese at Freezout; the strutting Sage Grouse of Winnet; the camouflaged Mountain Plovers and Piping Plovers of the C. M. Russell NWR; the elusive Sharp-tailed Sparrows of Medicine Lake; the disappearing, almost magical Merlins of the Long Pines area; the undulating Golden Eagles of Decker.

This book is primarily a birder's guide, and throughout the text I have tried to promote an ethical approach to birding. Birding is growing ever more popular, placing undue pressure on certain birds and their habitats. We should enjoy our resources, but protect them as best we can for future generations. In this book there is little mention of bird nests or nesting, and I have taken great care to avoid placing any particular species in jeopardy.

When discussing particularly vulnerable birds, I refrained from giving detailed viewing directions. In some cases, a birding site or a given species at a site has been omitted entirely. For most of the birds, the information presented in this book is detailed enough to get you to the right area, the right habitat, and the time of year when the bird should be present. Your success ultimately depends on birding skills, weather, timing, and luck.

This guide was designed to save you time, money, and energy, besides being a convenient tour guide with interesting highlights about Montana's history, geology, ecology, and culture. *The Birder's Guide To Montana* will save you thousands of miles of unnecessary travel; hundreds of hours of travel time; and a tremendous amount of money otherwise spent on phone calls, gasoline, and maps. I truly hope this book serves its purpose as *The Birder's Guide to Montana*. Wishing you the best of Big Sky birding!

Terry McEneaney

Yellowstone National Park
April 1993

FOREWORD—WESTERN MONTANA

This is a fine guide for both experienced and new-comers to bird watching. Terry's many years as a professional wildlife biologist, his strong love of birds, and his own detailed knowledge of the birds of Montana make him the best possible person to write this account.

He has solicited the help of well qualified local avian experts who know the forty-five sites he has described. Terry serves on the active Montana Bird Records Committee and is charged with keeping the official list of birds of the state; in this capacity, he has access to the most recent additions to the state's avifauna. Montana now has a number of highly qualified bird watchers who are scattered all over this vast state. He has known them all personally, and his knowledge is respected by them.

His selection of sites in western Montana is well chosen and most are areas I am personally well acquainted with. The species mentioned are appropriate ones. The maps of species destribution were prepared from the latest edition of the P. D. Skaar book on bird distribution.

I am happy to have taught Terry in my ornithology class more than twenty years ago and to have had him as a museum assistant where he had the unusual opportunity to study and handle hundreds of avian specimens.

This book should serve as a standard for other states to match in terms of thoroughness and overall usefulness.

Philip Wright
Emeritus Professor of Zoology
University of Montana

FOREWORD—EASTERN MONTANA

Eastern Montana is often loosely described as the two-thirds of the state lying east of the Rocky Mountains or roughly east of a line from Cut Bank to Livingston. And the image of this area projected in the minds of many is that of an expanse of sagebrush—grassland that is diversified only by equally large tracts of grainfields. Although both of these land types exist in large acreages, an abundance of habitat diversity is present and reflected in the wide spectrum of bird species to be found.

Although Montana is included in the area covered in Roger Tory Peterson's revised *Field Guide to Western Birds,* most of the eastern two-thirds is in what he refers to as the west-east "Blend Zone." Thus one can often find Eastern and Mountain Bluebirds, Brown and Sage Thrashers, Blue and Pinyon Jays or Rose-breasted and Black-headed Grosbeaks within short distances of one another. With island mountain ranges within the area, Great Gray, Long-eared, Short-eared and Burrowing Owls may be found on a single outing.

However, given the size of the area and its relatively sparse human population, a birder unfamiliar with the state could spend a lot of time and drive many unnecessary and unproductive miles seeking out productive birding sites or a particular species. Dave Skaar's classic *Montana Bird Distribution* provides birders with a geographical key to species location within degree blocks or "latilongs." However, latilongs averaging 47 x 69 miles may and frequently do extend over several different habitats and accompanying bird species. Terry McEneaney, in this guide, has more specifically identified these habitats and their expected bird components. These "Best Birding Areas" are conveniently grouped by broad geographic areas in such a way that sites can be readily located by resident or non-resident birders alike.

Terry McEneaney, with a background as a working professional in the natural resource field in different areas of Montana, is well equipped to author a guide of this type. He is the first to admit, however, that the size and diversity of the state is much too great for any one person to claim complete familiarity. Many competent birders familiar with different parts of the state have assisted in providing detail for specific areas.

Thus, in putting together this directional guide to birding in Montana, Terry McEneaney has provided a service to the casual as well as the serious birder and has provided this service in an informative and interesting fashion. Whether one is looking for a Yellow-breasted Chat along the cottonwood bottoms of the Yellowstone, or a McCown's Longspur on the grassy plains of central Montana, this book will greatly enhance the opportunity.

Robert L. Eng
Emeritus Professor
of Fish and Wildlife Program
Montana State University

Clark's Nutcracker. Discovered during the Lewis and Clark Expedition. The primary distributor of whitebark pine and limber pine seeds.

INTRODUCTION

The first birders in Montana were undoubtedly the native inhabitants. These people lived in close harmony with the land and had an intimate understanding of animal behavior and the environment, including the ecology of birds. Each tribe had names for every component of the natural world, and names and lessons were passed down by word of mouth and through symbolism and art. Tribal languages included special names for each bird species. Birds played an important role in most Native American cultures, as evidenced by the dances and pow-wow rituals that mimic the plumage and behavior of different species of Montana birdlife.

The first white explorers brought with them a new appreciation for the natural wonders they encountered. One of the greatest scientific and geographical explorations in history occurred in Montana when Meriwether Lewis and Captain William Clark led the Corps of Discovery across the continent between 1804 and 1806. Lewis, a naturalist and journalist, was appointed leader of this scientific team by President Thomas Jefferson. Lewis was accompanied by a group of adventurers, including his friend Clark who had no formal education but tremendous wilderness skills and talents as a communicator, cartographer, and chronicler.

The expedition set off May 14, 1804 from St. Louis, heading up the Missouri River to explore uncharted wilderness. Their primary mission was to record as much information as possible about the native inhabitants and natural resources encountered along their route. In April 1805, they entered what is today Montana, and recorded a number of impressive bird discoveries in their field journals.

Many of the species described by Lewis and Clark were new to science. The Sage Grouse for instance, was first noted in the vicinity of the Marias River. During the expedition, Capt. Clark sketched this bird in his journal and named it "Cock of the Plains." The Loggerhead Shrike was also first described by the explorers near the mouth of the Marias River. The list of birds grew as the expedition forged ahead. A Lewis' Woodpecker was first found near the Gates of the Mountains area, while Blue Grouse and Pinyon Jay were discovered near what is today the town of Whitehall. Clark's Nutcracker, formerly called Clark's Crow, was another bird first discovered in Montana. The number and diversity of birds, mammals, reptiles, amphibians, and plants documented for the first time during this expedition could never be duplicated. On the banks of the Missouri River, near the confluence of the Marias River, Lewis actually compiled the first bird list for Montana.

They not only recorded individual species, but found the time to record wildlife abundance. Their journals were saturated with accounts of wildlife, such as "game is becoming more scarce, particularly beaver of which we have seen few for several days." The expedition also contributed new knowledge of the geographical distribution of species not well understood, such as the

Black-billed Magpie. Found throughout a large portion of Montana, especially near human habitation.

now extinct Passenger Pigeon. The Corps of Discovery noted the most westerly extent of this species' range when they recorded Passenger Pigeons just southwest of Great Falls in July 1805, and in the Cutbank and Wolf Point areas in July 1806.

Cross-country travel in those days was extremely difficult. The Corps of Discovery proved as adaptable as the terrain was varied, at times relying on keel boats, pirogues, canoes, horses, and the moccasins on their feet. The obstacles they encountered were true tests of skill and daring, including raging rivers, hostile grizzly bears, hordes of mosquitoes, and the sharp-spined prickly pear cactus.

Although the Lewis and Clark Expedition went as far as the mouth of the Columbia River on the Pacific Coast, they still returned by way of Montana. Their last day in Montana was August 12, 1806. In total, approximately one-quarter of the total distance traveled during the entire expedition, and six months of time, was spent by the Corps of Discovery in Montana. They spent more time in Montana than in any other state. Upon return to St. Louis, the explorers ran into unforeseeable obstacles after completing such a successful journey. Lewis died in 1809, and Clark was unable to take on the difficult task of publishing the journals. The results of the expedition remained in limbo for years. Even though most of the specimens collected by the expedition were lost during museum exchanges and publication of the journals was long delayed, Lewis and Clark had paved the way for future scientific expeditions in the west. The opportunities for discovery had just begun.

The explorers came and so did the adventurers and birders. Of note was David Thompson, who explored western Montana. Then Prince Maximilian du Wied, accompanied by premier artist and painter Karl Bodmer, visited eastern Montana and the movement began. Next came the famous wildlife artist and naturalist John James Audubon, who visited only a small section of eastern Montana but was able to discover two important bird species, the "Sprague's Missouri Skylark" (now called Sprague's Pipit) and the Baird's Sparrow. These species were named after two of Audubon's close friends.

The age of adventure and discovery in Montana was in full force, and eventually included such notable birders/naturalists as J. A. Allen, F. M. Bailey, S. F. Baird, J. Burroughs, J. Cassin, Maj. Bendire, W. Brewster, E. S. Cameron, F. Chapman, J. Cooper, E. Coues, Earl of Dunraven, M. J. Elrod, G. B. Grinnell, E. Harris, F. V. Hayden, E. Mearns, C. H. Merriam, J. Muir, H. Oberholser, R. Ridgeway, T. Roosevelt, A. Saunders, D. Skaar, E. T. Seton, P. Silloway, and M. Skinner.

What drew these pioneer birders to Montana, and what continues to draw birders today, is the state's exceptional environment. Montana is Spanish for "mountainous," and mountainous it is. The western third of Montana is characterized by mountains and mountain valleys, the central third by plains and isolated mountain ranges, and the eastern third by plains country with rolling hills. The Continental Divide, the high dividing line that separates waters into the Atlantic or Pacific drainages, meanders from north to south

Steller's Jay. A bird most closely associated with spruce or fir forests in Montana. An accentuated crest is often the sign of an aggressive display or territorial defense.

though the western third of the state. Montana is the nation's fourth largest state, bordering four states and three Canadian provinces, and comprising a land area of approximately 93 million acres. On average, Montana measures 550 miles from east to west, and 275 miles from north to south. The highest point in Montana is 12,799-foot Granite Peak in the Beartooth Range, and the lowest point is where the Kootenai River enters Idaho at an elevation of 1,820 feet.

For all the space and scenery, Montana is comparatively uncrowded. The state is home to 800,000 people, including members of seven Native American tribes: the Assiniboine and Sioux, the Blackfeet, the Chippewa-Cree, the Confederated Salish and Kootenai, the Crow, the Assiniboine and Gros Ventre, and the Northern Cheyenne. With most of the state's population centered around Billings, Great Falls, Helena, Bozeman, Butte, Missoula, and the Kalispell area, there are thousands of wilderness acres still available for the original residents. Montana is the home to the largest grizzly bear population in the lower 48 states, several packs of timber wolves, and large herds of deer and elk. The state also abounds with dinosaur remains (most famous of which is the Maiasaura, the official state dinosaur and fossil). The natural resources found in this state are unique indeed, as evidenced by two world class national parks—Yellowstone and Glacier.

Nicknames are a sign of endearment, and Montana is known by more than one: the Treasure State, the Last Best Place, the Land of Shining Mountains, and of course the Big Sky. Anyone who travels through Montana will notice the sensational skyscapes of clouds and light and deep blue sky; perhaps no other name is as fitting as the Big Sky state.

Names can reveal a lot about a place. Some names are merely pleasant to the ears and eyes, while others have a story to tell. As a person lives and wanders among so many places, the sound of their names—like a certain smell or an old photograph—can bring back memories. Consider for a moment Montana's rivers, history's highways: the Missouri, Yellowstone, Madison, Gallatin, Jefferson, Clark Fork, Marias, Flathead, and Kootenai. Imagine mountains to match these names: the Beartooths, Crazies, Belts, Little Rockies, Bitterroots, Missions, Absarokas, Bridgers, Gravellys, Cabinets, and Tobacco Roots.

And relish just a handful of names from the list of Montana birds: Trumpeter Swan, Harlequin Duck, Northern Goshawk, Golden Eagle, Peregrine Falcon, Gyrfalcon, Prairie Falcon, Spruce Grouse, Blue Grouse, White-tailed Ptarmigan, Sage Grouse, Sandhill Crane, Piping Plover, Mountain Plover, Black-necked Stilt, Burrowing Owl, Great Gray Owl, Boreal Owl, Northern Saw-whet Owl, Black Swift, Vaux's Swift, Red-headed Woodpecker, Three-toed Woodpecker, Black-backed Woodpecker, Boreal Chickadee, Chestnut-backed Chickadee, American Dipper, Eastern Bluebird, Western Bluebird, Montain Bluebird, Varied Thrush, Townsend's Warbler, Western Tanager, Baird's Sparrow, Le Conte's Sparrow, McCown's Longspur, Rosy Finch, Pine Grosbeak, Red Crossbill.

Moments of bird discovery are still available in Montana today, particularly in the central and eastern regions of the state, which are often greatly underrated by birders unfamiliar with the sweeping expanse of plains and rolling hills. Nothing is more serene than springtime on the prairie. The sights and sounds of the birds characteristic of this area are extremely impressive. Narrow belts of vegetation lining the river drainages here are the places with the greatest diversity of birdlife. But no matter where you watch birds in Montana, if you find something that you feel might be rare or unusual, please report it. Our knowledge of Montana birds is the result of information gathered by people like yourselves actively birding in the field. Those birders interested in contributing to our knowledge of Montana birdlife should consult the agency addresses in the back of this book. The more detailed the bird information you provide, the more it will stand the test of time.

Birding Montana is an adventure. Follow the advice of Yogi Berra, "when you come to a fork in the road—take it." Get off the beaten path and discover this land on your own, and take your time. There is a feeling you get when you enter Montana, one that you will carry ever after, and that is wonder and respect for the land and its inhabitants.

How To Use This Guide

The purpose of this book is to guide readers to some of the best places in Montana to see and hear birds. This slender volume is not intended to present detailed life histories of all of the birds found in Montana, nor is this a book

Important birding items: Montana Highway Map, P. D. Skaar's Montana Bird Distribution, A List of Montana Birds *(Montana Department of Fish, Wildlife and Parks and the Montana Heritage Program),* Montana Wildlife Viewing Guide, *Rare Bird Report Form, Montana Latilong and Quarter Latilong Map.*

about how to identify birds. Think of *The Birder's Guide To Montana* as your tour guide to the state's birding hot spots, with a hearty sprinkling of geological, cultural, and ecological information guaranteed to make your birding trip (and reading this guide) more enjoyable.

No matter which season you visit Montana, or which corner of the state you are traveling, this book can guide you to a likely birding spot, a bit of roadside history, or a scenic vista. This format adds variety to the serious birder's itinerary, and the more casual birder can choose from any number of birding opportunities while on a vacation or business trip. **For best birding results, refer to the Montana Highway Map when using this guidebook**. Most of the good birding in Montana is conducted from or near a road. To obtain a copy of the map call Travel Montana at 1-800-541-1447 (outside Montana) or 444-2654 (in Montana).

Chapter 1 of *The Birder's Guide To Montana* covers the essentials for "Planning a Montana Birding Trip." Information includes when to go birding, what to wear, a checklist of essentials, where to stay, hazards likely to be encountered in the field, and birding ethics. Also included are names and addresses of organizations to contact when birding Montana. Also see Appendix III: Agency Index.

Chapter 2 orients the reader to "Montana's Varied Environments," with brief descriptions of the wonderfully dynamic Montana landscape, and the enviromental factors such as climate, topography, and vegetation that influence bird distribution and abundance. Sections about Montana's seasons and bird migration patterns add to the birder's understanding of annual cycles of bird distribution.

The body of the book, **Chapter 3**, describes in detail "Montana's Best Birding Areas." Forty-three major birding areas, each with numerous specific sites listed, are described here. The sites are distributed across the entire state, and have been grouped into six regions, beginning with northwest Montana, plus Glacier and Yellowstone national parks. The regions roughly correspond to major river drainages, each encompassing characteristic landforms, vegetation, habitat types, and, hence, birdlife.

The area descriptions are usually geared for birding in the summer, an ideal time for both birds and birdwatchers in Montana. Many sites offer interesting birding during other seasons, and this is indicated in the site description. Birds that are usually seen only during migration are listed accordingly. Many of the birds listed for a given site are more frequently heard than seen, but for brevity's sake this book relies upon the terms "look for," "watch for," and "seen" when listing a site's bird species. Despite this semantic bias, birders can greatly enhance their chances of identifying their quarry by learning to distinguish the songs and calls of particular species.

Each area description is formatted for easy reading and quick reference to specific sites and details without reading the entire text. Site names are printed in **boldface**, and characteristic birds to look for are generally listed together and grouped by their preferred habitat. Each birding area is presented in four parts:

• General information sidebar of interesting (historical, geological, cultural, ecological) information about the birding area.

• A detailed description of birding information for each area, how to get to it, and a list of its characteristic birds. Birds of special interest are highlighted here, as are other wildlife species of note, landmarks to aid in route-finding, and local hazards such as rough or fair-weather roads, heavy traffic, and—in a few places—rattlesnakes.

• A detailed birding map indicating specific sites and access roads. These maps are drawn to scale and often show features of interest to birders that are not found on other maps. They are best used in conjunction with the Montana State Highway Map, National Forest and Bureau of Land Management maps, and topographical maps available from the U.S. Geological Survey.

• A list of "Helpful Information" for quick reference to facts about the area, including where to find gas, food, lodging, and camping; and where to obtain additional information about the area.

Chapter 4 is a checklist of Montana birds, with a graphic respresentation of each bird's seasonal occurrence and relative abundance in the state.

Chapter 5 provides more in-depth information for about 137 of "Montana Bird Specialties." Included here are birds that are representative of Montana habitats, and that are much sought after by out-of-state birders.

A glossary of birding and ecological terms is provided on page 287, followed by a bibliography of selected books and articles. Birders interested in contributing their observations of birds to the general fund of knowledge will find in Appendix I on the section on "Reporting Montana Bird Information" quite helpful. Appendices II and III provide addresses for birding organizations and relevant land management agencies. Finally, indices are given for the bird species featured in this book, for all site names, and maps.

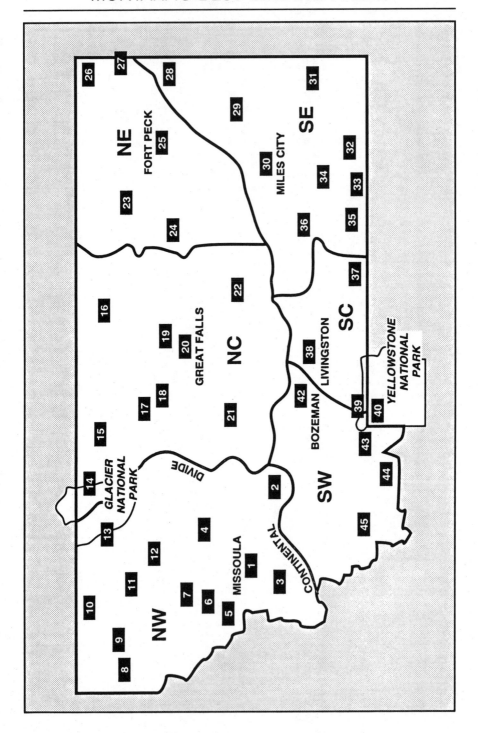

The horn of an adult American White Pelican drops off from the the beak immediately following the breeding season.

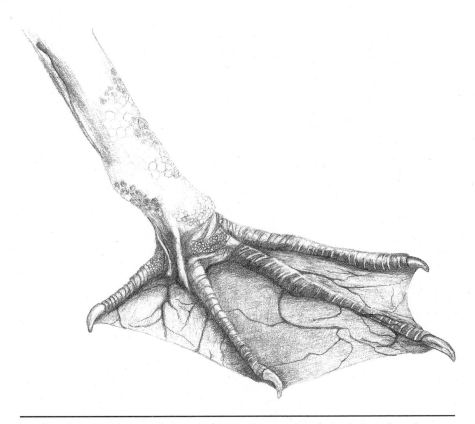

The foot of an American White Pelican showing the large number of veins in the webs and most notably a webbed hind toe.

The courtship display of a male Common Raven.

CHAPTER 1
PLANNING A MONTANA BIRDING TRIP

When To Go Birding

Choosing the best time of year to go birding in Montana depends on what birds you want to see and the elevation of the area you plan to visit. To a lesser extent, your favorite birding season in Montana may also depend on your threshold for enduring harsh weather.

To improve your chances of seeing a particular species, become familiar with that bird's distribution, breeding season, peak migration times, and winter range. To date, 388 bird species have been reported in Montana, but not all of these birds are found in large numbers, and some occur here only rarely or are difficult to see because of their behavioral habits. Some birds breed here in great concentrations for weeks at a time. Other species are present in Montana in significant numbers only during migration, and then only briefly. Several arctic species, notably the Gyrfalcon and Snowy Owl, visit Montana only in winter, and their presence is often irregular, influenced by distant weather patterns and availability of food. The better field identification guides provide such details for many species, but long-term personal experience is perhaps the best tutor. To get a head start, see the checklist and seasonal abundance tables for Montana birds in Chapter Four of this book.

On average, Montana's coldest winter months are December and January. But winter-like conditions usually come to Montana's high elevations early in the fall and may remain well into spring and early summer. Snowstorms may occur at higher elevations during any month of the year. Lower elevations enjoy a longer period of milder temperatures, hence large numbers of birds arrive earlier in the spring and remain later in the fall in Montana's intermountain valleys and on the plains. Successful birders factor in this lag time for different elevations. For example, to see the greatest diversity of birds, May through mid-July is best at lower elevations; at higher elevations try mid-June through August.

Spring migration in Montana is best observed from April through May, and autumn migration typically occurs from July through November. For rare, unusual, or difficult to find birds, try May through mid-June, and mid-August through December.

What to Wear

No matter what time of year, be prepared for unexpected weather changes. The best rule of thumb is to always dress for a variety of conditions, but most importantly, bring adequate cold-weather clothing. Even in mid-summer, the best birding hours around dawn and dusk can be uncomfortably cool, and at higher elevations sub-freezing temperatures may occur any day of the year. Pack a variety of clothing that can be worn in layers: wool or synthetics to wick away perspiration; wool, fleece, down, or pile for insulation; and an outer shell to fend off wind and water. Dressing in layers allows you to shed or add clothing depending on weather conditions and activity levels. If you plan to visit high elevations in the summer or travel anywhere in Montana during the fall, winter, or spring, be sure to bring warm hats, coats, gloves, and boots. At the other extreme, summer temperatures in the 90s F. and even 100s F. are not uncommon in the intermountain valleys and on the eastern plains.

Essentials For A Successful Birding Trip
The following is a checklist of items essential for a successful birding trip in Montana.

__Montana Highway Map
__Other maps
__Binoculars
__Spotting Scope
__Field identification guides
of birds
__*Montana Bird Distribution*
by P.D. Skaar
__Bird sound tapes
__Insect repellent and
sunscreen

__Toilet paper
__Drinking water (especially
for Eastern Montana)
__Ice Cooler for drinks
__Food
__Drinks
__Travel money
__Good Attitude
__Good traveling music
__Fun people

Optional:

__Camping equipment
__Field journal

__Camera and film
__Tape recorder

Where To Stay
Most of the birding sites listed in this book are within range of developed car campgrounds (for tents and RVs) or sizeable towns with the usual array of cabins, motels, hotels, and lodges. More adventurous birders will find that backcountry camping is excellent in Montana, with outstanding opportunities for solitude and a western wilderness experience. Public lands offer the widest choice of camping options, from primitive to improved, but remember that fully modern, resort-style camping facilities are few and far between. At best, the average public camping area in Montana has an outhouse and drinking water. Nevertheless, camping out allows birders to make the most of their days in the field, waking to the morning melodies of song birds and drifting to sleep with the hoot of an owl punctuating the night. Brochures listing campgrounds and lodging in Montana are available free from Travel Montana, Department of Commerce, 1424, 9th Avenue, Helena, MT 59620.

Please keep your campsite clean. Montanans take pride in leaving a

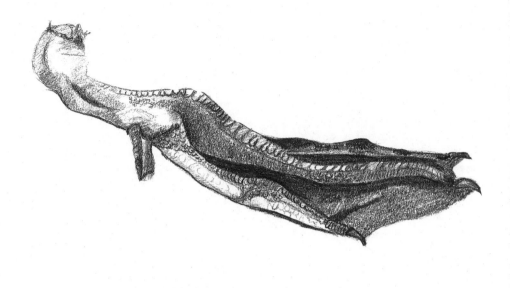

The foot of a Canvasback and lobed hind toe typical of diving ducks.

campsite cleaner than they found it. Trash cans are not provided at many sites, and campers should pack out their own trash. Where restroom facilities are **not** available, bury all excrement and toilet paper six inches deep and at least 200 feet from the nearest surface water. Nothing is more unpleasant than looking at someone else's mess.

Field Hazards

Montana has such a varied landscape that it presents a visitor with a wide range of field hazards. Foremost in many visitors' minds are wild animals, particularly bears.

Both grizzly and black bears are found in Montana, primarily in the western third of the state. But encounters between people and bears are rare, and serious confrontations rarer still. If you do happen to see a bear, remember that all bears are potentially dangerous and should be treated with respect. When camping or hiking in bear country, never grow complacent. Make a habit of the following simple precautions, and you will greatly lessen the risk of an unpleasant encounter.

Some bears make a habit of roaming campgrounds at night, so keep a clean camp and store all food in air-tight containers **in your vehicle**. Backcountry campers should hang food, cooking utensils, and all clothes with food odors from a tree, at least twenty feet off the ground and eight feet from the trunk of the tree. These same precautions also reduce the likelihood of property damage by raccoon, ground squirrel, marmot, or porcupine. Ground squirrels, as cute as they look, can bite holes in tents or cut into radiator hoses. Porcupines and other small mammals are notorious for eating the straps off backpacks or destroying a good pair of hiking boots or shoes in search of the salt residue of human sweat. Never feed wildlife. Wild animals habituated to humans are more vulnerable to malnutrition and predation, and they may cause trouble for the next people they encounter.

Traveling the roads of Montana can be a challenge. Deer, elk, and free-roaming livestock sometimes browse along highways and bound into oncoming traffic unexpectedly, especially between sunset and sunrise. It's best to avoid long-distance travel at night in Montana. National Parks and other heavily visited areas of Montana offer frustrating traffic conditions during the summer and on holiday weekends. In fall, winter, and spring, snow-packed or icy roads can drastically slow your travel. When traveling the roads of western Montana, be extremely careful of logging trucks. Birders need to take special heed on busy highways or roads with limited sight-distances, and should pull well off the roadway when actively watching or searching for birds.

There are many more dirt roads in Montana than there are paved roads. Recently graded dirt roads are often responsible for flat tires due to nails, sharp rocks, and other debris that resurfaces. Poor quality tires on gravel or dirt roads usually are responsible for the bulk of flat tires. Cattle guards, those steel grates across roads to keep livestock out, can cause flat tires. Most large cattle guards have a seam, and if a tire comes in contact with this seam it can rip a tire apart. Throughout Montana (especially eastern Montana), there are a number of dirt roads that look fine in fair weather but become impassible at the first taste of rain, hail, or snow. Even four-wheel-drive vehicles can quickly mire in Montana's gumbo, so it's often best to wait out the storm. Most muddy roads dry up very quickly with just a little wind or sun. If dirt or gravel roads show old ruts when dry, it is a sure sign these roads are terrible when wet.

In the summer there are a number of natural field hazards that deserve mention. Thunderstorms and heat prostration are extremely dangerous and require close monitoring. Mosquitoes, gnats, horse flies, and ticks can be a nuisance in some areas. In the drier regions of Montana, keep a lookout for rattlesnakes.

Being aware of the elevation is also a serious consideration for senior citizens or people with heart problems. Visitors should get acclimated to higher altitudes before performing any type of physical activity. Sudden visits to high elevations without resting or acclimatizing can result in shortness of breath, dizziness, nausea, and in some cases increased risk of heart attacks. This is particularly true for Glacier and Yellowstone national parks, Red Rock Lakes, the Beartooth Plateau, and numerous mountain passes in Montana.

An Ethical Approach to Birding

As a group, birders are growing increasingly aware that their hobby can have a negative influence on birdlife, especially in areas that are heavily visited such as city parks, national parks, and national wildlife refuges. While selecting sites for this book, the author was mindful of the danger of popularizing sensitive areas, and a few locales were intentionally down-played or omitted from the text entirely.

Readers will also notice that the words "nest" and "nesting" are rarely mentioned in the text. Nesting sites are better left unpublicized to protect birds and their offpsring during this critical time in their life cycle. Nesting birds are especially sensitive to disturbances, and birders should never approach too close to nesting sites. Read as much as you can about the species you want to watch in the field, and learn what time of year these birds nest, breed, and fledge. Learn to recognize nesting behavior so you can minimize pressure on individual nest sites and colonies. Remember, many nest sites will be used year after year if they remain secure from human intrusion. Please be responsible in all of your birding actions, and politely educate others who, out of ignorance or carelessness, endanger the security or survival of birds in the wild.

Anyone can watch birds, but the real test of a responsible birder is to observe birds without disturbing them. Outdoor recreation is on the rise in Montana, placing added pressure on wildlife. The following tips will help preserve the bird resources that mean so much to us:

1. The welfare of the bird is the most important consideration, above and beyond our personal desires.
2. Always ask permission before entering private land.
3. When traveling through gates or over fences, always leave them as you found them.
4. Use binoculars or spotting scopes to observe birds, and long lenses when photographing birds; this reduces the chance of disturbance.
5. Understand bird behavior; if a bird **changes** its behavior because of your presence, then you are too close.
6. Never disturb birds on or near nests; always avoid touching bird nests, eggs, or young. Mammalian or reptilian predators key in on human scent.
7. Splitting up family groups of birds only increases their chances of mortality.
8. Learn to identify birds through use of your own skills and not by relying on pre-recorded calls played on a tape recorder. Remember, attracting birds with tape-recorded calls is illegal in Glacier and Yellowstone national parks. Visitors have been fined $100 for violating these regulations.
9. Also see the American Birding Association Code of Ethics (Appendix IV).

Maps

Always keep a Montana Highway Map handy. *The Birder's Guide To Montana* is designed to accompany the Montana Highway Map. This free map can be obtained by contacting Travel Montana, Department of Commerce, Helena, MT 59620, phone: 444-2654. Non-residents can call 1-800-541-1447.

A number of regional maps can be purchased from the U.S. Forest Service and Bureau of Land Management. See the agency index in the back of this book for further details.

An assortment of detailed U.S. Geological Survey maps (7.5 and 15 minute series) covering the state of Montana can be obtained by writing USGS, Denver Federal Center, Lakewood, CO 80225. Request an index and price list of maps covering Montana. These same maps can be obtained at outdoor equipment shops throughout Montana.

Birding Organizations

American Birding Association

For serious birders, one organization stands out. The non-profit American Birding Association (ABA) is dedicated to all aspects of birding, including identification, bird finding, conservation, and publishes an informative bimonthly magazine and monthly newsletter. For further information contact the American Birding Association, P.O. Box 6599, Colorado Springs, CO 80934, or telephone 1-800-634-7736.

Audubon Society

Birders interested in birding with other people in Montana should contact the Montana Audubon Council. The address is P.O. Box 595, Helena, MT 59624. For further information on Montana Audubon Chapters, see the index of organizations and agencies in the back of this book.

Montana Audubon Chapters conduct field trips, Breeding Bird Surveys, and Christmas Bird Counts. Christmas Bird Counts are conducted in Bigfork, Billings, Bowdoin NWR, Bozeman, Chester, Clark Canyon Dam, Ennis, Fort Peck, Glacier National Park, Great Falls, Hamilton, Helena, Lewistown, Libby, Little Rocky Mountains, Livingston, Miles City, Missoula, Ninepipe NWR, North Fork Flathead River, Stevensville, Three Forks, Troy, Warm Springs, and Yellowstone National Park. Christmas Bird Counts (usually held around mid-December or early January) are a lot of fun. If you are interested in participating in these outings, please contact the local Audubon Chapter.

Montana Rare Bird Alert

To find out about recent rare bird sightings in Montana, or to report a rare bird, telephone: (406) 721-2935.

Crossbills are best identified by the wing pattern. Field identification guides fail to mention Red Crossbills can have faint wing bars (left), whereas White-winged Crossbills reliably have bold wing bars (right).

Lewis' Woodpecker. Has the unique ability of catching insects on the wing and often resembles the flight of a Flycatcher.

CHAPTER 2
MONTANA'S VARIED ENVIRONMENTS

The Montana Landscape

The terrain we see today in Montana is the result of complex geological forces that shaped the landscape over time. Although difficult to imagine, eons ago a large portion of Montana was actually below sea level and was flooded with shallow inland seas. Other areas of Montana consisted of small islands and coastal plains just slightly above sea level. Fossil evidence found in sedimentary rock formations around the state led scientists to these discoveries about the geological history of Montana.

The first dinosaurs appeared 240 million years ago and died out somewhat abruptly 65 million years ago, probably due to a sudden cataclysmic event. During the age of dinosaurs, known as the Mesozoic Era, Montana remained below sea level. Shallow inland seas covered the eastern two thirds of the state and large portions of western Montana. At the end of the Mesozoic Era, the Rocky Mountains began to form and a variety of complex geological processes interacted to shape the land. The valley, mountain, and plains landscapes that we see today in Montana are the result of the shifting of the earth's crust, volcanic activity, igneous intrusions, glaciation, and extensive erosion.

Glaciation had a profound influence on the landscape, particularly in northern Montana, where the massive Laurentide Ice Sheet rested. During the Pleistocene Era, numerous isolated mountain glaciers carved the jagged peaks and U-shaped valleys found in western Montana. Evidence of past and current glaciation is obvious on the landscape even today. Active mountain glaciers are still visible in places such as Glacier National Park, the Mission Mountains, and the Beartooth Mountains.

Topography

The most striking natural features of this state are its mountains. In western Montana where mountains are most prominent, the landscape was primarily formed through folding and faulting of the earth's crust. Many of the isolated mountain ranges found in central and eastern Montana are the result of either resurgent domes, igneous intrusions, or volcanic activity.

Mountain building continues in Montana even today. The area around Quake Lake, Hebgen Lake, and West Yellowstone remains the most active earthquake zone in the Northern Rockies. Near the northeast corner of Yellowstone National Park, the Beartooth Mountains are home to some of the oldest rocks on Earth. The Earth is approximately 4.3 billion years old. The rocks found in the Beartooth Mountains date back as far as 3.9 billion years.

Elevation is an important consideration in understanding Montana's varied environments. In northwestern Montana the mountain ranges parallel each other on a northwest-southeast axis, and are usually lower and more continuous. Montana west of the Continental Divide is characterized by numerous mountains and mountain valleys. At 10,665 feet, Mount Haggin (in the Anaconda-Pintler Range) is the highest peak on the west side of the Continental Divide, whereas the place where the Kootenai River leaves Montana and enters Idaho is the lowest point in Montana west of the Continental Divide at 1,820 feet. The mountain ranges in southwest and south central Montana present more of a scrambled arrangement of mountains and much wider valleys. The mountains are highest in the south central section of the state, as are the valleys, but the distance between summits and valleys is surprisingly the same relief ratio found in northwestern Montana. Granite Peak (12,799 feet) is the highest mountain in Montana, and is naturally the highest peak east of the Continental Divide. The lowest point east of the Continental Divide lies near the confluence of the Yellowstone and Missouri rivers at 1,875 feet.

The topography in central Montana is characterized by plains and isolated mountain ranges such as the Highwoods, Sweet Grass Hills, Bear Paws, Little Rockies, Judiths, and the Big Snowy's. These mountains stand in sharp contrast to the gently rolling plains that surround them. Much of these plains have been turned into farmland, particularly a large swath north of Great Falls to the Canadian border.

The eastern third of Montana is primarily plains and rolling hills. The terrain is hilly as a result of rivers cutting through what once was a relatively flat area. In some cases the rivers and streams cut close together, leaving heavily eroded, steep-walled, gullied "badlands" similar to those found in the Dakotas. The terrain around Terry and at Makoshika State Park south of Glendive are classic examples of badland topography in Montana. Evidence of past glaciation can be found on the plains, particularly north of the Missouri River in the northeast corner of the state. The terrain is a much smoother, gentle surface interspersed with isolated potholes, marshes, ponds, and lakes. A good example of this is the Medicine Lake area. Because of the relatively flat terrain, rich soils, and good climate, a large portion of this land has been transformed into farmland.

Montana is a large, relatively undeveloped state, but even here the landscape changes: new roads are built, prairie becomes cropland, forests are cleared. In selecting sites for this guide, every attempt was made to choose sites that are not likely to be greatly altered in the foreseeable future.

Climate

Climate is defined by four important components: wind, air pressure, temperature, and precipitation. These components are referred to when comparing the climate of one area to another. In Montana the climate is dictated by the mountains, wind directions, storm patterns, distance from the equator, proximity to large bodies of land and water, the elevation above sea level, and localized weather patterns. Temperature and precipitation follow general trends influenced by these forces and factors.

A look at Montana's average monthly temperatures readily shows how important these factors are. The only areas that have an average January temperature over twenty-four degrees Fahrenheit are the Flathead, Clark Fork, and Bitterroot valleys of northwest and west central Montana. Winters are typically colder in eastern Montana, particularly in the northeast corner, where the annual January temperature averages less than eight degrees F. Other cold temperature areas include West Yellowstone and Cutbank. The coldest winter winds that approach Montana usually arrive from Canada, most often east of the Continental Divide. The mountains west of the Continental Divide tend to obstruct these excessive cold fronts, but once in a while a surge of arctic air manages to muscle over the divide.

The high elevation mountains of western Montana influence the much lower average summer temperatures that typify this area. Bordered to the east by the Continental Divide, northwest Montana is also closer to the Pacific Ocean, producing cooler summer temperatures, averaging in some areas under fifty-six degrees F. in July. Of particular note are the high mountain areas of Glacier, the Cabinets, and the Missions. Higher elevations also mean cooler summers in the Pintler's, Yellowstone National Park, the Beartooths, and numerous high points along the Continental Divide. Southeastern Montana is the hottest part of the state. Average July temperatures in this area are in excess of seventy-two degrees F.

Moist air masses typically move from the Pacific Ocean to Montana and deposit snow, rain, sleet, or hail. During fall and winter, air masses and winds enter Montana from the northwest and carry with them moisture from the Pacific Northwest. In spring and summer, air masses enter the state from the south carrying moisture from the Gulf of Mexico and the Gulf of California. Some areas of Montana have their own localized weather patterns, which vary slightly from the prevailing wind.

Montana is a relatively arid state. Ninety percent of the state receives less than eighteen inches of moisture annually, and fifty percent of the state receives less than fifteen inches of moisture annually. Some places receive less than ten inches of annual precipitation. Of particular note is the rainshadow just east of the Beartooth Mountains and another low precipitation zone just south of Bannack. Heavy annual precipitation in excess of thirty-five inches occurs in extreme northwest Montana, and accounts for the more humid conditions west of the Continental Divide. This arid climate is striking in contrast with the average annual precipitation amounts of other regions of the U.S.: the Pacific Northwest, 100+ inches; the Mid West, thirty to fifty inches; and the East, forty to sixty inches.

Vegetation

The Big Sky state can be broken down into three general vegetation zones: forested areas (continuous and savannah), riparian areas (dominated by tall and medium-sized deciduous vegetation), and open areas (grasslands, sagebrush, saltbrush, and alpine).

The most apparent zone is the forested areas of the state, best recognized by the presence of conifers. The continuous forests found at high elevations (referred to as subalpine) are composed of tree species of little economic value such as whitebark pine, larch, subalpine fir, spruce, and limber pine. Most of the wilderness areas in Montana are composed of a high percentage of these species of trees. The continuous forests found at moderate elevations of the mountains (referred to as montane) consist of many tree species including one or more of the following: Douglas fir, lodgepole pine, and spruce and fir mixed with scattered stands of aspen. In the continuous forests west of the Continental Divide, certain localized sites with high precipitation can support grand fir, white spruce, western white pine, pacific yew, western red cedar, western hemlock, and paper birch. Ponderosa pine is usually found on drier sites at slightly lower elevations. Ponderosa pines form continuous forests in northwest Montana, but the savannah or open woodland surrounded by grasslands is more characteristic of ponderosa pines in north central, south central, and southeast Montana.

The riparian zones in Montana vary from east to west. West of the Continental Divide, where much of the surface water is available year-round, deciduous vegetation is composed of either one or a combination of black cottonwood, willow, and alder, sometimes mixed with pines and firs. Deciduous vegetation in western Montana can cover large tracts of land.

East of the Continental Divide, the riparian zones change dramatically the further east one travels. In central Montana the riparian zones are of moderate size and are charged by both intermittent surface runoff and year-round groundwater. Deciduous species characteristic of the riparian zones of central Montana include black cottonwood, eastern cottonwood, and willow. In eastern Montana, the riparian zones serve as an oasis for birdlife. Though surface runoff occurs during a short period of time, groundwater is available in river and stream gravels. The zones of deciduous vegetation are restricted to narrow greenbelts along rivers and streams. Some characteristic vegetation includes American elm, eastern cottonwood, green ash, boxelder, and willow.

The majority of the state is dominated by vegetation characteristic of open areas. The open grasslands above timberline, or alpine zones, comprise a much smaller area compared to other vegetation types. The harsh wind and weather conditions associated with this zone are consistently found on higher, more exposed mountain ranges in Montana.

Sagebrush is an important plant in open areas, especially for Sage Grouse and Sage Thrasher. It is found primarily east of the Continental Divide, and may be mixed with grassland vegetation and saltbrush. Grasslands are the largest vegetative zone in all of Montana. These open grassland areas can be further subdivided into shortgrass prairie, palouse prairie, tallgrass prairie, general range land, weedy fields, and farmland. These differences are pointed out only to help the reader realize that these open areas are more complex than they appear, and are critical for certain species of birdlife.

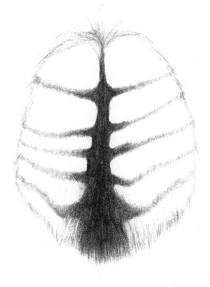

Breast feather comparisons of the Eastern (left) versus Western Screech-Owl (right).

Birds of Montana's Varied Environments

Because each of Montana's regions feature different habitats and environmental conditions, certain birds are more characteristic of any one given region. Some of the more interesting birds likely to be found in each region include:

Northwest Montana
Common Loon
Red-necked Grebe
Common Goldeye
Hooded Merganser
Bald Eagle
Northern Goshawk
Spruce Grouse
Blue Grouse
Flammulated Owl
Westerm Screech-Owl
Northern Pygmy Owl
Barred Owl
Boreal Owl
(cont. next page)

Glacier National Park
Harlequin Duck
Golden Eagle
Spruce Grouse
Blue Grouse
White-tailed Ptarmigan
Barred Owl
Black Swift
Vaux's Swift
Rufous Hummingbird
Pleated Woodpecker
Steller's Jay
Boreal Chickadee
Chestnut-backed Chickadee
(cont. next page)

Northwest Montana (cont.)

Northern Saw-whet Owl
Black Swift
Vaux's Swift
Black-chinned Hummingbird
Calliope Hummingbird
Rufous Hummingbird
Lewis' Woodpecker
Red-naped Sapsucker
Three-toed Woodpecker
Black-backed Woodpecker
Pileated Woodpecker
Gray Jay
American Dipper
Brown Creeper
Winter Wren
Western Bluebird
Mountain Bluebird
Varied Thrush
Nashville Warbler
Northern Waterthrush
Rosy Finch
Cassin's Finch
Red Crossbill
White-winged Crossbill

Northcentral Montana

Horned Grebe
Red-necked Grebe
American White Pelican
Snow Goose (migration)
Ross' Goose (migration)
Ferruginous Hawk
Golden Eagle
Sharp-tailed Grouse
Black-necked Stilt
Upland Sandpiper
Sprague's Pipit
Clay-colored Sparrow
Baird's Sparrow
Grasshopper Sparrow
Mountain Bluebird
McCown's Longspur
Chestnut-collared Longspur

Glacier National Park (cont.)

American Dipper
Winter Wren
Golden-crowned Kinglet
Varied Thrush
Townsend's Warbler
Northern Water Thrush
McGillivray's Warbler
LeConte's Sparrow
Fox Sparrow
White-crowned Sparrow
Rosy Finch

Northeast Montana

Piping Plover
Mountain Plover
Upland Sandpiper
Least Tern
Sage Grouse
Sharp-tailed Grouse
Black-billed Cuckoo
Eastern Screech-Owl
Burrowing Owl
Common Poorwill
Chimney Swift
Red-headed Woodpecker
Least Flycatcher
Say's Phoebe
Eastern Bluebird
Brown Thrasher
Loggerhead Shrike
Clay-colored Sparrow
Field Sparrow
Lark Bunting
Baird's Sparrow
Grasshopper Sparrow
Sharp-tailed Sparrow
Chestnut-collared Longspur
Orchard Oriole
Northern Oriole

Southeast Montana

Golden Eagle
Merlin
Prairie Falcon
Sage Grouse
Sharp-tailed Grouse
Upland Sandpiper
Black-billed Cuckoo
Yellow-billed Cuckoo
Eastern Screech-Owl
Burrowing Owl
Long-eared Owl
Common Poorwill
Lewis' Woodpecker
Least Flycatcher
Say's Phoebe
Cassin's Kingbird
White-breasted Nuthatch
Canyon Wren
Eastern Bluebird
Mountain Bluebird
Sage Thrasher
Loggerhead Shrike
Solitary Vireo
Yellow-breasted Chat
Field Sparrow
Lark Bunting
Grasshopper Sparrow
Chestnut-collared Longspur
Red Crossbill

Southwest Montana

Tundra Swan (migration)
Trumpeter Swan
Ferruginous Hawk
Peregrine Falcon
Prairie Falcon
Blue Grouse
Sandhill Crane
Long-billed Curlew
Great Gray Owl
Boreal Owl
American Dipper
Sage Thrasher
Green-tailed Towhee
Red Crossbill

South Central Montana

Golden Eagle
Prairie Falcon
Blue Grouse
Red-naped Sapsucker
Pinyon Jay
American Dipper
Mountain Bluebird
American Pipit
Green-tailed Towhee
Rosy Finch

Yellowstone National Park

Common Loon
American White Pelican
Trumpeter Swan
Harlequin Duck
Barrow's Goldeneye
Osprey
Bald Eagle
Swainson's Hawk
Peregrine Falcon
Blue Grouse
Sandhill Crane
Great Gray Owl
Williamson's Sapsucker
Three-toed Woodpecker
Gray Jay
Clark's Nutcracker
Common Raven
American Dipper
Mountain Bluebird

Seasons

Birders will find it important to know that the four seasons in Montana are not of equal duration and are highly dependent on the elevation of the landscape. In general, Montana is noted for its long winters and short summers. However, at higher elevations winter lasts even longer, and the summer season is shorter still. There also seems to be a quick transformation, especially at higher elevations, from winter to summer and back to winter again. At these elevations, spring may be almost non-existent, whereas fall seems to be slightly more noticeable but very short in duration. In the mountains, snow can occur during any month of the year, but the bulk of snow falls from October/November through March/April. During winter the best birding is confined to lower elevations where there is a diversity of food and shelter, and also milder weather. The only exception to this is birding for forest owls at higher elevations, which seems to be best during the winter months.

The spring season entices most Montanans outside after the long winter, and is also the time birds become most noticeable. Harbingers of spring such as the American Robin, Mountain Bluebird, Western Meadowlark, and Sandhill Crane make their presence well known first at lower elevations, and then slowly progress to higher elevations. Their beautiful songs and calls and the many birds to follow make this season a special event for Montana. In early spring the weather is very unsettled, but the weather improves as the days grow longer, and bird migration becomes more apparent. The landscape comes alive with bird activity as the skies above the eastern plains and the sweet air of western valleys fill with the flash of wings and the melodious peal of bird songs.

The summer season is a great time to watch birds in Montana. Snowmelt from the mountains, coupled with rain from thunderstorms, provides the fountain of life to the lower elevations. The long summer days in Montana add a bonus, and are reminiscent of long arctic days found further to the north. Birds are singing, calling, displaying, breeding, nesting, and rearing and fledging young. The fall season is quite different from summer, and birding is not as dramatic. Most birds are not as colorful as in the spring, and the weather is often more settled earlier in the fall and becomes less so as winter approaches. Bird migration has begun, and winter is not far away.

Migration

Migration is the regular, extensive, seasonal movement of birds between their breeding range and their wintering area. Birds are forced to migrate for different reasons, but food and weather undoubtedly play an important role. Not all birds migrate, but the majority of species found in Montana do migrate in some form or another.

Some birds leave Montana and travel long distances to reach their wintering grounds. For example, the Upland Sandpiper and Swainson's Hawk, which breed throughout much of Montana, both winter on the pampas of Argentina. The American Pipit begins its migration from the

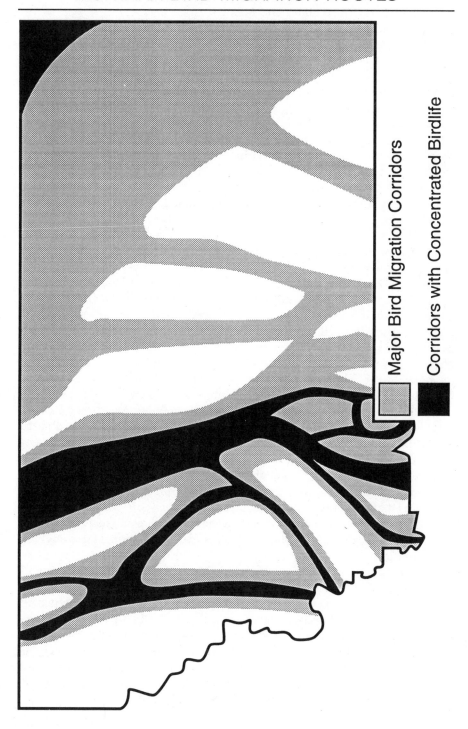

timberline and alpine areas of Montana's high peaks after the first killing frost or first major snowstorm, and winters in open areas at lower elevations in the southern United States and Mexico.

The Snow Goose migrates through Montana from nesting sites in the high Canadian Arctic and Wrangel Island in Siberia to its primary wintering area in the Central Valley of California. Other arctic birds, such as the Lapland Longspur, Snowy Owl, Gyrfalcon, and Rough-legged Hawk, summer in the far north and winter in the open landscapes of Montana.

A few Montana species migrate altitudinally—that is, from high elevations to lower, more temperate regions—within the state. The American Dipper is one such hardy bird, a resident of fast-moving streams with rock or cobble beds and bottom-dwelling aquatic insects. The Dipper may remain on a stream year-round or migrate to lower elevations as streams freeze over.

Spring bird migration differs from the fall flights in that it is more direct, more closely timed, and often more channeled or focused on specific stopover sites. Lingering snowpack often forces birds to bypass or overfly mountainous and foothill areas. As lakes and ponds thaw, spring migration sets in motion, usually running from mid-March through May and sometimes extending into early June at higher elevations.

In contrast, fall migration seems to be less direct, more loosely timed, and more widespread. The first killing frosts in open valleys and freeze-out on lakes are signals that force many birds to head south. Lakes freeze early at high elevations, typically in September or October, but at lower elevations freeze-out may not occur until November or December. Intermittent thawing often allows birds to delay migration despite shorter days and a paucity of food.

Birds migrate through Montana on a north-south axis, concentrating in a number of corridors formed by the broad intermountain valleys on either side of the Continental Divide and following somewhat less defined paths across the eastern plains. Much of the migration funnels through three major corridors. The Flathead and Bitterroot valleys form a primary corridor west of the Continental Divide. Immediately east of the divide, large numbers of migrants converge along the Rocky Mountain Front and along the Missouri River and its headwater tributaries. The third major corridor in Montana is found in the extreme northeast corner of the state, where a great diversity of birds cross the plains each spring and fall, offering exceptional birdwatching opportunities.

During migration, birds are found in nearly every conceivable type of habitat, and it becomes especially difficult to predict what species might be found in any given place. In particular, passerines pop up in unexpected places, seeking shelter and food wherever these are available. Large numbers of migrating shorebirds and waterfowl are drawn to ponds, lakes, rivers, and other wetlands. Many of the National Wildlife Refuges in Montana serve as migration stopovers—and excellent birding sites—for a great number and variety of ducks, geese, cranes, grebes, gulls, swans, shorebirds, and raptors.

Some species of raptors, notably Peregrine Falcon, follow migrating flocksof waterfowl and shorebirds. Bald Eagles also rely on concentrations of their prey—waterfowl and fish—to fuel migration. Each fall, hundreds of Bald Eagles congregate to feed on abundant fish supplies at Lake Koocanusa near Libby and on the Missouri River below Canyon Ferry Dam near Helena.

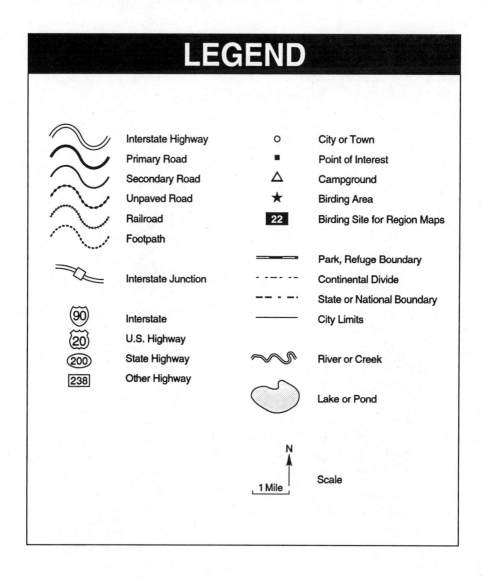

LEGEND

Interstate Highway	○ City or Town
Primary Road	■ Point of Interest
Secondary Road	△ Campground
Unpaved Road	★ Birding Area
Railroad	22 Birding Site for Region Maps
Footpath	
Interstate Junction	Park, Refuge Boundary
	Continental Divide
	State or National Boundary
90 Interstate	City Limits
20 U.S. Highway	
200 State Highway	River or Creek
238 Other Highway	
	Lake or Pond

N
1 Mile Scale

Beargrass. The flower most closely identified with Glacier National Park.

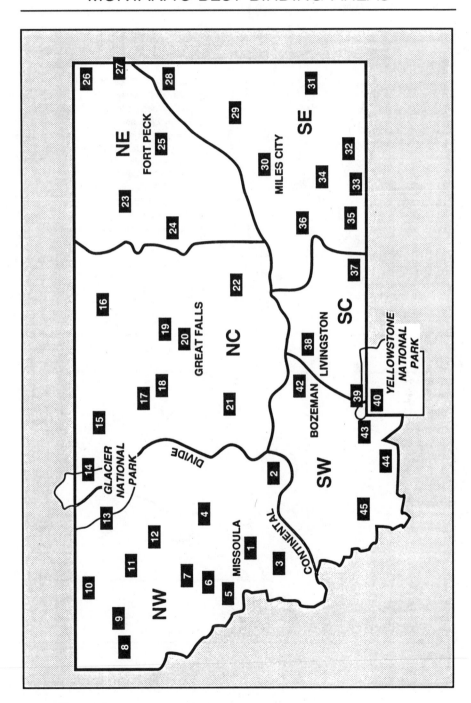

NORTHWEST MONTANA

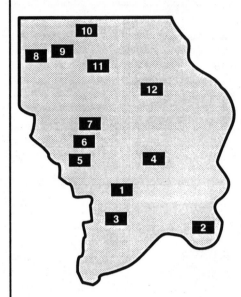

1. Missoula and Vicinity
2. Butte and Vicinity
3. Lee Metcalf National Wildlife Refuge
4. Seeley Lake and Vicinity
5. National Bison Range
6. Ninepipe National Wildlife Refuge
7. Polson and Vicinity
8. Troy and Vicinity
9. Libby and Vicinity
10. Fortine and Eureka
11. Kalispell and Vicinity
12. Swan River/Swan Lake

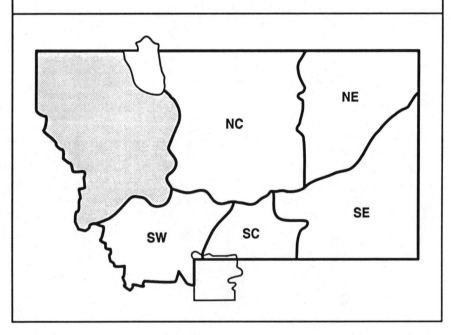

1 MISSOULA AND VICINITY

General Information: *Missoula is the largest city in western Montana. It is popularly known as the "garden city" due to the abundance of trees and shrubs in town. The Missoula valley was a popular area for the Salish and Blackfeet tribes in the years before white settlers arrived. Missoula takes its name from the Salish word "Lm-i-sule-tiku," which means "by or near the cold, chilling waters." The city rests on the bed of an ancient, glacial lake, now the central convergence for five mountain valleys. Lewis and Clark camped along the Bitterroot River just south of present-day Missoula in 1805 and 1806. Missoula became a natural trading place and even a strategic point for the military during the war with the Nez Perce Indians, thus Fort Missoula was established.*

Birding Information: Missoula is one of the few places in Montana where the birding is excellent year-round. Particularly good birding exists on the **University of Montana campus,** especially near the oval at the center of campus. The grounds have a variety of native and exotic trees and shrubs harboring a diversity of birds. Evening Grosbeak are easy to find on campus in summer, and Bohemian Waxwing, Northern Pygmy-Owl, and Merlin are seen in winter. All three races of Merlin (*richardsonii, columbarius,* and *suckleyi*) have been observed in town in winter. The 0.75-mile hike from campus up to the "M" is steep but can be productive. Scan this slope for Rufous Hummingbird, Calliope Hummingbird, Vesper Sparrow, and Lazuli Bunting in summer.

A less urban setting is found immediately northeast of campus in Hellgate Canyon. The tree-lined **Kim Williams Nature Trail** follows an old railroad grade above the south bank of the Clark Fork River, offering glimpses of waterfowl, Common Raven, and the occasional Osprey and Bald Eagle in the fall. Late spring through summer, Nashville Warbler favor the deciduous shrubs between the river and the old Hellgate forest fire burn. Hike on the nature trail one mile east from the Van Buren Street foot bridge to a junction with the newly established **Hellgate Canyon Trail**. This two-mile trail is strenuous, but leads through the old burn to the 5,158-foot summit of Mount Sentinel. Three-toed Woodpecker have been sighted on snags in the burn area, and deer, coyote, black bear, and even cougar frequent the forest on top. Return by the same route or follow the trail west two miles to the "M" above the university campus and the switchbacks into town.

On the northeast end of Missoula between the city and Mount Jumbo, Rattlesnake Creek is a favorite haunt for local birders. The lower end of the creek runs through **Greenough Park**, a forty-two acre pocket of deciduous trees and shrubs sprinkled with conifers. The main park entrance is at the corner of Duncan Drive and Vine Street, and off-street parking is available at two other trailheads on Monroe Street along the east side of the park. All

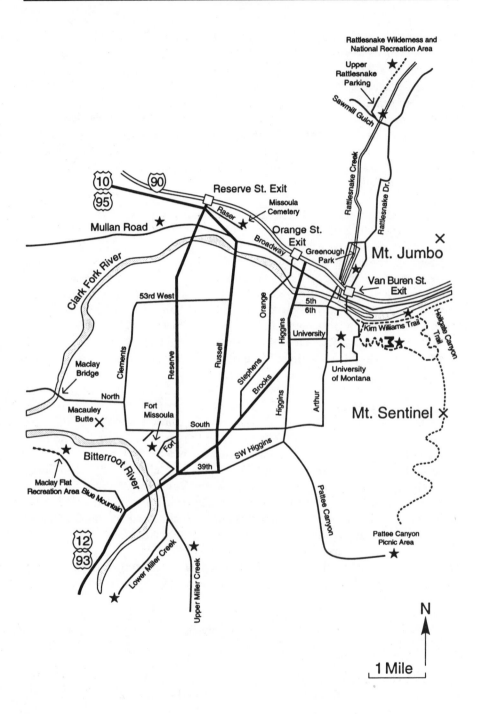

of these entrances provide access to Greenough's interpretive birdwatching trail. In summer, look for Black-headed Grosbeak, Lewis' Woodpecker, and a variety of warblers. In winter, the park teems with Winter Wren, Pine Grosbeak, and Bohemian Waxwing. Look for American Dipper along the rushing creek. In the fall, keep an ear tuned for the drumming of a Pileated Woodpecker; a rare sight in the Rockies, this bird is a frequent visitor to Greenough Park.

The headwaters of Rattlesnake Creek rise in the **Rattlesnake Wilderness and National Recreation Area** just twelve miles north of Missoula. From the east end of Broadway, take Van Buren Street north under I-90 and follow the main road north about five miles to a narrow dirt road marked with a Forest Service sign on the left. Drive a half mile down the dirt road and across Rattlesnake Creek to the parking area and trailhead.

Birders face a wide choice of trails and habitats here. Stay on the two-track that parallels **Rattlesnake Creek** through lush meadows and riparian thickets to see Northern Flicker, Gray Jay, and Black-billed Magpie.

A foot path up **Sawmill Gulch** wanders beneath ponderosa pine and beside a narrow corridor of riparian vegetation. Watch for Pygmy Nuthatch, Red-breasted Nuthatch, Mountain Chickadee, and American Dipper. **Spring Gulch** forks off the main two-track and climbs northwest through Douglas fir and lodgepole pine toward Stuart Peak. Look for Dark-eyed Junco and Ruffed Grouse in the undergrowth, Northern Saw-whet Owl perched in the firs, and Cooper's Hawk and Common Raven in flight over the forest. Mule deer are common in spring on the open, south-facing slopes.

The **Missoula Cemetery,** also north of town, is an especially good migrant trap for passerines.

The **Mullan Road,** the first wagon route over the northern Rockies, runs west of town to the paper mill at Frenchtown. Head west along Mullan Road, especially in the winter, to see a large number and variety of raptors and passerines in the open fields. Watch for Gray Partridge, Red-tailed Hawk, American Kestrel, Prairie Falcon, Rough-legged Hawk, and on rare occasion, Gyrfalcon. Six miles out on the Mullan Road, turn north through hilly country on **Deschamps Lane** for possible sightings of Northern Shrike and Long-eared Owl. Deschamps eventually turns into Roller Coaster Road and ends at U.S. Highway 93 one mile north of I-90.

From Higgins Avenue at the southeast end of Missoula, a scenic, winding four-mile drive up **Pattee Canyon** offers excellent birding for species that prefer coniferous forests. Look for Northern Saw-whet Owl, Calliope Hummingbird, Hammond's Flycatcher, Dusky Flycatcher, Red-breasted Nuthatch, Swainson's Thrush, Orange-crowned Warbler, Yellow-rumped Warbler and Western Tanager here. These species are easier to spot from the Lolo National Forest trails that leave from the **Pattee Canyon Picnic Area** where the paved road turns to dirt. An old dirt two-track climbs north from the picnic area through meadows and stands of ponderosa to the summit of Mount Sentinel. A series of short loop trails (groomed for cross-country skiers in winter) threads through Douglas-fir and lodgepole pine from the small parking lot fifty yards beyond the end of the pavement.

South of Missoula, the eight-mile loop along **Miller Creek** is a popular birding drive. The loop passes stands of ponderosa pine, grasslands, and weedy fields, returning by way of Lower Miller Creek. Watch for Pygmy Nuthatch, Western Meadowlark, Northern Shrike, Bobolink, and Common Redpoll.

Also south of town, heading west on Blue Mountain Road, an impressive list of birds can be found at the **Maclay Flat Recreation Area and Nature Trail**. Cottonwood and aspen mixed with ponderosa pine flank the Bitterroot River here, offering cover to Wood Duck, Hooded Merganser, Common Merganser, Pileated Woodpecker, Downy Woodpecker, Red-naped Sapsucker, Great Horned Owl, Western Screech-Owl, Warbling Vireo, Lazuli Bunting, Vaux's Swift, and Yellow Warbler. Trails also wander among the conifers on **Blue Mountain** to the southwest, providing glimpses of forest bird species, including the diminutive Flammulated Owl.

Back in city limits, the weedy fields and rows of cottonwoods at **Fort Missoula** attract a large number of passerines and raptors. Various sparrows are abundant, Black-billed Magpie are common, and summer days find American Kestrel hunting from powerlines.

Helpful Information:
Elevation: Missoula, 3,200 ft; upper Rattlesnake drainage, 4,000 ft; Mount Sentinel, 5,158 ft.
Habitat(s): Urban, riparian, grassland, ponderosa parkland, forest.
Best Birding Season(s): Year-round.
Best Birding Month(s): January, May, June, September, December.
Montana Highway Map Location: 2-D.
Hazards: Icy winter streets, mosquitoes.
Nearest Food, Gas, Lodging: Missoula.
Camping: Charles Waters, Blodgett, Lake Como (Bitterroot National Forest).
Land Ownership: Private, state, USFS.
Recommended Length of Stay: 1 to 2 days.

2 BUTTE AND VICINITY

General Information: *Butte is famous as the richest hill on earth, due to the bountiful copper deposits found in this area. The town was started by an Irishman by the name of Marcus Daly, also referred to as the "Butte Copper King." The city's name is derived from a 6,369-foot mountain, known as Big Butte, on the west side of town. Of all Montana's cities, Butte is closest to the Continental Divide and it regularly sets cold temperature records.*

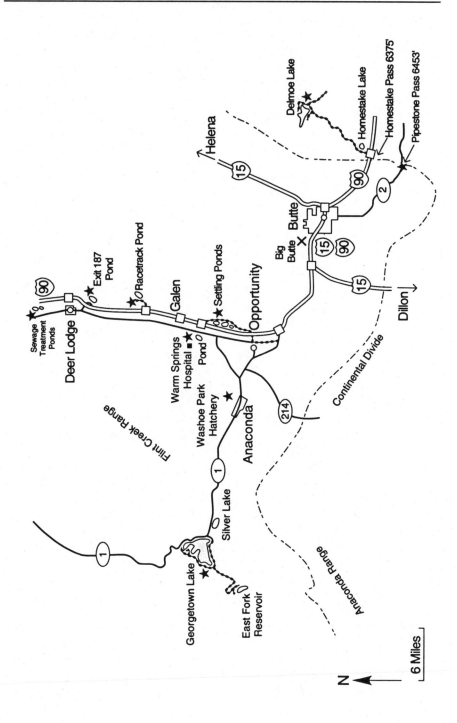

Birding Information: The birding here, so near the divide, can be very unpredictable. The area is good for waterfowl, especially in the spring, but fall waterfowl watching is often complicated by waterfowl hunting and weather conditions that cause birds to overfly the area on their journey south.

Birding around **Butte** is very limited. Rosy Finch (Gray-crowned race) and Bohemian Waxwing are found at bird feeders throughout town in winter. At Homestake Pass, east of Butte and north of I-90, try birding **Homestake Lake** and **Delmoe Lake**. These areas are good places to find Red Crossbill, Gray Jay, Red-breasted Nuthatch, Cassin's Finch, and Dark-eyed Junco. The lakes are also fair migrant traps for passerines during fall migration. Another interesting place for passerines is **Pipestone Pass**, on Highway 2 southeast of Butte toward Whitehall.

The Warm Springs/Deer Lodge area west of Butte offers the best variety of places to view local birdlife. At the **Warm Springs Hospital Pond** look for Wood Duck and Barrow's Goldeneye in the summer. Four other areas are worthwhile birding stops, including **Warm Springs Settling Ponds, Racetrack Pond, Exit 187 Pond**, and the **Deer Lodge Sewage Treatment Ponds**. The Settling Ponds are not accessible by vehicle, but can be approached on foot. Racetrack Pond and Exit 187 Pond are both on private property, yet birds can easily be observed from the road. The Deer Lodge Sewage Treatment Ponds are approached by walking a half mile west of frontage road (parallel to I-90) just north of Deer Lodge. Some species likely to be encountered during spring migration include Ring-necked Duck, Northern Shoveler, Snow Goose, Tundra Swan, and the rare Ross' Goose and Trumpeter Swan. Shorebirds are most noticeable during July and August and can include Western Sandpiper, American Avocet, Marbled Godwit, Baird's Sandpiper, Pectoral Sandpiper, Least Sandpiper, Lesser Yellowlegs, and Greater Yellowlegs.

Washoe Park Trout Hatchery, in Anaconda, is a good place to observe songbirds during the spring, summer, and fall. **Georgetown Lake**, named in honor of George Cameron, an early miner, is one of the best places in Montana to see Red-necked Grebe in summer. To reach Georgetown Lake, drive west fourteen miles from Anaconda on Highway 1. The highway skirts the east shore, and a good gravel road loops around to a number of Forest Service campgrounds on the west shore of the lake. Gray Jay and Steller's Jay can be found year-round along the south end of Georgetown Lake, while Spruce Grouse and Great Gray Owl have been reported in this same area, particularly in winter. The perimeter drive around Georgetown Lake is worthwhile birding, given enough time, as is East Fork Reservoir.

Helpful Information:
Elevation: Butte, 5,549 ft; Anaconda, 5,288 ft; Deer Lodge, 4,531 ft.
Habitat(s): Primarily lakes and ponds; riparian; coniferous forests.
Best Birding Season(s): Spring.
Best Birding Month(s): May, June; July through August for shorebirds.
Montana Highway Map Location: 3-F, 4-F.

Hazards: Mosquitoes.

Nearest Food, Gas. Lodging: Butte, Anaconda, Deer lodge.

Camping: Georgetown Lake; Delmoe Lake.

Land Ownership: Private; state; USFS; BLM.

Additional Information: MDFWP, 1420 E. 6th Ave., Helena, MT 59620 ph: (406) 444-2535.

Recommended Length of Stay: 1 to 2 days.

---

3 LEE METCALF NWR

General Information: *The bitterroot is the state flower of Montana and was first collected and described by Captain Meriwether Lewis of the Lewis and Clark Expedition. Stevensville takes credit as being the site of the first permanent white settlement in the Big Sky state. In 1841, Jesuit missionary Father DeSmet established the St. Mary Mission in Stevensville, now a historic site. Father Ravalli eventually took over the mission in 1845, and the county is named in his honor. In 1963, the Ravalli National Wildlife Refuge was established and was later changed in 1978 to the Lee Metcalf National Wildlife Refuge. The late Senator Metcalf was a strong supporter of Montana wildlife and was instrumental in acquiring land for several national wildlife refuges.*

Birding Information: The 2,800-acre **Lee Metcalf National Wildlife Refuge** is located one mile north of Stevensville between the East Side Highway (Route 203) and the Bitterroot River. This is a small refuge encircled by private land, so public access is quite limited. Short hiking trails do exist, but birdwatching from a vehicle often produces the most satisfactory results. **Wildfowl Lane**, off of the East Side Highway north of Stevensille, is the principal route through the refuge. Species to look for here include American Bittern, Osprey, Bald Eagle, Blue-winged Teal, Cinnamon Teal, Virginia Rail, Sora, Great Horned Owl, Lewis' Woodpecker, Pileated Woodpecker, and Marsh Wren. Wood Duck, always a sought after species, are best observed near the picnic area.

Waterfowl gather here in large numbers and are the primary birds found in the area. Canada Geese are often found nesting in abandoned osprey nests, and no other birding area in Montana has a higher Osprey density than this refuge. Spring is the best season for birding. Tundra Swan are more easily found here then. Fall also offers exciting birding, but the overall waterfowl numbers are nowhere as spectacular as viewed from the road due to waterfowl hunting pressure. However, shorebird numbers appear to be best in the fall due to lower water levels. Snow Geese visit the refuge occasionally during migration, and most often show up in large numbers during snowy, foggy, or rainy weather. White-fronted Geese stop here on occasion. Odd migrants such as the Eurasian Wigeon (primarily during March and April)

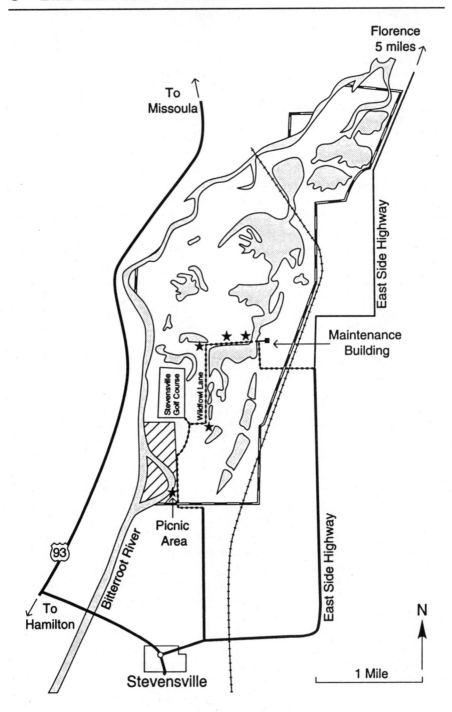

and the White-winged Scoter (mostly in the fall) have been known to stop here. Winter bird specialties include Mallard, Common Snipe, Bald Eagle, Peregrine Falcon, Prairie Falcon, and Golden Eagle. This refuge has high densities of Short-eared Owl during winters when prey populations are high.

A drive from Lolo (eleven miles south of Missoula) west (thirty-three miles) to 5,235-foot Lolo Pass on U.S. 12, is worth the trip for those interested in the history of the Lewis and Clark Expedition and the travels of Chief Joseph. Near the junction of U.S. 12 and 93, at a campsite called Traveler's Rest, the Lewis and Clark expedition split into two parties on their return trip east in 1806. En route to Lolo Pass, Fort Fizzle is where Chief Joseph evaded the calvary in 1877. Lewis and Clark bathed in Lolo Hot Springs in 1806, and a hot soak can still be had today for a modest price. **Lolo Pass** is one of the best places in Montana to find Boreal Owl. February and March are the best months, and the first two hours after sunset are the best time to listen for their calls, which sound similar to the winnowing of a Common Snipe. Search for these owls along the edges of meadows and clearcuts. Steller's Jay, Gray Jay, Pine Grosbeak, and Red Crossbill can be found here more easily throughout the year. However, birding this area in the winter can be difficult due to weather, throngs of cross-country skiers, and short daylight period.

Helpful Information:
Elevation: Lee Metcalf NWR, 3,370 ft.
Habitat(s): River bottom (wetlands, riparian, dry conifers, cultivated fields).
Best Birding Season: Spring, Fall.
Best Birding Month(s): March, April, October, November.
Montana Highway Map Location: 2-E.
Hazards: Mosquitoes, ticks.
Nearest Food, Gas, Lodging: Stevensville.
Camping: Blodgett Canyon, Bass Creek (USFS), both located in the Bitterroots.
Land Ownership: USFWS.
Additional Information: Lee Metcalf National Wildlife Refuge, P.O. Box 257, Stevensville, MT 59870 ph: (406) 777-5552. Refuge Headquarters is located at W. 3rd St. in Stevensville.
Recommended Length of Stay: 2 to 8 hours.

4 SEELEY LAKE AND VICINITY

General Information: *Highway 83, popularly known as the Seeley-Swan road, traverses some of Montana's most scenic country from Clearwater Junction to Bigfork. The highway links a beautiful chain of lakes that includes Salmon Lake, Seeley Lake, Lake Inez, Lake Alva, Rainy Lake, Summit Lake, and Swan Lake. Seeley Lake is reportedly named after J.B. Seeley, the first white person to live in the area.*

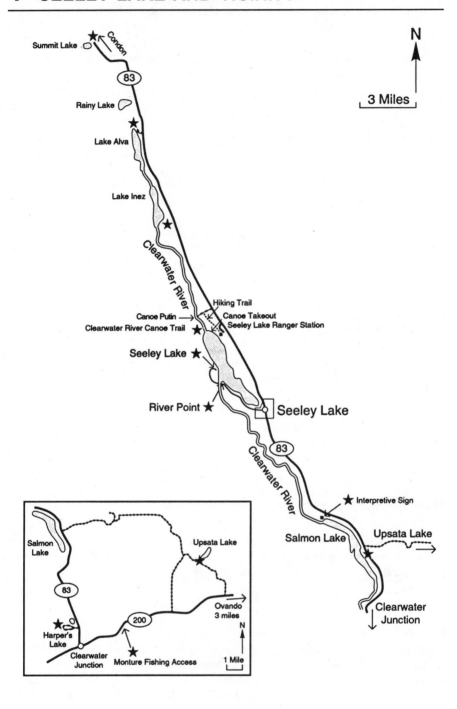

Blackfoot River in the Lincoln/Ovando area.

Birding Information: Starting at Clearwater Junction (intersection of Highway 200 and 83), drive one mile north on Highway 83 and turn west on the gravel road that leads to **Harper's Lake**. The habitat here is a combination of riparian, lake, and ponderosa pine. Harper's is a good place to camp, and birders will enjoy the company of Bald Eagle, Great Horned Owl, Red-breasted Nuthatch, Pygmy Nuthatch, Yellow Warbler, Yellow-rumped Warbler, and Western Tanager.

    Salmon Lake harbors waterfowl and passerines. A campground and several pull-outs along the highway offer good viewing. Near the lake's mid-point, a gravel road heads east and south for eleven miles back to Highway 200 near Ovando. The birding is interesting, especially in the pothole country near Upsata Lake. Birders should also try the Blackfoot Waterfowl Production Area (nine miles east of Ovando) and Monture Fishing Access (five miles west of Ovando).

    Returning to Salmon Lake, stop at the interpretive sign on the north end of the lake to look for Common Loon, Red-necked Grebe, Great Blue Heron, Bald Eagle, Yellow Warbler, and American Redstart.

    Continue north on Highway 83 to the small town of Seeley Lake. Where the slower speed zone begins, watch for the road on the left for the West Shore recreation areas. Drive past the lumber mill and two miles west to the Lolo National Forest's **Riverpoint Recreational Area**. Campgrounds and picnic areas with connecting trails offer good birding and views of Seeley Lake and the placid Clearwater River. Watch for Common Loon, Red-necked

Grebe, Common Raven, Belted Kingfisher, Clark's Nutcracker, Red-breasted Nuthatch, and Dark-eyed Junco.

The **Seeley Lake Ranger Station** at the north end of the lake on Highway 83 also offers excellent birding. Walk behind the ranger station to the lakeshore and follow the Clearwater River upstream. Common Loon and Red-necked Grebe are regularly found here. May to early June is the best time to bird this area. A short trail leads back to the ranger station through spruce-larch forest, home to Pileated Woodpecker and Brown Creeper. Back near the ranger station, visit the viewing blind by the marsh for a closer look at waterfowl, Yellow-headed Blackbird, Common Yellowthroat, and the shy Virginia Rail and American Bittern.

For birders who enjoy boating, the 3.5-mile **Clearwater River Canoe Trail** begins one mile north of the ranger station. From the river, birders are likely to see American Bittern, Great Blue Heron, Osprey, Bald Eagle, Rufous Hummingbird, Red-naped Sapsucker, Willow Flycatcher, Gray Catbird, Yellow Warbler, American Redstart, Northern Waterthrush, Common Yellowthroat and Song Sparrow.

North on Highway 83, Stop at **Inez and Alva lakes** to see Common Loon. The small campsite and boat ramp on the north end of Lake Alva offers the best access to the lake. Five miles north, pause at Summit Lake for excellent views of the lake and the Mission Mountains to the west. Also look for Hooded Merganser and Bufflehead on the lake.

Helpful Information:
Elevation: Seeley Lake, 3,993 ft.
Habitat(s): Riparian, lake, conifers.
Best Birding Season: Late spring, summer.
Best Birding Month(s): May, June, July.
Montana Highway Map Location: 3-D.
Hazards: Mosquitoes.
Nearest Food, Gas, Lodging: Seeley Lake, Holland Lake, Condon.
Camping: River Point, Seeley Lake, Lake Alva.
Land Ownership: USFS, state, private.
Additional Information: Seeley Lake Ranger Station, Seeley Lake, MT 59868 ph: (406) 677-2233.
Recommended Length of Stay: 3 hours to 1 day.

5 NATIONAL BISON RANGE

General Information: *The Bison Range is one of the oldest big-game refuges in the U.S., and was established in 1908 with the help of Teddy Roosevelt and the American Bison Society. The original purpose for the Bison Range was to preserve and maintain a representative herd of American bison or buffalo. Today this 18,541-acre refuge has an assortment of big-game wildlife, including white-tailed deer, mule deer, pronghorn, elk, bighorn sheep, and even mountain goats. The range was eventually designated as a refuge for native birds in 1921. It is one of the best places to view a mixture of big game and birds. The scenery is also sensational, with the broad Flathead Valley to the north and the majestic Mission Mountains to the east. The St. Ignatius Mission in St. Ignatius, Montana, (five miles north of Ravalli) is well worth the stop. Established in 1854 for the Flathead Indians by Father DeSmet, this church is the second oldest mission in Montana (the first being the St. Mary Mission in Stevensville). The paintings inside the church are truly a Montana treasure.*

Birding Information: The National Bison Range is located forty-five miles north of Missoula on the Flathead Indian Reservation. Three primary habitat types are found here: riparian (vegetation along Mission Creek, Jocko River); palouse prairie (wheatgrass-fescue mixture similar to that found in eastern Washington); and montane forest (Douglas fir, ponderosa pine). The only entrance to the Bison Range is found in the small town of Moiese on Highway 212, and if you are not paying attention you can drive right by it. Stop at the visitor center to see excellent exhibits about bison management and to find out which roads are open. The visitor center is open from 8 a.m. to 8 p.m. seven days a week during summer and 8 a.m. to 4:30 p.m. on weekdays in winter. Inquire at the visitor center for more specific birding information.

There are two options for birding the Bison Range, depending on the time of day and season: the short tour and the long tour. The short loop, also known as **Buffalo Prairie Drive**, is a narrow gravel road through grassland habitat near the visitor center. Watch for Gray Partridge, Mourning Dove, Mountain Bluebird, Vesper Sparrow, and Western Meadowlark. The grassland swales or gullies on the short loop are the best places on the Bison Range to see the Grasshopper Sparrow (especially during late spring-summer).

In the riparian corridor along Mission Creek, stops at the nature trail, picnic area, and educational group area usually produce satisfactory results. Great Horned Owl, Northern Pygmy-Owl, Long-eared Owl, and Northern Saw-whet Owl have an affinity for this riparian habitat. Double-crested Cormorant, Common Merganser, Belted Kingfisher, Western Kingbird, Eastern Kingbird, Northern Rough-winged Swallow, Marsh Wren, and Common Yellowthroat also can be found here during the appropriate season. Townsend's Solitaire are easily found here in fall and winter.

The long tour, a one-way nineteen-mile loop on the **Red Sleep Moun-**

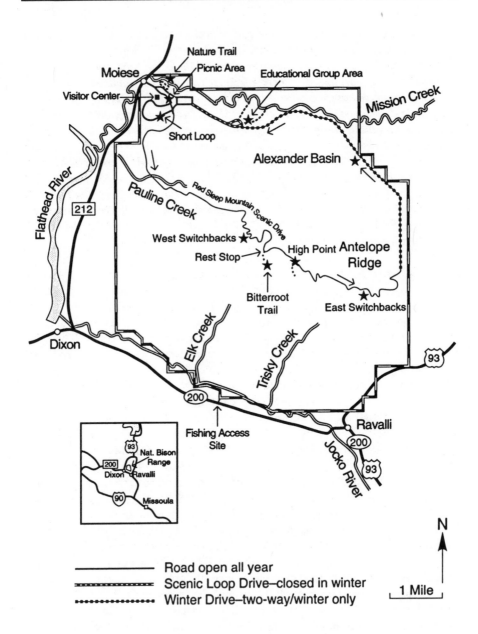

Road open all year

Scenic Loop Drive—closed in winter

Winter Drive—two-way/winter only

N

1 Mile

National Bison Range and Mission Mountain in background.

tain Scenic Drive, takes two to three hours to complete. This drive is closed in winter, except the out-and-back ten-mile drive through Alexander Basin. The Red Sleep Mountain Scenic Drive is gravel and very winding, with outstanding scenic and wildlife viewing opportunities. Visitors are not allowed to hike away from the road, except on two short designated trails at Bitterroot Trail rest stop and High Point. A word to the wise—don't get out of your car with bison nearby. Bison are unpredictable and dangerous.

The long, scenic loop drive begins in grasslands, where Western Meadowlark and Vesper Sparrow are the predominant species. Mountain Bluebird can also be found here, while the Dusky Flycatcher favors shrub vegetation (snowberry) in the smaller draws. Along Pauline Creek, Yellow-breasted Chat and MacGillivray's Warbler are the predominant species. Lazuli Bunting, Yellow Warbler, and Wilson's Warbler can be found in the medium height vegetation. Red-eyed Vireo and Northern Oriole are typically found in the taller deciduous trees. The west switchback area is another place to look for the Dusky Flycatcher.

On the edge of the timber, look for Warbling Vireo, Cassin's Finch, Chipping Sparrow, and Dark-eyed Junco in summer. In the timber, notice how the Douglas fir is found primarily on the wetter north-facing slopes, while ponderosa pine occurs on the drier south-facing slopes. Watch for Yellow-rumped Warbler and Mountain Chickadee. At the **Bitterroot Trail rest stop**, look for Clark's Nutcracker, Lewis' Woodpecker, Northern Flicker (red-shafted race), and on occasion Pygmy Nuthatch. Blue Grouse can also be found in the timber here. For a nice view, try taking the short walk on the Bitterroot Trail from the rest stop.

At **High Point**, Golden Eagle and an occasional Red-tailed Hawk can be observed. On the east switchbacks, Rock Wren can be found singing in the rock outcrops. Golden Eagle are also seen here, as are mountain goats on occasion. In **Alexander Basin**, besides viewing Vesper Sparrow and Western Meadowlark, look for Short-eared Owl and Northern Harrier. The road returns by paralleling Mission Creek, completing the scenic loop.

Two nearby birding areas are worth mentioning. The **Ravalli Potholes** are 1.5 miles north of Ravalli on U.S. Highway 93. These potholes lie within the Bison Range on the north side of the St. Ignatius divide. Depending on the water levels of the ponds, birding can be excellent for waterfowl and shorebirds, especially during migration. Tundra Swan may be sighted here during migration. The other area is the **Jocko River Fishing Access Site** three miles west of Ravalli on Highway 200 (mile marker 113). A short walk on the trail to the river through cottonwood and dense shrubs offers excellent viewing of passerines. Black-capped Chickadee, Red-breasted Nuthatch, and Pileated Woodpecker are some of the species found here.

Helpful Information:
Elevation: 2,585 ft (riparian); 4,885 ft (High Point).
Habitat(s): Riparian, palouse prairie, montane forest.
Best Birding Season(s): Spring, summer.
Best Birding Month(s): Mid May to mid June.
Montana Highway Map Location: 2-D.
Hazards: Bison, rattlesnakes.
Nearest Food, Gas, Lodging: Moiese, Ravalli, St. Ignatius.
Camping: Numerous (inquire at the National Bison Range). A tribal permit is required when camping on the Flathead Indian Reservation.
Land Ownership: USFWS.
Additional Information: National Bison Range, 132 Bison Range Road, Moiese, MT 59824 ph: (406) 644-2211.
Recommended Length of Stay: 3 to 8 hours.

6 NINEPIPE NATIONAL WILDLIFE REFUGE

General Information: *The Ninepipe National Wildlife Refuge was established in 1921 around an existing irrigation reservoir on the Flathead Indian Reservation and is administered by the U.S. Fish and Wildlife Service. The adjacent wetlands are managed by the Montana Department of Fish, Wildlife and Parks and the Confederated Salish and Kootenai Tribes. Drawdowns for irrigation on Ninepipe Reservoir do occur and are more obvious during drought years and in the fall. No hunting is allowed on the refuge, though it is allowed on adjacent state-owned lands.*

The landscape here is an ancient glacial moraine pocked with thousands of potholes or kettle ponds. The potholes formed when large masses of ice buried in the glacial moraine melted out, leaving a water-filled hole in the ground. The abundance of ponds make Ninepipe one of the most important wetland areas in western Montana. The jagged wall of the Mission Mountains dominates the eastern horizon of this scenic birders paradise.

Birding Information: This 5,037-acre refuge located about five miles south of Ronan on U.S. 93 offers relatively easy birding year-round. Parts of the refuge are closed during nesting season, and during hunting season access is limited to the secondary county roads and paved highways that surround the refuge.

The network of roads crosses a variety of habitats, most offering excellent birdwatching opportunities. From late fall through early spring, look for Northern Shrike perched atop the tallest shrubs as they hunt for mice, insects, and small birds. Ring-necked Pheasant, year-round residents, favor fields, shelterbelts, and dense reed beds. Bobolink are occasionally seen in roadside fields. On warm, still summer evenings, rare Black Swift sometimes venture from their nesting sites in the Mission Mountains to feed over the refuge.

Try **Olsen Road** for good views of waterfowl in summer and a strong fall and winter contingent of Long-eared and Great Horned Owls; Rough-legged and Red-tailed Hawks; and Prairie and Peregrine Falcons. Lucky birders may glimpse a rare winter visitor from the arctic, the Gyrfalcon. **Duck Road** is excellent for ducks and pheasants; also watch for Short-eared, Long-eared, and Great Horned Owls. The rare Snowy Owl is known to winter on the refuge and adjacent farmlands.

The most abundant nesting waterfowl species include Canada Goose, Mallard, Redhead, Northern Pintail, American Wigeon, Northern Shoveler, Blue-winged Teal, Green-winged Teal, Ruddy Duck, Gadwall, and Common Merganser. Colonial nesting birds include Double-crested Cormorant, Great Blue Heron, California Gull, and Ring-billed Gull. Other spring and summer species to look for are Western Grebe, Red-necked Grebe, American Coot, and American Avocet. Bald Eagle are present year-round, though more

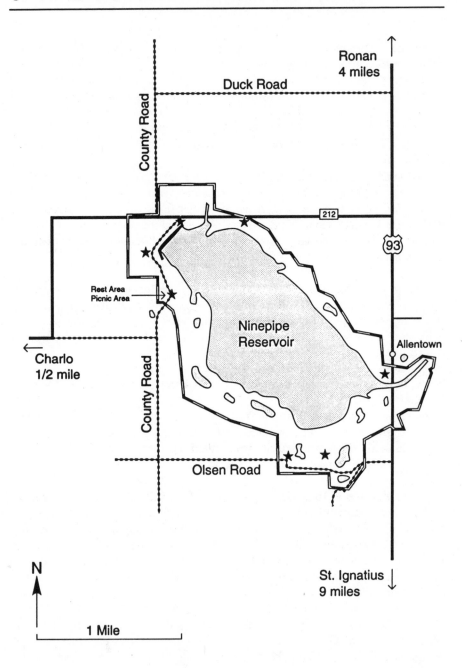

Ronan
4 miles

Duck Road

County Road

212

93

Rest Area
Picnic Area

Ninepipe
Reservoir

Allentown

Charlo
1/2 mile

County Road

Olsen Road

N

St. Ignatius
9 miles

1 Mile

Ninepipe NWR.

plentiful during migration periods. Tundra Swan and shorebirds also stop-over at Ninepipe during migration.

Wildlife checklists and information on local wildlife watching sites for the Flathead Indian Reservation are available by contacting the Wildlife Management Program, Confederated Salish and Kootenai Tribes, P.O. Box 278, Pablo, MT 59855 ph: (406) 675-2700. Bird checklists for the refuge are available from the National Bison Range (see Helpful Information for address).

Helpful Information:
Elevation: 3,100 ft.
Habitat(s): Wetlands, cultivated fields, shelterbelts.
Best Birding Season(s): Good year-round; winter for raptors.
Best Birding Month(s): April, May, June, September, October.
Montana Highway Map Location: 2-C.
Hazards: Flies, mosquitoes.
Nearest Food, Gas, Lodging: Ronan, St. Ignatius.
Camping: MacDonald Lake (inquire for a listing at the National Bison Range).
Land Ownership: Confederated Salish and Kootenai Tribes, USFWS, MDFWP.
Additional Information: National Bison Range, 132 Bison Range Rd. Moiese, MT 59824 ph: (406) 644-2211.
Recommended Length of Stay: 1 to 5 hours.

7 POLSON AND VICINITY

General Information: *The town of Pablo and Pablo Reservoir were named for Michel Pablo, a Flathead Indian rancher who raised wild bison and was credited for saving the bison from extinction. While hunting the Milk River country years ago, a man by the name of Walking Coyote caught and brought back a few wild bison calves to the Flathead Valley. When Walking Coyote raised thirteen bison calves on his own, he sold them to Michel Pablo and Charles Allard. The wild bison eventually formed the nucleus of the herd that now roams the National Bison Range. Polson received its name from David Polson, a prominent stockman who lived in the Mission Valley. Polson Hill lies on an ancient glacial moraine created during the last ice age.*

Birding Information: Both the **Pablo National Wildlife Refuge** and the town of **Polson** are located on the Flathead Indian Reservation. Pablo National Wildlife Refuge is administered by the U.S. Fish and Wildlife Service and receives its water primarily by pumping from the Flathead River. The reservoir is drawn down in the fall, making birding difficult since birds are observed from long distances. May and June are the best months to bird here. The south and west sides of the refuge are closed to public access year-round. The only roads that offer year-round birding are the county roads and

South shore of Flathead Lake.

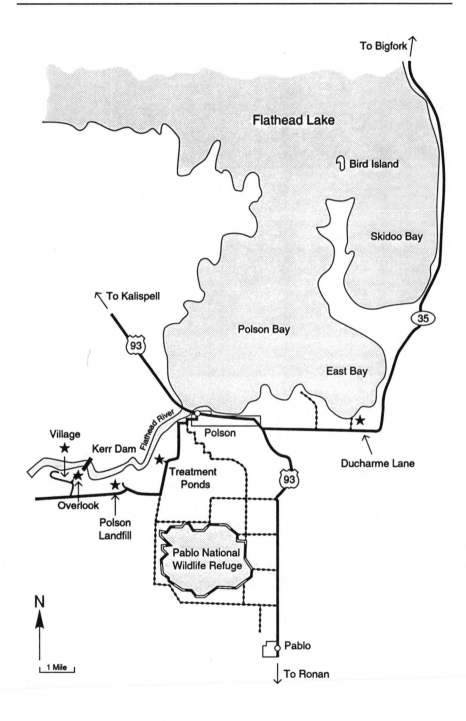

To Bigfork

Flathead Lake

Bird Island

Skidoo Bay

To Kalispell

93

Polson Bay

East Bay

35

Flathead River

Village

Kerr Dam

Polson

Ducharme Lane

Treatment
Ponds

93

Overlook

Polson
Landfill

Pablo National
Wildlife Refuge

N

1 Mile

Pablo

To Ronan

Polson Landfill and Denver Holt.

the Dike Road. Waterfowl and shorebirds are the primary birdlife attracted to the area, but raptors and songbirds are reliably found here also.

The **Polson Landfill**, 3.5 miles southwest of Polson, can be approached either by way of a paved road southeast of Polson or a gravel county road around Pablo National Wildlife Refuge. The Polson Landfill is one of the best areas in western Montana to find rare and unusual species of gulls, thanks to the abundant food source and the close proximity to the Flathead River and Flathead Lake. Spring, fall, and winter are the best times to look for rare species. Herring Gull, Thayer's Gull, and Glaucous Gull, Mew Gull, Glaucous-winged Gull have been reported here. It takes time and attention to detail to separate the odd bird from the numerous California Gulls and Ring-billed Gulls that frequent the dump. Stay clear of the traffic and the bulldozer moving the garbage. Flat tires are always a possibility when visiting any landfill.

Seven miles southwest of Polson, **Kerr Dam** and the adjacent village has a manicured area sprinkled with many exotic tree species, and is a fairly good birding area for songbirds. Look for Cedar Waxwing, Yellow Warbler, Townsend's Solitaire, Western Tanager, and Northern Oriole in summer. Birding is even better during spring and fall migration. At the Kerr Dam Overlook, watch for Rock Wren, Violet-green Swallow, Cliff Swallow, and White-throated Swift.

Back near Polson on the same road, the **municipal treatment ponds**, though not the prettiest of settings, is a good place to see both common and

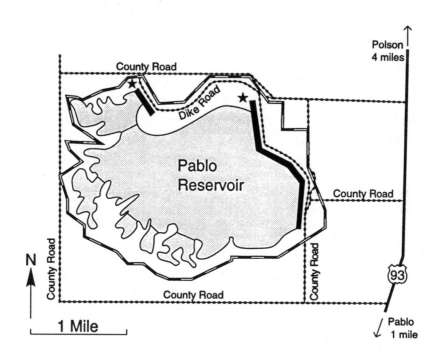

unusual waterfowl during migration. Barrow's Goldeneye are frequently found here during fall migration.

Drive down **Ducharme Lane**, off Highway 35 east of Polson, for fair viewing of waterfowl throughout most of the year. Large rafts of Redheads and American Coots can be found on East Bay during migration. Tundra Swan are often seen here in early spring. In summer, look for Common Yellowthroat, Song Sparrow, and Red-winged Blackbird. Bird Island Sanctuary on Flathead Lake is off limits to the public to protect colonial nesting birds.

Note: Ninepipe and Pablo National Wildlife Refuges are superimposed on Tribal lands. For bird checklists see section on Ninepipe NWR.

Helpful Information:
Elevation: Pablo National Wildlife Refuge, 3,320 ft; Polson, 2,931 ft.
Habitat(s): Wetlands, cultivated fields, riparian, juniper.
Best Birding Season(s): Spring, fall.
Best Birding Month(s): April, May, September, October, November.

Montana Highway Map Location: 2-C.

Hazards: Gnats.

Nearest Food, Gas, Lodging: Polson.

Camping: Numerous (especially on the west shore of Flathead Lake).

Land Ownership: Confederated Salish and Kootenai Tribes, USFWS, City of Polson, Lake County (dump).

Additional Information: National Bison Range, Moiese, MT 59824 ph: (406) 644-2211.

Recommended Length of Stay: 4 to 8 hours.

8 TROY AND VICINITY

General Information: *Translated, Kootenai means "people of the lakes," an apt name for these masters of fishing and navigation on the big water of this river. The Kootenai tribe developed the sturgeon-nosed canoe, a combination canoe/ kayak that could be easily maneuvered in whitewater.*

Birding Information: One region of Montana often overlooked by the traveler is the area around Troy in the extreme northwest corner of the state. This rolling, heavily timbered country is drained by the Kootenai River, named after the Kootenai Indian tribe.

Fourteen miles northwest of Troy, the **Kootenai River** leaves Montana at the lowest point in the state, 1,820 feet above sea level. To bird this area, travel northwest from Troy on U.S. Highway 2 and turn west at mile marker 2 onto the graveled Forest Road 408. A 1.4-mile drive down this narrow road offers enjoyable birding for Common Merganser, Osprey, Mountain Chickadee, Chestnut-backed Chickadee, Ruby-crowned Kinglet, and Townsend's Warbler. The road ends at an old dilapidated bridge, and across the river is the old railroad siding, **Leonia**. Walk 400 yards downstream on either side of the river to stand at the lowest point in all of Montana.

Leonia also makes a good take-out point for birders who want to canoe the lower Kootenai. Boats can be launched at the confluence with the Yaak River, "Kootenai Vista" (mile marker 10 on U.S. 2), and at Troy, giving a choice of six-, ten-, and fifteen-mile river runs respectively. Birding is good here, especially for the abundant passerines in the riparian vegetation. Stops along the river to bird are very worthwhile. The river attracts many Ospreys and the occasional Bald Eagle.

Seven miles east of Troy on U.S. 2, stop at **Kootenai Falls**, "the Niagara Falls of Montana." Here, the mighty Kootenai breaks and plummets 200 feet over two cascades and a rough set of rapids. David Thompson, the explorer/ geographer of northwest Montana, made his first portage around the falls in 1808. On his fourth portage here in 1810, he wrote the first detailed scientific

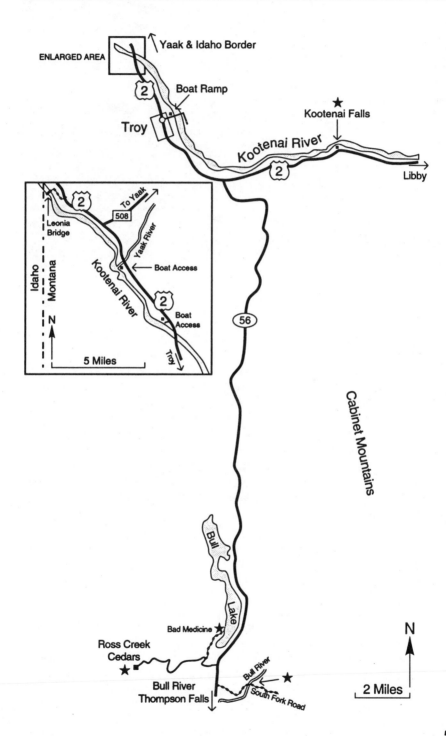

Kootenai Falls.

account of the American Dipper, a species still found on the falls today.

The Lion's Club maintains a picnic area by the falls. A trail down to the falls eventually leads upriver to the brink of Kootenai Falls. Look for Harlequin Duck above the falls in April and May. The hike down to the falls, although strenuous for some people, offers a close-up view of this spectacular torrent. On the trail downriver, look for Golden-crowned Kinglet. Crossing the cascading Kootenai River on a swinging foot suspension bridge is the grand finale to this hike. Now that is birding!

Bull Lake is a beautiful, forested lake located fifteen miles south of Troy on Highway 56. A stop near the south end of the lake can be worthwhile for species such as Ring-necked Duck, Red Crossbill, Pine Siskin, and Steller's Jay. Campers can stay at the Bad Medicine Campground on the southwest shore.

About one mile south from Bull Lake on Highway 56, turn west at mile marker 16 and follow the signs for 4.2 miles to the **Ross Creek Cedars**. A short hike through the tall, old-growth western red cedars, western white pines, and western hemlocks offers excellent birding. Look and listen for Pileated Woodpecker, Steller's Jay, Chestnut-backed Chickadee, Brown Creeper, Winter Wren, Golden-crowned Kinglet, Varied Thrush, Red Crossbill, and White-winged Crossbill. Birding can also be good in the parking lot and in the picnic area across the creek. The drive back out to Highway 56 affords excellent views of the Cabinet Mountains Wilderness to the east.

Heading south on Highway 56, birding is excellent from Bull Lake

South Fork Bull River and Cabinet Mountains.

downstream along the **Bull River** for the next eleven miles. Roughly two miles from the south end of Bull Lake, turn east on the **South Fork Road** to watch and listen for birds. This gravel road crosses the Bull River riparian zone and a swamp, with willows and alders prevailing. Less than four miles up the South Fork Road look for a clearcut that harbors a large number of Mountain Bluebirds. Back on Highway 56, drive south to the junction with Highway 200. Likely sightings along the way include Willow Flycatcher, Swainson's Thrush, Solitary Vireo, Warbling Vireo, Red-eyed Vireo, Orange-crowned Warbler, Townsend's Warbler, American Redstart, MacGillivray's Warbler, and Fox Sparrow. Bobolink can be found in the hay fields on the lower reaches of the Bull River.

Helpful Information:
Elevation: Bull River, 2,356 ft.
Habitat(s): Riparian, mixed-deciduous, old-growth conifer forest.
Best Birding Season(s): Late spring, early summer.
Best Birding Month(s): May, June.
Montana Highway Map Location: 1-B.
Hazards: Logging trucks.
Nearest Food, Gas, Lodging: Troy.
Camping: Bull Lake.
Land Ownership: USFS, private.
Additional Information: Troy Ranger Station, 1437 N. Highway 2, Troy, MT 59935 ph: (406)295-4693.
Recommended Length of Stay: 2 to 3 days.

9 LIBBY AND VICINITY

General Information: *Libby is named for the daughter of George Davis, an early white settler in the area. The Kootenai Indians and white explorers such as David Thompson used the Kootenai River system quite extensively in the years before Montana became a state. Steamships eventually took over as the primary means of transportation on the river, only to be replaced by a series of forest roads.*

Birding Information: Libby is located along the Kootenai River in northwestern Montana. Birding around Libby can be quite good, since there is an excellent diversity of birdlife only a short distance from town. However, birding for waterfowl during migration months is not very good, and only the Kootenai River and Libby Dam are recommended.

One of the better birding areas is **Libby Creek** south of town. Drive eleven miles south (east) of Libby on U.S. Highway 2, and head southwest on Libby Creek Road, a good gravel route. The first four miles offer the best birding, through western hemlock, western red cedar, western white pine, cottonwood, and western larch. Look for Pileated Woodpecker, Red-breasted Nuthatch, Winter Wren, Golden-crowned Kinglet, and Varied Thrush, . Turn around at the four-mile point and return to U.S 2. Libby Creek Road continues across the highway, heading north along the creek to a dead-end in about five miles. Watch for Black Swift, Olive-sided Flycatcher, Black-headed Grosbeak, and Fox Sparrow.

Return to town on U.S. 2 and stop at the **confluence of Libby Creek and the Kootenai River**, an excellent place to watch birds. To reach the confluence, turn east off Mineral Avenue onto 5th Street; go slightly beyond the Champion Lumber Mill to the bridge over Libby Creek about a half mile east of town. Willow Flycatcher, Red-eyed Vireo, and American Redstart are found here in summer.

The **Champion Haul Road** is also a good place to bird, but it can be dangerous. Logging trucks haul timber at high speeds on this road. Go early in the morning, make sure you stay alert for these trucks, and pull completely off the road when stopped. This private haul road owned by Champion International parallels the Kootenai River east of Libby, and eventually ends up on Highway 37 just below Libby Dam.

Other birds likely encountered in the Libby area include Great Blue Heron, Bald Eagle, Black-chinned Hummingbird, Rufous Hummingbird, Red-naped Sapsucker, Williamson's Sapsucker, Northern Flicker, Solitary Vireo, Warbling Vireo, Red-eyed Vireo, Orange-crowned Warbler, Nashville Warbler, Townsend's Warbler, American Redstart, Northern Waterthrush, MacGillivray's Warbler, Wilson's Warbler, and Cassin's Finch. Osprey are easily found along the Kootenai River in the summer. A large number of Osprey nests can be found in the forest fire burn across from Canoe Gulch.

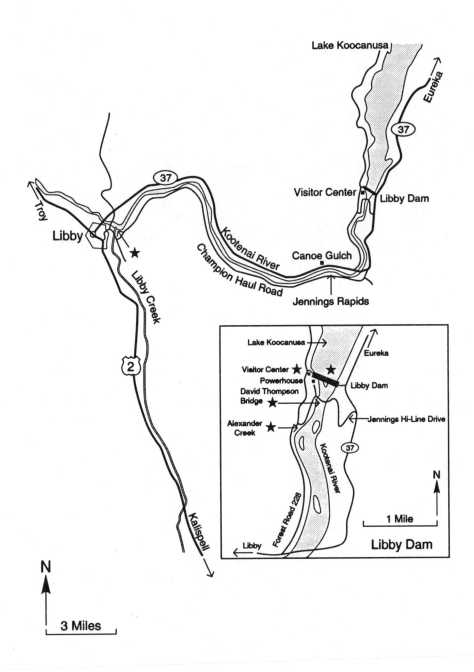

Libby Dam.

Harlequin Duck have been known to show up at Jennings Rapids during April and May.

Libby Dam is located thirteen miles east of Libby on Highway 37. This massive dam blocks the Kootenai River, forming Lake Koocanusa, a huge body of water that extends forty-five miles into British Columbia. Birding on and below Libby Dam can be fun. Recommended birding areas include the brink of the dam, Jennings Hi-line Drive, Wildlife Viewing Area, David Thompson Bridge, Alexander Creek, and the visitor center. Lake, riparian, and coniferous forest habitats are found here. Species likely to be encountered include Common Loon, Great Blue Heron, Canada Goose, Green-winged Teal, Mallard, American Wigeon, Common Merganser, Osprey, Bald Eagle, Ruffed Grouse, Spotted Sandpiper, California Gull, Northern Saw-whet Owl, Common Nighthawk, Black Swift, Calliope Hummingbird, Rufous Hummingbird, Northern Rough-winged Swallow, Common Raven, Boreal Chickadee, Chestnut-backed Chickadee, Red-breasted Nuthatch, Orange-crowned Warbler, Northern Waterthrush, MacGillivray's Warbler, Rufous-sided Towhee, Dark-eyed Junco, and Red Crossbill. Birding for passerines is best near the visitor center and the small campground at Alexander Creek.

Libby Dam is noted for its Bald Eagle concentration in late fall. Large numbers of Bald Eagles stop here from October through December, with peak numbers usually occurring in November. If you are having troubles spotting eagles, try searching for them perched in trees on the hillside near David Thompson Bridge. California Gull also show up in larger than normal numbers, joining the eagles to take advantage of the stunned kokanee salmon that manage to make their way through the turbines of the dam. Directly below the dam is also a good place to look for rare and unusual gulls during migration.

Helpful Information:
Elevation: Libby, 2,066 ft.
Habitat(s): Deciduous, coniferous, and mixed forests, riparian, lake.
Best Birding Season(s): Late spring, early summer.
Best Birding Month(s): May, June, and November (Libby Dam only).
Montana Highway Map Location: 1-B.
Hazards: Logging trucks.
Nearest Food, Gas, Lodging: Libby.
Camping: Alexander Creek (Libby Dam), Lake Koocanusa.
Land Ownership: (Libby Dam) U.S. Army Corps of Engineers, other: USFS, private.
Additional Information: U.S. Army Corps of Engineers, 17115 Highway 37, Libby, MT 59923 ph: (406)293-5577.
Recommended Length of Stay: 1 to 2 days.

10 FORTINE AND EUREKA

General Information: *Fortine, twelve miles south of Eureka, was named for Octave Fortine, an early settler here. Eureka is nine miles south of the British Columbia boundary in northwest Montana. The town was first named Deweyville and was situated along the banks of the Tobacco River. In 1904, postmaster Emma Dimmick suggested the name change to Eureka.*

The Tobacco Plains form a unique and expansive grassland surrounded by heavily forested mountains north of Eureka. In prehistoric times, this valley was filled with an enormous ice sheet. The hills and potholes found here today are the result of this glaciation. The Tobacco Plains were so named by the Indians who harvested a tobacco-like plant in this area for religious purposes. During the fur trapping and trading days in the early part of the last century, this remote corner of the state was inaccessible from customary trapping grounds and operating bases of the Americans. Representatives of the British and Canadian companies came in from the north and established posts along the Kootenai River.

Birding Information: Fortine is a good place to start birding the Tobacco Valley. Two miles south of Fortine on U.S. 93 is **Murphy Lake**, where Common Loon are consistently found. Check at the ranger station on the north end of the lake for the most up-to-date loon information. Around **Fortine,** be on the lookout for American Kestrel, Black-chinned Humming-

Tobacco Plains looking south.

bird, Calliope Hummingbird, Rufous Hummingbird, Red-naped Sapsucker, Mountain Bluebird, Red-eyed Vireo, Yellow Warbler, the rare Pine Siskin, and Western Bluebird.

The surrounding high mountains can be reached via a gravel road 6.5 miles southeast of Murphy Lake that travels east up the Stillwater River to Mount Marston; via a logging road east of Fortine; or via Grave Creek. **Grave Creek Road**, 2.5 miles north of Fortine on U.S. 93, is a pleasant drive and is the easiest to find. A wide variety of habitat types and, consequently, bird species can be encountered here. Trees have been cleared in the valley for pasture, adding to the habitat diversity of the area. Along Grave Creek look for American Dipper, Common Merganser, Calliope Hummingbird, and on very rare occasions, Harlequin Duck. A slow 28.5-mile drive up Grave Creek from the valley to the subalpine zone leads to the scenic, subalpine **Therriault Lakes**. Forest species likely to be encountered on this ascent to the high mountains include Steller's Jay, Boreal Chickadee, Chestnut-backed Chickadee, Brown Creeper, Golden-crowned Kinglet, Ruby-crowned Kinglet, Winter Wren, Swainson's Thrush, Hermit Thrush, Varied Thrush, Yellow-rumped Warbler, Townsend's Warbler, Pine Grosbeak, Red Crossbill, and, on occasion, White-winged Crossbills. On the open slopes of the higher mountains look for Rufous Hummingbird, Olive-sided Flycatcher, Gray Jay, Clark's Nutcracker, Mountain Bluebird, MacGillivray's Warbler, Chipping Sparrow, and Fox Sparrow.

The **"string of lakes"** drive offers good birding in June and July. This

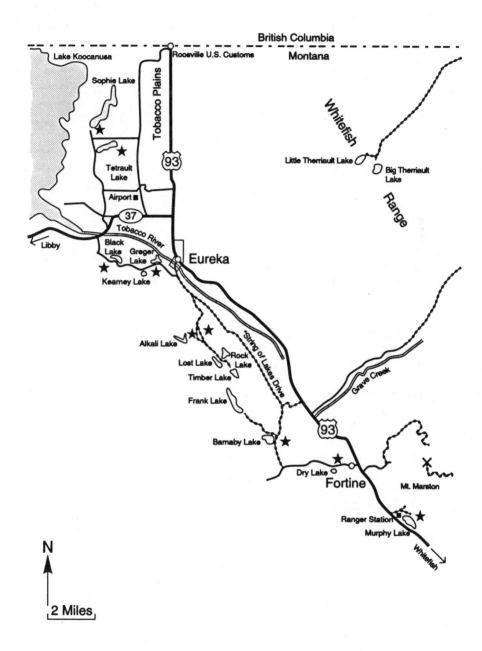

British Columbia

Montana

Lake Koocanusa

Roosville U.S. Customs

Sophie Lake

Whitefish

Tobacco Plains

93

Little Therriault Lake

Big Therriault Lake

Tetrault Lake

Range

Airport ■

37

Tobacco River

Libby

Black Lake

Greger Lake

Eureka

Kearney Lake

Alkali Lake

String of Lakes Drive

Lost Lake

Rock Lake

Grave Creek

Timber Lake

Frank Lake

93

Barnaby Lake

Dry Lake

Fortine

Mt. Marston

Ranger Station ■

Murphy Lake

Whitefish

N

2 Miles

road is best reached by driving west through Fortine 2.8 miles and turning north toward Eureka. Barnaby and Dry lakes are also good places for observing Tundra Swans (late March, October and November) and various species of shorebirds during migration in late summer and fall. Stops at the following lakes will produce good results: Dry Lake (a half mile west of Fortine), Barnaby Lake, Frank Lake, Alkali Lake, Lost Lake, Rock Lake, Timber Lake, Greger Lake, Kearney Lake, and Black Lake. Species likely to be encountered include Common Loon, Pied-billed Grebe, Red-necked Grebe, Eared Grebe, American Bittern, Canada Goose, Redhead, Ring-necked Duck, Lesser Scaup, Common Goldeneye, Bufflehead, Ruddy Duck, American Coot, Killdeer, Red-naped Sapsucker, Marsh Wren, Mountain Bluebird, Cedar Waxwing, and Red-winged Blackbird.

A drive through the grasslands of the **Tobacco Plains** can be productive for American Kestrel, Long-billed Curlew, Horned Lark, Western Bluebird, Vesper Sparrow, Grasshopper Sparrow, and Western Meadowlark. Look for Northern Shrike here in winter. Columbian Sharp-tailed Grouse from Canada have been experimentally introduced into this area to help bolster the dangerously low local population. Due to the sensitivity of this project, the exact location of this species cannot be given. One route worth traveling for grassland species is the back road from Rooseville to the Eureka airport. A sidetrip to Sophie Lake and Tetrault Lake can be productive for waterfowl and species that prefer conifers.

Helpful Information:
Elevation: Eureka, 2,566 ft; Fortine, 2,965 ft; Tobacco Plains, 2,833 ft.
Habitat(s): Coniferous-deciduous forests, riparian, lakes, marshes, subalpine.
Best Birding Season: Summer.
Best Birding Month(s): June, July.
Montana Highway Map Location: 1-A.
Hazards: Logging trucks.
Nearest Food, Gas, Lodging: Eureka, Fortine.
Camping: Tetrault Lake, Sophie Lake.
Land Ownership: USFS, private.
Additional Information: Murphy Lake Ranger Station, USFS, P.O. Box 116, Fortine, MT 59918 ph: (406) 882-4451.
Recommended Length of Stay: 6 hours to 2 days.

11 KALISPELL AND VICINITY

General Information: *A massive ice age glacier was responsible for the landscape patterns seen today in the Flathead Valley. The magnificent mountain ranges to the northeast (Whitefish Range, Glacier National Park), east (Swan Range), and southeast (Mission Range) of Kalispell resisted the power of this large glacier and are a testimonial to that era. Kalispell is named after the Kalispell Indians, relatives of the Flathead Indians. The area around Kalispell was first settled in 1881, when Angus McDonald of the Hudson's Bay Company established a post here.*

Birding Information: The area around **Kalispell** is a fun place to watch birds. Vaux's Swift is one species you can find right in the middle of town. At the north end of Main Street, three-quarters of a mile north of U.S.Highway 2 and just east of U.S. Highway 93, is a great birding spot called **Lawrence Park**. The Stillwater River meanders through the park, and the riparian vegetation here is in excellent condition. This is one of the most natural city parks in all of Montana and should serve as a model for other cities and towns if we are to preserve habitat for birds. Breeding species likely to be encountered in Lawrence Park include Common Merganser, Ruffed Grouse, Spotted Sandpiper, Red-naped Sapsucker, Downy Woodpecker, Hairy Woodpecker, Pileated Woodpecker, Least Flycatcher, Northern Rough-winged Swallow, Black-capped Chickadee, Warbling Vireo, Red-eyed Vireo, Northern Water-thrush, and MacGillivray's Warbler. Wood Ducks are easily found in this park. The area is also a migrant trap for birds during spring and fall.

    Smith Lake is another productive birding area that is convenient to Kalispell. To get there, drive nine miles west of town on U.S. 2 and take Kila Road south, then follow the signs to the fishing access site. Smith Lake has a wide array of habitat— marsh, cattail, bulrush, extensive cover, cultivated fields— surrounded by ponderosa pine and Douglas-fir with scattered stands of aspen. It is a great area for waterfowl, particularly during migration. Some species likely to be encountered during the breeding season (May through August) include Pied-billed Grebe, Red-necked Grebe, Great Blue Heron, Osprey, Northern Harrier, Red-tailed Hawk, American Coot, Sandhill Crane, Black Tern, Marsh Wren, Red-winged Blackbird, and Yellow-headed Blackbird. A loop on a rough dirt road (east and north) around the lake leads back to U.S. 2. Bluebird nest boxes abound on this road. Mountain Bluebird, Violet-green Swallow, and Tree Swallow are easily found here, and so is the less common Western Bluebird.

    Drive eleven miles west of the Smith Lake turnout on U.S. 2 to a paved road on the right that passes through the town of Marion. A five-mile drive down this road leads to a boat launch at **Little Bitterroot Lake State Park** where Common Loon and Red-necked Grebe can be found spring through fall. Look and listen for Townsend's Warblers in the conifers en route to the lake.

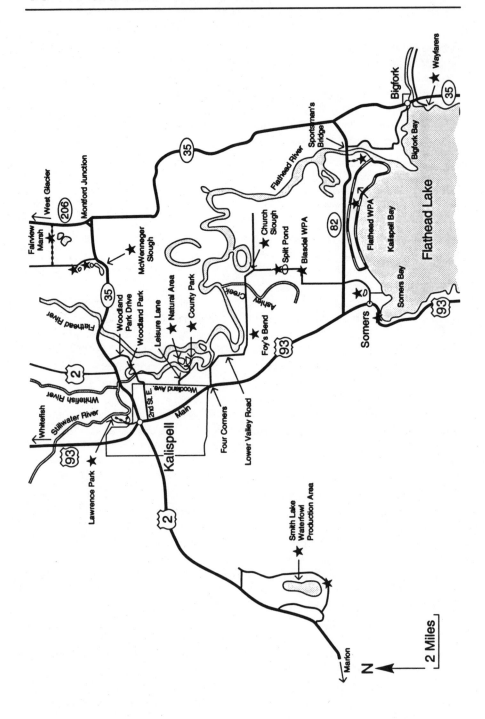

Back in Kalispell, **Woodland Park** is a beautiful, manicured park in the middle of town. From U.S. 93, take 2nd Street East to Woodland Park Drive. This park is unique in that it has a large number of exotic waterfowl from all over the world. It is a good place to test your waterfowl skills. Wild Canada Geese, Mallards, and Wood Ducks often join the flock; most other species should be considered part of the collection. During migration, scan the Ring-billed Gull flocks here for California Gull and Herring Gull, or rarer species. The exotic species are pinioned to prevent escape into the wild.

Also from 2nd Street East, a drive south on Woodland Avenue to Willowglen leads to a small road to the east called Leisure Lane. Watch for a small sign on the right, opposite the turn. The lane goes for 0.6 mile and crosses a narrow wooden bridge, then turns left to the **Owen Sowerwine Natural Area** or right to a **County Park** (boat access), both located along the banks of the Stillwater River. The Natural Area is not signed; park at the posted signs indicating private land and head left to the river. Both areas feature beautiful, riparian vegetation with slow-flowing water. Species found breeding in these two areas include Wood Duck, Hooded Merganser, Spotted Sandpiper, Vaux's Swift, Belted Kingfisher, Pileated Woodpecker, Willow Flycatcher, Eastern Kingbird, Bank Swallow, Veery, Cedar Waxwing, Warbling Vireo, Red-eyed Vireo, Yellow Warbler, Black-headed Grosbeak, and Song Sparrow.

A drive along the **Lower Valley Road**, which heads east from U.S. 93 at Four Corners and then south to Somers, is another fun birding route. One mile down this road, the **confluence of the Stillwater and Flathead rivers** is an excellent place for ducks and geese in the spring and fall. Bald Eagle, Osprey, and Wild Turkey can usually be found around **Foy's Bend**, and Wood Duck, Hooded Merganser, and various species of songbirds can be found by stopping at the bridge on **Ashley Creek**. **Church Slough** is an excellent waterfowl staging area especially in March and April. Waterfowl by the thousands (including some Tundra Swans) and various species of gulls congregate here, as do Bald Eagle and Osprey. Look for Eurasian Wigeon and Greater Scaup, particularly in March and early April. After Church Slough, head south 0.8 mile on North Somers Road to **Split Pond**. Keep a close watch for Savannah Sparrows and Gray Partridge. Also look for Ruddy Duck, Lesser Scaup, Ring-necked Duck, Common Goldeneye, Yellow-headed Blackbird, Marsh Wren, and occasionally Barrow's Goldeneye. Rarities such as Old Squaw and White-winged Scoter have been found here on occasion during migration (particularly April and November). In summer, Short-eared Owl, Sora, and Virginia Rail can be found at the **Blasdel Waterfowl Production Area** one mile south of Split Pond and near the Grange Hall. In winter, look for Rough-legged Hawks, Red-tailed Hawks, and Northern Shrikes. Hike into the WPA in fall or spring to see a variety of waterfowl and shorebirds. This is also one of the better local spots for migrating Peregrine Falcon (particularly May and October).

Continue south on the North Somers Road, crossing U.S. 2, and enter **Somers** from the north. Watch for Cedar and Bohemian Waxwings in the

Russian olives along this road in the winter. A stop along the slough in Somers is good for ducks and swallows in the spring, shorebirds in the fall, and Black Terns in the summer.

Drive through Somers and turn left (or south) on U.S. 93 to bird **Somers Bay** on Flathead Lake. The bay is a great place to observe migrant waterfowl. Diving ducks, grebes, loons, gulls, and mergansers abound here, and rarities are seen here on occasion. The best time to visit this area is spring, fall, and early winter. Summer is much too busy due to large numbers of boaters that congregate at the paved boat ramp.

To continue birding, head east on **Highway 82**. From Somers to Bigfork, this road offers good viewing for raptors, especially Bald Eagles and Ospreys. At mile marker 4, head south down a dirt road to the **Flathead Lake WPA** on Kalispell Bay. Pygmy Nuthatch can be found in the ponderosa pines to the east. From the parking lot 0.7 mile from U.S. 2, walk out on the dike to see Canada Goose, Tundra Swan, Bald Eagle, and Red-tailed Hawk during fall and spring. The dike trail is closed during the nesting season (March through June) and early winter. Unlike on the Lower Valley Road, a spotting scope is necessary to scan for waterfowl flocks on Flathead Lake.

Immediately west of Sportsman's Bridge on Highway 82, head south on the side road toward the **Flathead River outlet**. Osprey can be easily found here in the summer as can a variety of ducks in winter. Another back road 100 yards east of Sportsman's Bridge leads four miles to Bigfork. Wild Turkey can be found on this road in the vicinity of the **Eagle Bend Golf Course**. **Wayfarers State Recreation Area** just south of Bigfork on Highway 35 is a nice place to camp and birdwatch. Townsend's Solitaire and a variety of other songbirds can be found here; look for diving ducks in Bigfork Bay.

On Highway 206, one mile north of Montford Junction (intersection of highways 35 and 206), a dirt road 0.3 mile to the west leads to **Fairview Marsh**. Cinnamon Teal, Ruddy Duck, Northern Shoveler, Yellow-headed Blackbird, and Marsh Wren can be found here, particularly during wet springs. Continue further on this road, then head south on the Columbia Falls Road. At a dangerous bend in the road, pull completely off the road and look down on the marsh. This is an excellent place to see Wood Duck and Ring-necked Duck. The road then joins with Highway 35 (Old Highway 2). A pullout on the north side of the road allows good views of the **McWenneger Slough**. Look for Red-necked Grebe, Sora, and a variety of songbirds.

Helpful Information:
Elevation: Kalispell, 3,084 ft; Flathead Lake, 2,893 ft.
Habitat(s): Riparian, lake, pond, river, marsh, cultivated fields.
Best Birding Season(s): Spring, summer, fall.
Best Birding Month(s): March-June, September-December.
Montana Highway Map Location: 2-B.
Hazards: Poison ivy (Lawrence Park), mosquitoes, black flies.
Nearest Food, Gas, Lodging: Kalispell, Whitefish, Columbia Falls, Bigfork.
Camping: Wayfarers, Ashley Lake, Echo Lake, and others.

Land Ownership: city, state, federal, private.

Additional Information: Flathead Audubon Society, P.O. Box 715, Bigfork, MT 59911.

Recommended Length of Stay: 1 to 2 days (in addition to a trip to Glacier!).

12 SWAN RIVER NWR/SWAN LAKE

General Information: *The place names of Swan Lake and Swan River have two possible origins. One story says the features are named after Emmett Swan, an early resident of the valley. Another plausible explanation is the report, by E.S. Camecon, of nesting Trumpeter Swans on Swan Lake in 1881. Tundra Swans have traditionally migrated through this area during spring and fall migration. Whatever the explanation, Swan River, Swan Lake, Swan Valley, and the Swan Mountains are beautiful nonetheless.*

Birding Information: This 1,568-acre refuge is nestled in the picturesque Swan Valley between the Swan Range to the east and the Mission Range to the west. To reach the refuge, drive thirty-eight miles southeast from Kalispell on Highway 83 to the south end of Swan Lake. Drive through the hamlet of Swan Lake and watch for Bog Road, the main refuge access, on the right. The interior of the refuge is closed from March 1 to July 1 to protect nesting birds, and birding is somewhat unpleasant in the fall during hunting season.

Access to this small refuge is very limited, but in July a walk down **Bog Road** can offer productive birding. A canoe trip through the refuge on the **Swan River** provides excellent birding opportunities spring through fall. The canoe route is open to the public throughout the summer. Put-in at the Swan River bridge on Porcupine Road about two miles south of Bog Road on Highway 83. The take-out point is the boat ramp at the town of Swan Lake.

Species likely to be encountered in the summer include Common Loon, Red-necked Grebe, Horned Grebe, Great Blue Heron, American Bittern, Wood Duck, Ruddy Duck, Bald Eagle, Black Tern, Vaux's Swift, Calliope Hummingbird, Willow Flycatcher, Marsh Wren, Varied Thrush, Red-eyed Vireo, Warbling Vireo, Savannah Sparrow, and Song Sparrow. In the spring and fall this is a good place to observe Tundra Swan. The larger expanse of Swan Lake has a similar complement of birds. Two areas worth birding include the boat ramp at Swan Lake and the access site to Loon Lake near the northwest end of Swan Lake (see map).

Helpful Information:

Elevation: Swan Lake, 3,066 ft.

Habitat(s): Riparian, wetland, lake.

Best Birding Season: Late spring, summer.

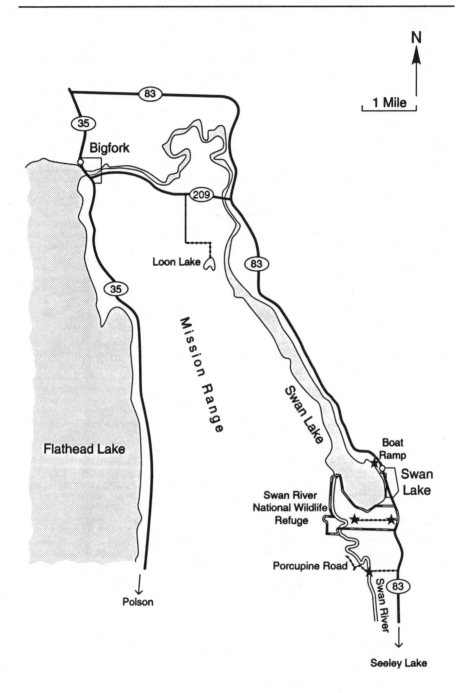

N

1 Mile

83

35

Bigfork

209

Loon Lake

83

35

Mission Range

Swan Lake

Flathead Lake

Boat
Ramp

Swan
Lake

Swan River
National Wildlife
Refuge

Porcupine Road

83

Swan River

Polson

Seeley Lake

Swan Lake.

Best Birding Month(s): May, June, July.
Montana Highway Map Location: 3-C.
Hazards: Mosquitoes, black flies.
Nearest Food, Gas, Lodging: Swan Lake.
Camping: Swan Lake, Cedar Creek.
Land Ownership: Swan River NWR (USFWS); Swan Lake (private, state, USFS).
Additional Information: Northwest Montana Wetlands, 280 Creston Hatchery Road, Kalispell, MT 59901 ph: (406) 755-4375.
Recommended Length of Stay: 2 to 4 hours.

GLACIER NATIONAL PARK

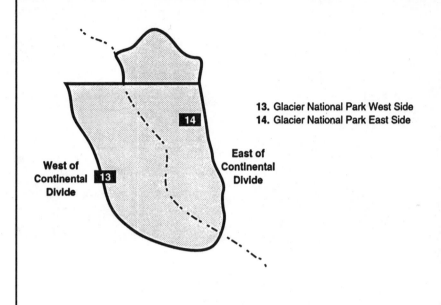

13. Glacier National Park West Side
14. Glacier National Park East Side

14

13

West of Continental Divide

East of Continental Divide

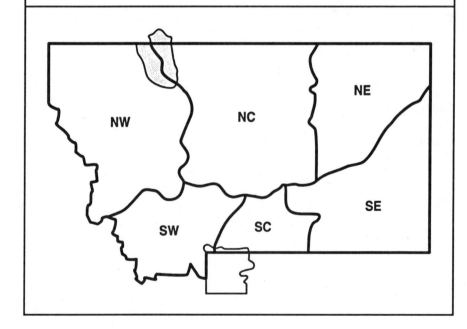

GLACIER NATIONAL PARK

Straddling the Continental Divide from the Canadian border south to Marias Pass is the most picturesque landscape in Montana, Glacier National Park. As the name implies, this land was formed by ancient glaciers, and many glaciers are still present here today. Fifty to sixty sizeable glaciers and many smaller glaciers are found close to the crest of the Continental Divide, usually on north-facing slopes. Glacier is known as the "Switzerland of the United States" due to the magnificent glaciers and jagged, lofty peaks. The architecture of the buildings in the park is a mixture of western atmosphere and swiss style.

In July 1806, explorer Meriwether Lewis and his party camped twelve miles northeast of Browning, coming within twenty miles of what is today Glacier National Park. Their exploration of the Marias River to its source in the mountains was cut short due to inclement weather, inadequate food, and possible confrontation with the much feared Blackfeet Indians. In 1815, Hugh Monroe, a Hudson's Bay fur trapper known to the Blackfeet Indians as "Rising Wolf," saw the Glacier country and stayed to explore it in detail. In 1846, Monroe guided Father DeSmet to two mountain lakes on the edge of the prairie which DeSmet named St. Mary. The "gap through the mountains" so often talked about by the Indians—Marias Pass—was first reconnoitered by Major Baldwin in 1889. Dr. Sperry, a geologist, explored the inner reaches of the park, including Avalanche Lake and a glacier that bears his name. It was Dr. Sperry who convinced the Great Northern Railroad to take advantage of the lucrative tourist potential, which eventually led to the construction of rail lines, hotels, and chalets in the area. George Bird Grinnell, a well-rounded naturalist, explorer, and early conservationist, and John Willard Schmitz (a long-time friend of the Blackfeet) advocated the establishment of this area as a national park. In 1910, their wish came true. Waterton Lakes National Park in Canada borders Glacier to the North. In 1932, the Canadian and U.S. governments established the first international peace park. Waterton/Glacier International Peace Park symbolizes the bonds of goodwill, friendship, and peace between the people of both countries.

For birding purposes, Glacier National Park should be considered as two distinct areas: the west side and the east side, separated by the Continental Divide. This natural barrier running from north to south neatly bisects Glacier into two nearly equal halves. The birdlife found on either side of the divide can be quite different because the weather, vegetation, and adjoining habitats are so different.

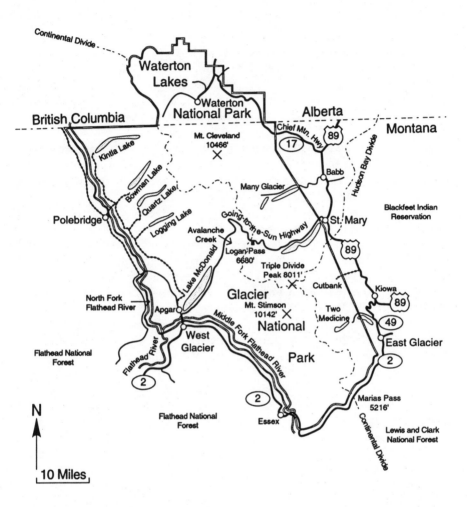

13 GLACIER NATIONAL PARK—WEST SIDE

General Information: *The west side of Glacier is typically forested, gradually sloping terrain with an elevation gain of 7,032 feet from the lowest point (at 3,110 feet) to the highest point (10,142-foot Mount Stimson). Since the base elevation is considerably lower on the west side, and is situated in a mountain valley where temperature inversions do occur, birds have been known to arrive at lower elevations two to three weeks earlier in the spring than on the east side. The west side is also slightly warmer, with mild winds, and has a moist, humid climate reminiscent of Pacific Coast rainforests. Characteristic vegetation here includes lodgepole pine, Engelmann spruce, western white pine, western larch, western red cedar, grand fir, black cottonwood, western hemlock, pacific yew, Douglas fir, subalpine fir, whitebark pine and an incredible variety of deciduous shrubs. Only half as many active glaciers are found on the west side of the Continental Divide.*

Birding Information: Beginning in the hamlet of West Glacier on U.S. Highway 2, follow the park entrance road west. Drive about 200 yards past the West Entrance Station and turn left on the side road, past the Horse Corrals, to the **Quarter Circle Bridge**, about a mile from the entrance road. This is one of the lowest elevations in the park to watch birds. The forest here holds a variety of deciduous trees and shrubs such as cottonwood, alder, and willow, and a beautiful riparian zone borders McDonald Creek. Hillsides across the creek are blanketed by a mix of deciduous and coniferous trees. Species likely to be encountered include Spotted Sandpiper, Willow Flycatcher, Violet-green Swallow, Cedar Waxwing, Warbling Vireo, Red-eyed Vireo, Yellow Warbler, American Redstart, Northern Waterthrush, Wilson's Warbler, Western Tanager, Black-headed Grosbeak, Song Sparrow, Brown-headed Cowbird, and Pine Siskin.

Drive back to the main road and go left for less than a mile to Apgar Junction. Turn right and go one mile to the Apgar Village road on the left. Stop at the picnic area on **Lake McDonald** immediately on the right. Footpaths lead to the pebble beach for outstanding views of the lake and not-so-distant high peaks. Common Loons pause at this lake during fall migration; also watch for Common Merganser and other waterfowl. Continue west on the Apgar road to the campground entrance and **Apgar Village**. The birds found here range from Warbling and Red-eyed Vireo to Western Tanager.

From Apgar Village, go west and turn right onto the **Camas Creek Road**. Several stops along this road offer worthwhile birding; don't pass up the McDonald Creek Bridge (a five minute stroll from the Apgar Ranger Station), Fish Creek, McGee Meadow, and the Forest Fire Exhibit. Watch for Red-tailed Hawk, Red-naped Sapsucker, Golden-crowned Kinglet, Swainson's Thrush, Varied Thrush, Solitary Vireo, Northern Waterthrush, MacGillivray's Warbler, Common Yellowthroat, Black-headed Grosbeak, Chipping Sparrow, Song Sparrow, Red Crossbill, and sometimes even White-winged Crossbill.

About seven miles from Apgar, stop at **McGee Meadow Overlook**, well-marked with an interpretive sign. Try searching and listening for the elusive LeConte's Sparrow here. McGee is a wet meadow, and tramping out into the bog is disruptive for both birds and vegetation. Be prepared to spend a lot of time at the McGee pull-out if you are determined to see or hear LeConte's Sparrow. June seems to be the best month to bird here. Other species to watch and listen for at McGee include Mallard, Sora, Common Snipe, Tree Swallow, Swainson's Thrush, Varied Thrush, Warbling Vireo, Northern Waterthrush, Chipping Sparrow, Lincoln's Sparrow, and Red-winged Blackbird.

Other good birding stops on the Camas Creek Road are **Huckleberry Mountain Trailhead** and the **Wildlife Exhibit**, both marked by signs. Also try **Edge of Meadow**, about 1.5 miles north of the Huckleberry Mountain trailhead. Besides those species mentioned above, watch for Dark-eyed Junco, American Robin, Common Yellowthroat, and Yellow-rumped Warbler here. The road leaves Glacier at the **North Fork Bridge**, about eleven miles northwest of Apgar. Look just east of the bridge, around the clumps of spruce, for Townsend's Warbler, Steller's Jay, and Pine Siskin. Cliff Swallow and Spotted Sandpiper may be seen from the bridge.

Back near Apgar, about 300 yards north of the McDonald Creek Bridge, the road to **Fish Creek Campground** drops down toward the west shore of Lake McDonald. Between the Camas Creek Road and the campground, look for Chestnut-backed Chickadee. Birding can be good at the picnic area, amphitheater, and campground. Species likely to be encountered include Vaux's Swift, Pileated Woodpecker, Northern Flicker, Barn Swallow, Common Raven, Red-breasted Nuthatch, Swainson's Thrush, Solitary Vireo, Warbling Vireo, Orange-crowned Warbler, Townsend's Warbler, Western Tanager, and Fox Sparrow. The adventurous birder can continue beyond Fish Creek on the rough, gravel **Inner North Fork Road**. Again, the wet meadows (five and seven miles up this road) are productive for Le Conte's Sparrow. This road continues to Polebridge (thirty miles from Apgar) and up the North Fork of the Flathead. Average driving speed is twenty mph on this rutted, winding road, so set aside a lot of time if you plan to travel this section of Glacier National Park.

The **Going-to-the-Sun Road** heads east from Apgar Junction along the shore of Lake McDonald, eventually climbing to Logan Pass on the Continental Divide. The Park Service is following a long-term plan to improve and maintain this road, so expect construction delays on some sections. The route over the pass itself is winding and narrow, much of it walled in by a rock cliff on one side and a sheer drop on the other. Vehicles longer than thirty feet are not permitted on the road between Avalanche Creek (on the west side) and Sun point (on the east side) from July 1 to August 31. During the rest of the year, vehicles are limited to a maximum length of thirty-five feet. No vehicle may exceed eight feet in width, including side mirrors. Trailers can be parked temporarily at Sun Point or in one of the west-side campgrounds. The Going-to-the-Sun Road is closed in winter, usually from mid-November until May.

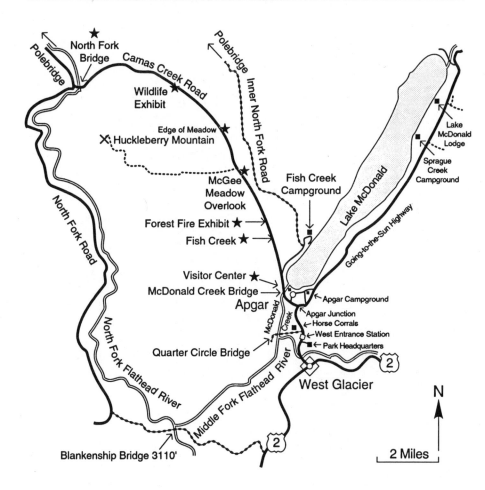

As the road winds along the east shore of Lake McDonald, watch for pullouts and take every opportunity to scan the water's edge for Common Merganser and Spotted Sandpiper. Stop at the **Sprague Creek Campground and Picnic Area** about eight miles from Apgar, which at times can be productive for Barred Owl, Tree Swallow, Violet-green Swallow, Barn Swallow, Swainson's Thrush, American Robin, Varied Thrush, Solitary Vireo, Warbling Vireo, American Redstart, Northern Waterthrush, MacGillivray's Warbler, Chipping Sparrow, Song Sparrow, Red Crossbill, and Pine Siskin. Look for these same birds at **Lake McDonald Lodge** one mile up the lake and on the hiking trails across the road. An occasional Bald Eagle is seen from the lodge's dock on the lake.

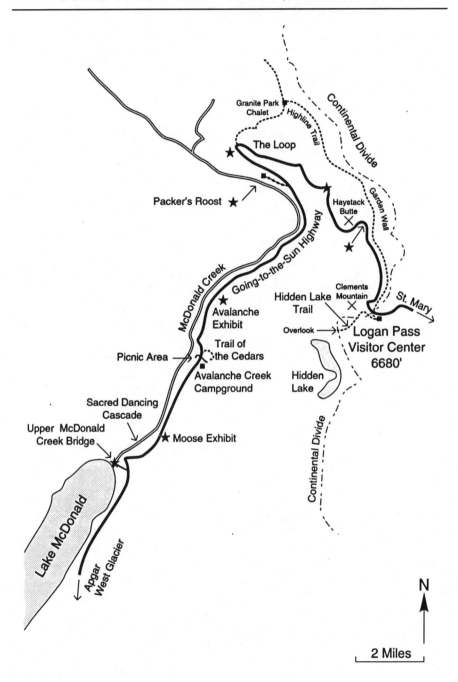

One and a half miles north of Lake McDonald Lodge, turn left and go one-quarter mile to the **Upper McDonald Creek Bridge**. This spot can be good for American Dipper, Vaux's Swift, Belted Kingfisher, and Common Merganser. In May and June, look along McDonald Creek for Harlequin Duck. American Dipper can also be found at Sacred Dancing Cascade. Pull off the road at the **Moose Country Exhibit** to watch for MacGillivray's Warbler, Townsend's Warbler, and Red-breasted Nuthatch.

Five miles north of Lake McDonald Lodge, the **Avalanche Creek Picnic Area** is good for Harlequin Duck, Spotted Sandpiper, Great Horned Owl, Black Swift, Calliope Hummingbird and at times Broad-tailed Hummingbird, Northern Rough-winged Swallow, Common Raven, and Swainson's Thrush. Other species likely to be encountered include Chestnut-backed Chickadee, Red-breasted Nuthatch, Brown Creeper, Winter Wren, Golden-crowned Kinglet, Swainson's Thrush, American Robin, Varied Thrush, Townsend's Warbler, MacGillivray's Warbler, and Pine Siskin. Across from the picnic area on the east side of the road, the **Trail of the Cedars** is well worth the hike. This half-mile, handicap-accessible boardwalk leads to a footbridge over Avalanche Creek and loops back through the campground to the parking lot. Varied Thrush are most apparent here, and Golden-crowned Kinglet, Brown Creeper, American Dipper, and Winter Wren are slightly more difficult to find.

Stops at the **Avalanche Exhibit**, **Packer's Roost**, and the road's first big switchback known as **The Loop** are also pleasant places to bird. From The Loop, the road winds its way along the impressive Garden Wall, climbing hard to Logan Pass at a slant that reveals how the Going-to-the-Sun Road received its name. Look for Blue Grouse and Steller's Jay along this section of road. Major pullouts on either side of Haystack Butte are good spots to look for Golden Eagle, Common Raven, and, of course, mountain goats.

The summit of 6,680-foot **Logan Pass** is at timberline atop the Continental Divide, surrounded by absolutely spectacular scenery. Here are jagged peaks, snow, ice, sky, waterfalls, wildflowers, and tenacious alpine shrubs shaped by the wind. A stop at the Logan Pass Visitor Center is a must, even just to smell the fresh air. The pass is also a good place to look for migrant birds in the fall. From the parking lot, watch for Golden Eagle, Common Raven, Fox Sparrow, and White-crowned Sparrow.

If you have time, there are two hikes from Logan Pass that are fun to bird. The 1.5-mile boardwalk and footpath to the **Hidden Lake Overlook** heads southwest from the visitor center. Rolling through fields of alpine wildflowers, this trail is the best place in Montana to see American Pipit, Rosy Finch (Gray-crowned Race), and White-tailed Ptarmigan. The alpine plants here are very sensitive to trampling—please stay on the boardwalk. If birds are around, hikers can see them right from the boardwalk.

The **Highline Trail** leads north from the parking lot at Logan Pass, contouring at a fairly constant elevation along the Garden Wall to Granite Park Chalet. Birders can get a taste of the trail by hiking a mile or two and retracing their steps back to Logan Pass. Heartier souls can hike 7.6 miles to Granite Park

Chalet and then another four miles to trail's end at The Loop. Either leave a car at The Loop on the way up to Logan Pass, or arrange for a shuttle. Blue Grouse, Common Raven, Steller's Jay, Fox Sparrow, and Golden Eagle are seen on this trail, as are mountain goats and the occasional grizzly bear.

Helpful Information:
Elevation: 3,110 ft - 10,142 ft.
Habitat(s): Lake, riparian, mixed deciduous-coniferous, coniferous, alpine.
Best Birding Season(s): Late spring-summer.
Best Birding Month(s): June and July.
Montana Highway Map Location: 2-A, 2-B.
Hazards: Mosquitoes, grizzly bears.
Nearest Food, Gas, Lodging: West Glacier, Apgar, Lake McDonald Lodge.
Camping: Apgar, Fish Creek, Sprague Creek, Avalanche Creek.
Land Ownership: NPS.
Additional Information: Glacier National Park, West Glacier, MT 59936 ph: (406) 888-5441.
Recommended Length of Stay: 1 to 2 days.

14 GLACIER NATIONAL PARK—EAST SIDE

General Information: *The east side of the park features less forested, more abrupt terrain, with an elevation gain of 5,925 feet from the lowest point (4,541 ft) to the highest point (10,466-foot Mount Cleveland). Here the jagged mountains come in close contact with the rolling prairie. Fingers of the prairie actually reach the park in major river drainages bordering the Blackfeet Reservation. Since the base elevation is considerably higher on the east side and somewhat cooler, birds have been known to arrive here in the spring two to three weeks later than on the west side. The east side is typically cooler with extremely strong winds and a semi-arid climate. Characteristic vegetation found here includes subalpine fir, whitebark pine, Douglas fir, lodgepole pine, limber pine, Engelmann spruce, aspen, and black cottonwood. Twice as many active glaciers are found on this side of the park.*

Birding Information: From Logan Pass, follow Going-to-the-Sun Road down and eastward, through the Tunnel to **Siyeh Bend**. This is a good area to look for Golden Eagle, Blue Grouse, and White-crowned Sparrow, as well as grizzly bears and mountain goats. At the **Jackson Glacier Overlook**, watch for Townsend's Warbler, MacGillivray's Warbler, and Hermit Thrush. **Sunrift Gorge** and the 0.3-mile hike to Baring Falls are excellent places for American Dipper, Ruby-crowned Kinglet, Gray Jay, and MacGillivray's Warbler. The **Sun Point Picnic Area** above St. Mary Lake is a good place to take a break and view Western Tanager and Ruby-crowned Kinglet. At the

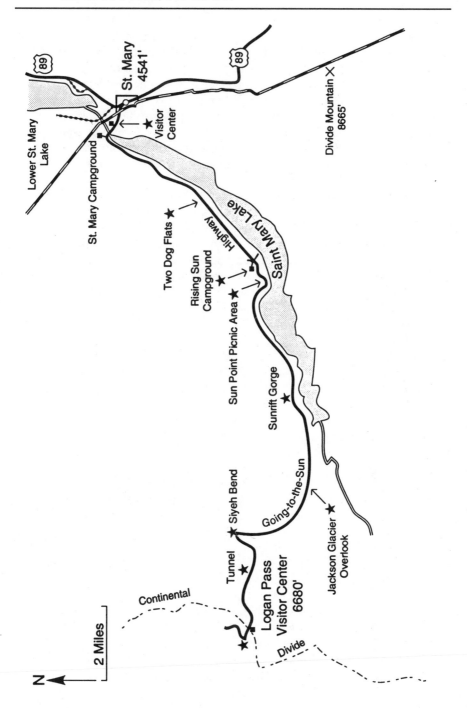

Rising Sun campground and boat launch, look for Clark's Nutcracker, Red-tailed Hawk, and Osprey. **Two Dog Flats** is a grassland bordered by aspen and Douglas fir, and frequented by Red-tailed Hawk, Prairie Falcon, Ruffed Grouse, American Crow, Black-capped Chickadee, Yellow Warbler, Lazuli Bunting, Chipping Sparrow, Vesper Sparrow, Savannah Sparrow, and Western Meadowlark. Keep an eye open for Common Loon as the road passes close to the shore of **St. Mary Lake** en route to the town of St. Mary.

The town of St. Mary is on the Blackfeet Indian Reservation. Turn north out of St. Mary and drive seven miles on U.S. 89 toward Babb to the north end of **Lower St. Mary Lake**. Watch for a pull-out on the west side of the road with excellent views of the lake. This is always a good place to view American White Pelican, Double-crested Cormorant, Canada Goose, Common Merganser, Belted Kingfisher, Yellow Warbler, California Gull, and an assortment of waterfowl. **Duck Lake**, four miles to the east, has a similar array of birdlife.

Nine miles north of St. Mary, turn west at Babb and drive to **Many Glacier**. Just 0.8 mile from Babb there is a beaver pond on the north side of the road. Look for Bufflehead, Red-naped Sapsucker, Western Wood-Pewee, Tree Swallow, House Wren, Northern Waterthrush, Wilson's Warbler, Western Tanager, and Red-winged Blackbird. The boundary of the park, the Many Glacier Entrance Station, and along the shores of Lake Sherburne are places to see Sharp-shinned Hawk, Cooper's Hawk, Swainson's Hawk, Red-tailed Hawk, Ruffed Grouse, Red-naped Sapsucker, Western Wood-Pewee, House Wren, Yellow Warbler, MacGillivray's Warbler, Common Yellowthroat, and Lazuli Bunting.

Around the Many Glacier area, species to watch for include Barrow's Goldeneye, Common Merganser, American Crow, American Dipper, and Calliope Hummingbird. Sometimes Boreal Chickadee, White-winged Crossbill, Red Crossbill, and Pine Grosbeak are sighted on the **Iceberg Lake Trail**. To find the trailhead, drive west from the Many Glacier Hotel one mile to the Swiftcurrent Motor Lodge and park at the end of the road. A short connecting trail leads to the Iceberg-Ptarmigan trailhead sign just north of the lodge. It's a 4.5-mile hike to Iceberg Lake, with a gain in elevation of nearly 1,200 feet. Brewer's Sparrows have been found on the lower end of this trail.

Returning to the Blackfeet Indian Reservation, head north out of Babb on U.S. 89 five miles to the Chief Mountain Turnoff. Birders looking for Savannah Sparrow and Black Tern should continue straight ahead on U.S. 89 for four miles toward the border town of **Piegan**. Otherwise, turn northwest onto Highway 17 at the Chief Mountain Turnoff and enjoy the scenic drive toward Waterton Lakes National Park in Canada. This beautiful stretch of highway takes its name from the lone obelisk of a mountain that dominates the view west of the road.

Views from the **Chief Mountain Highway** are impressive in all directions. Stop at the **Crusher Hill Overlook**, five miles from U.S. 89, for an excellent panorama of the mountains and the prairies of Montana and Alberta. The Chief Mountain Highway also has the most extensive views of aspen stands in all of Montana. Birding stops at beaver ponds along the way,

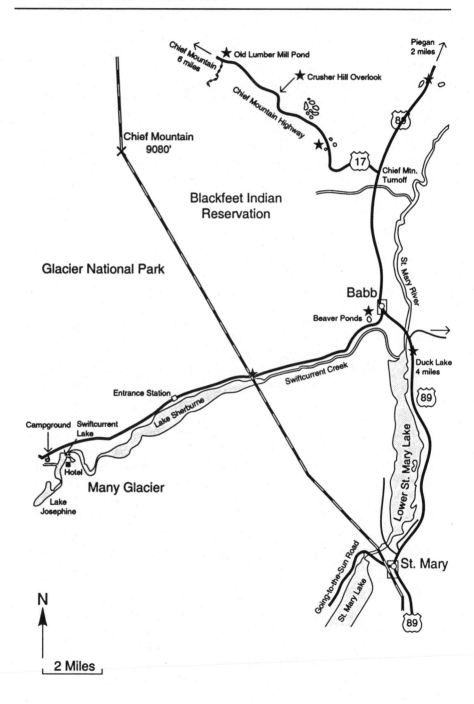

especially the **Old Lumber Mill Pond** eight miles from U.S. 89, can be very productive. Look for Canada Goose, Bufflehead, Least Flycatcher, House Wren, Cedar Waxwing, Orange-crowned Warbler, Northern Waterthrush, Wilson's Warbler, White-crowned Sparrow, Pine Siskin, Veery, Yellow Warbler, and Marsh Wren. The Chief Mountain border crossing is open only from mid-May through mid-September. Inquire in St. Mary, Babb, or Piegan for the specific hours that the Chief Mountain border crossing is open. For the energetic birder, a hike from the Chief Mountain Customs Station in Glacier National Park into the **Belly River** country can be rewarding. Spruce Grouse, Steller's Jay, Boreal Chickadee, Chestnut-backed Chickadee, Brown Creeper, Winter Wren, Golden-crowned Kinglet, Bohemian Waxwing, Townsend's Warbler, Pine Grosbeak, Red Crossbill, and White-winged Crossbill are species that can be encountered on this trail.

The Belly River, St. Mary, and Swiftcurrent drainages are unique in that they are the only areas in Montana that drain into Hudson Bay. Triple Divide Peak (8,011 ft), astride the Continental Divide south of St. Mary Lake, is a one-of-a-kind place. Water melting from this summit drains into the Pacific Ocean, the Atlantic Ocean, and Hudson Bay. The Hudson Bay Divide, several miles south of St. Mary, is the dividing line between Hudson Bay to the northeast and the Atlantic Ocean to the east. A variety of birds can be found in this Hudson Bay basin.

Heading south on U.S. 89 through the Blackfeet Indian Reservation from **St. Mary to Kiowa Junction**, the road passes through a variety of habitats including spruce-fir, lodgepole, Douglas-fir, limber pine, aspen, willow, and a series of beaver ponds. Stops at the Hudson Bay Divide, a series of unnamed beaver ponds, Cutbank Creek, and the South Fork of the Milk River can be good for Mountain Chickadee, Ruby-crowned Kinglet, Veery, Northern Waterthrush, Common Yellowthroat, Lazuli Bunting, Lincoln's Sparrow, and American Goldfinch.

On Highway 49, from Kiowa to East Glacier, a stop at **Two Medicine Ridge** is usually good for raptors and a stretch. Head into Glacier Park on the **Two Medicine Road** to see Common Loon, Common Merganser, Ruffed Grouse, Belted Kingfisher, Warbling Vireo, Orange-crowned Warbler, MacGillivray's Warbler, Lazuli Bunting, and Chipping Sparrow. A 0.3-mile hike to **Running Eagle Falls** will usually yield American Dipper, Spotted Sandpiper, Golden-crowned Kinglet, and Ruby-crowned Kinglet, plus a view of the gorgeous falls. At **Two Medicine Lake**, the campground is an excellent area for finding Steller's Jay, Yellow-rumped Warbler, MacGillivray's Warbler, Fox Sparrow, White-crowned Sparrow, Pine Grosbeak, and Red Crossbill. Harlequin Ducks are sometimes found on **Pray Lake**, just below the outlet of Two Medicine Lake, in May-early June. Rufous and Calliope Hummingbirds are often seen near the camp store. A half-mile hike out to **Paradise Point** along the south shore of Two Medicine Lake will sometimes yield Three-toed Woodpecker. The boat tour across Two Medicine Lake can be good for Pileated Woodpecker and Varied Thrush.

In East Glacier, look for the elusive Blue Jay especially on the north side

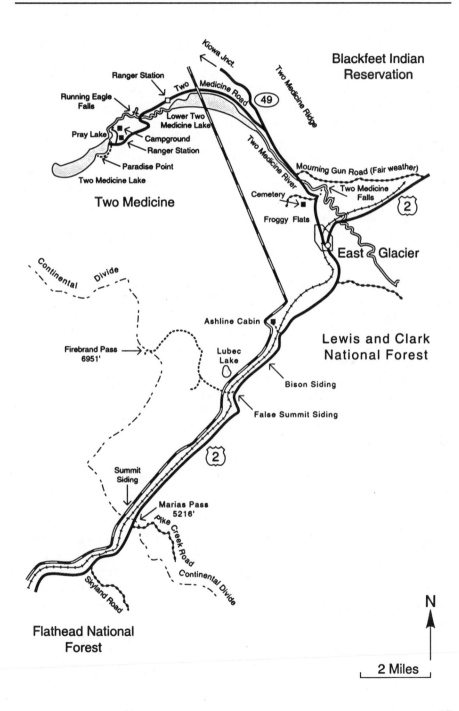

Kiowa Jnct.

Blackfeet Indian Reservation

Ranger Station

Two Medicine Ridge

Running Eagle Falls

Two Medicine Road

49

Lower Two Medicine Lake

Pray Lake

Campground

Ranger Station

Two Medicine River

Mourning Gun Road (Fair weather)

Paradise Point

Two Medicine Lake

Cemetery

Two Medicine Falls

2

Two Medicine

Froggy Flats

East Glacier

Continental Divide

Ashline Cabin

Lewis and Clark National Forest

Firebrand Pass 6951'

Lubec Lake

Bison Siding

False Summit Siding

2

Summit Siding

Marias Pass 5216'

Pike Creek Road

Continental Divide

Skyland Road

Flathead National Forest

N

2 Miles

of the railroad tracks. Calliope Hummingbird and Rufous Hummingbird are regulars at the Restaurant Thimbleberry and East Glacier Hotel, attracted there by the many flowers and feeders. One mile north of town on Highway 49 the birding can be good at **Froggy Flats**, a wet meadow on either side of the road. Pull well off the highway; traffic can be dangerous and hectic at times. Look for Sora, Northern Waterthrush, Common Yellowthroat, Savannah Sparrow, and Lincoln's Sparrow on **Froggy Flats** in the summer. A quarter mile farther north on Highway 49, a 0.3-mile hike leads east to **Two Medicine Falls** and good birding for American Dipper, Veery, and Western Tanager. The cemetery road, which heads west from Highway 49 across from the Two Medicine Falls trailhead, offers fair birding if you have the time.

Follow U.S. 2 from East Glacier to 5,216-foot **Marias Pass**, the lowest crossing of the Continental Divide in Montana. The name "Marias" was first mentioned in the diary of Captain Meriwether Lewis in 1805, and refers to his cousin Maria Wood. Native Americans called this pass Backbone Pass. Salish and Kootenai Indians used to cross here en route to the plains to hunt bison. Marias Pass still serves as an important route through the mountains, but be sure to stop at a few of the decent birding areas along the way. Across the railroad tracks about one mile west of the boundary of Glacier National Park, the small abandoned **Ashline Cabin** is visited by American Redstart, Veery, and Northern Waterthrush.

At mile marker 203 on U.S. 2, **Lubec Lake** and **Firebrand Pass Trail** offer good birding within the park. This is not an easy area to approach; be especially careful when crossing the railroad tracks as trains move through here quite often. Lubec Lake is a nice place for finding Willow Flycatcher, Wood Duck, Blue-winged Teal, and Red-necked Grebe. The five-mile Lubec Trail to Firebrand Pass is good for those that like to combine exercise with birding. Species likely to be encountered on this hike include the occasional Short-eared Owl, Rufous Hummingbird, Willow Flycatcher, Veery, Orange-crowned Warbler, Wilson's Warbler, Brewer's Sparrow, Fox Sparrow, Song Sparrow, and Lincoln's Sparrow. Spruce Grouse are occasionally seen in the spruce-fir zone closer to Firebrand Pass.

Spruce Grouse and Great Gray Owl have been reported at the Forest Service campground near the **Summit Siding**. Immediately west of the pass, the **Pike Creek** logging road meanders south of U.S. 2 on Forest Service land. A three-mile drive up this road provides glimpses of Spruce Grouse, Swainson's Thrush, Cedar Waxwing, Warbling Vireo, Townsend's Warbler, Fox Sparrow, Dark-eyed Junco (Montana Oregon Race), Red Crossbill, and even White-winged Crossbill. The **Skyland Road**, another logging road two miles west of Marias Pass, can be productive for Pine Grosbeak and Red Crossbill, as well as the occasional Spruce Grouse, White-winged Crossbill, and Northern Pygmy-Owl.

Helpful Information:
Elevation: 4,541 ft - 10,466 ft.
Habitat(s): Lake, riparian, mixed deciduous-coniferous, coniferous, alpine.
Best Birding Season(s): Summer.
Best Birding Month(s): July and August.
Montana Highway Map Location: 3-A, 3-B.
Hazards: Mosquitoes, grizzly bears.
Nearest Food, Gas, Lodging: St. Mary, East Glacier, Many Glacier.
Camping: Rising Sun, St. Mary, Many Glacier, Two Medicine.
Land Ownership: NPS. Additional Information: Glacier National Park, West Glacier, MT 59936 ph: (406) 888-5441. Or Glacier Park, Inc., East Glacier, MT 59434.
Recommended Length of Stay: 1 to 2 days.

NORTHCENTRAL MONTANA

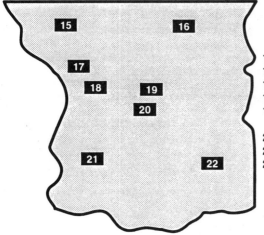

15. Blackfeet Indian Reservation
16. Havre and Vicinity
17. Pine Butte Swamp Preserve
18. Freezout Lake
19. Benton Lake National
    Wildlife Refuge
20. Great Falls and Vicinity
21. Helena and Vicinity
22. Lewistown and Vicinity

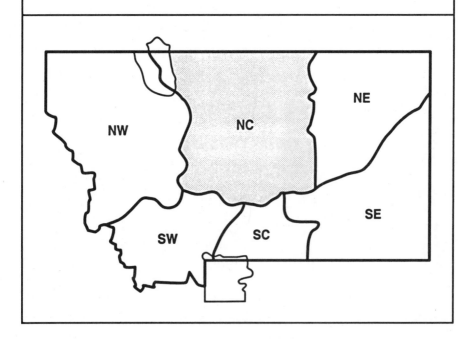

15 BLACKFEET INDIAN RESERVATION

General Information: *The Blackfeet tribe, also known as the "Siksiksa," had a reputation among other tribes and early explorers of being warlike, and therefore were much feared by early white settlers. Tribal legend holds that an old man had a vision and sent his sons on the plains in search of game. They found large numbers of bison, but could not get close enough to kill them. Then the Sun told the old man to rub the feet of the eldest in the village with black medicine. The old man did so and his sons then easily overtook the bison. The old man decreed that his descendants from then on would be called Blackfeet. Another legend suggests the name "Blackfeet" was given to the tribe after they walked across the charred, burned prairies between the Canada and Montana plains.*

In July 1806, Meriwether Lewis camped twelve miles northeast of what is today Browning, Montana. This marked the northernmost point reached by the Lewis and Clark Expedition. A large flock of Passenger Pigeons happened to roost in the cottonwoods around the camp, providing the party with food during their stay. Lewis' band was forced to turn back due to poor weather, shortage of food, and fear of meeting the Blackfeet. After camping here for three days Meriwether Lewis called this area Camp Disappointment.

Blackfeet Indian Reservation.

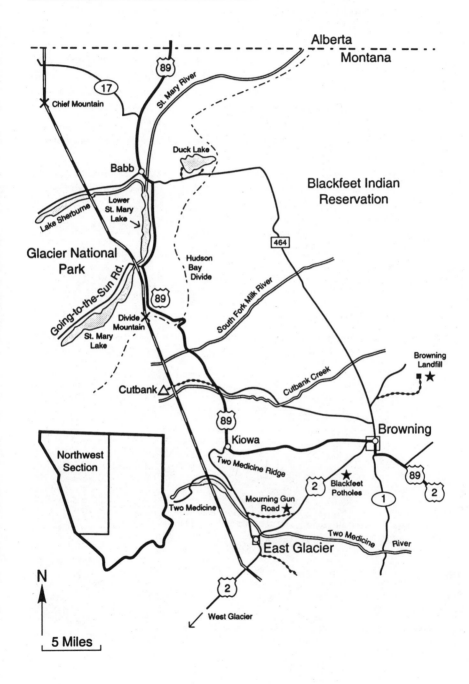

Alberta
Montana

89

17

✗ Chief Mountain

St. Mary River

Duck Lake

Babb

Blackfeet Indian
Reservation

Lower
St. Mary
Lake

Lake Sherburne

464

Glacier National
Park

Hudson
Bay
Divide

Going-to-the-Sun Rd.

89

South Fork Milk River

Divide ✗
Mountain

St. Mary
Lake

Browning
Landfill
■ ★

Cutbank △

Cutbank Creek

89

Browning

Kiowa

Northwest
Section

Two Medicine Ridge

89

2

2

Two Medicine

Mourning Gun
Road ★

Blackfeet
Potholes ★

1

2

Two Medicine
River

East Glacier

N

2

West Glacier

5 Miles

Lou Bruno checking Bluebird boxes on the Blackfeet Indian Reservation.

Birding Information: Contrary to Lewis' sentiments, birding on the Blackfeet Indian Reservation can be a very pleasant experience. However, strong winds are always a factor when birding the east side of the Rocky Mountain Front. The west side of the reservation borders Glacier National Park and Lewis and Clark National Forest. The western third of the reservation is characterized by rolling foothills, mountains, and open parkland

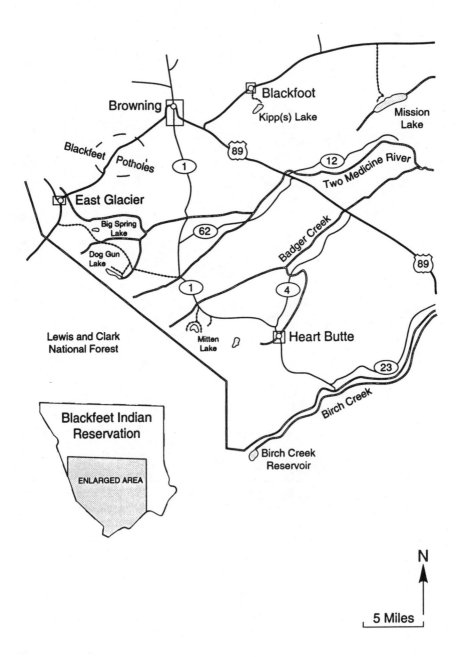

Blackfoot

Browning

Kipp(s) Lake

Mission Lake

Blackfeet Potholes

89

12

Two Medicine River

East Glacier

Big Spring Lake

Dog Gun Lake

62

Badger Creek

1

89

4

Lewis and Clark National Forest

Mitten Lake

Heart Butte

23

Birch Creek

Blackfeet Indian Reservation

ENLARGED AREA

Birch Creek Reservoir

N

5 Miles

Blackfeet Potholes.

similar to the landscape of east side of Glacier National Park. The eastern two-thirds of the reservation are primarily prairie cut by rivers flowing from the mountains. For birding information on the northwest section of the reservation (Chief Mountain Highway, Lower St. Mary Lake, Duck Lake, Hudson Bay Divide, Two Medicine Ridge, and East Glacier) consult the section "Glacier National Park—East Side."

Any birding trip on the Blackfeet Reservation begins in **Browning**. In town look for House Sparrow and Black-billed Magpie. Also stop in at the Museum of the Plains Indian, open from June through September, on the north end of town. North and east of town, the **Browning Landfill** is seldom visited by birders but offers good opportunities for viewing gulls (Ring-billed Gull, California Gull) and corvids (American Crow, Common Raven) besides Horned Lark and Northern Shrike during migration. Along U.S. 2 between Browning and East Glacier, the **Blackfeet Potholes** harbor a diversity and abundance of birds. Species likely to be seen here include Horned Grebe, Eared Grebe, Mallard, Northern Shoveler, American Wigeon, Canvasback, Redhead, Ring-necked Duck, Lesser Scaup, Ruddy Duck, Northern Harrier, Virginia Rail, Sora, American Coot, Common Snipe, Wilson's Phalarope, Black Tern, Barn Swallow, Sprague's Pipit, Western Meadowlark, and Yellow-headed Blackbird.

The **Mourning Gun Road**, just three miles north of East Glacier, also provides good birding, though the road is terrible if it gets wet. Species to watch for on this road include American Kestrel, Upland Sandpiper, Long-billed Curlew, Western Wood-Pewee, Eastern Kingbird, Black-capped Chicka-dee, Mountain Bluebird, Lazuli Bunting, Vesper Sparrow, and Savannah Sparrow.

Just one mile west of East Glacier off of U.S. 2, a gravel road leads to the town of Heart Butte. Along the way, birding at **Big Spring Lake** is good for waterfowl and songbirds. The side road going to **Dog Gun Lake** is very good for Red-necked and Pied-billed Grebes. Continuing on the back road to Heart Butte watch for Ruffed Grouse, Mountain Bluebird, Cedar Waxwing, Warbling Vireo, Black-headed Grosbeak, Vesper Sparrow, and American Goldfinch. At **Mitten Lake**, look for Red-necked Grebe, American White Pelican, American Bittern, Lesser Scaup, Black Tern, Cedar Waxwing, Yellow-headed Blackbird, American Goldfinch, and Rock Wren. Near **Heart Butte** look for Clark's Nutcracker in the limber pine and Eastern Kingbird, Northern Rough-winged Swallow, and Brewer's Blackbird along Birch Creek.

Mission Lake, about twenty miles east of Browning at mile marker 240 on U.S. 2, can be good birding. Access to the lake is not for those who prefer smooth roads. Mission Lake is home to Red-necked Grebe, Western Grebe, American White Pelican, Canada Goose, Lesser Scaup, Long-billed Curlew, California Gull, Northern Harrier, Horned Lark, Sprague's Pipit, Vesper Sparrow, McCown's Longspur, Chestnut-collared Longspur, and Western Meadowlark. The Camp Disappointment monument (mile marker 233) is worth a stop for the history and the view as well as Vesper Sparrow, Western Meadowlark, and Northern Harrier.

Just south of the town of Blackfoot (nine miles east of Browning on U.S. 2) is a birding area called **Kipps Lake**. At mile marker 228 head south on a dirt road for roughly two miles. Clay-colored Sparrow frequent the riparian vegetation. Other species found here include Red-necked Grebe, Eared Grebe, American White Pelican, Double-crested Cormorant, Redhead, Barrow's Goldeneye, Northern Harrier, Willet, Killdeer, Black Tern, and Common Nighthawk. This is also a good place to view migrant shorebirds in July and August.

Helpful Information:
Elevation: 3,500 ft to 9,066 ft.
Habitat(s): Mountains, foothills, grassland, riparian.
Best Birding Season(s): Summer.
Best Birding Month(s): June, July, August.
Montana Highway Map Location: 3-A, 3-B, 4-A, 4-B.
Hazards: Mosquitoes, grizzly bears, fair-weather roads.
Nearest Food, Gas, Lodging: Browning, East Glacier.
Camping: Summit (Marias Pass), Mission Lake, Two Medicine Lake.
Land Ownership: Blackfeet Tribe.
Additional Information: Blackfeet Fish and Game Department, P.O. Box 850, Browning, MT 59417 ph: (406) 338-7207.
Recommended Length of Stay: 1 to 2 days.

16 HAVRE AND VICINITY

General Information: *Havre (pronounced "HAV-er") is a railroad town on the Hi Line of Montana, just north of the Bear Paw Mountains. The city was named after the french hometown of one of the original homesteader's parents. Fort Assiniboine was built here in 1879 to prevent local Indian tribes from fleeing to Canada, which met with limited success. The term Assiniboine is derived after a tribe of Indians whose name equates with "stone boilers." These people reportedly boiled their meat by dropping heated stones in water until the meat was cooked. Southeast of Havre is the Chief Joseph Battlefield where on October 5, 1877, Chief Joseph surrendered to Colonel Miles and spoke the famous words "I will fight no more forever."*

Birding Information: One of the finest birding areas in northern Montana is **Beaver Creek County Park**, ten miles south of Havre on Secondary Road 234 (Beaver Creek Road). A popular recreation area for local residents and visitors alike, this mile-wide park runs for seventeen miles along a lush stream bordering the north slope of the Bear Paw Mountains. Encompassing 10,000 acres, it is one of the largest county parks in the nation, and is an excellent example of how county (and city) parks can accommodate recreational use while protecting wildlife at the same time. This is truly a birder's paradise!

The vegetation in Beaver Creek Park ranges from box elder, dogwood, chokecherry, alder, willow, wild rose, and buffaloberry on the north end to cottonwood, aspen, ponderosa pine, lodgepole pine, and Douglas-fir on the south end. Gray Partridge, Sharp-tailed Grouse, and Ring-necked Pheasant are found here, as are a wide variety of raptors, including Golden Eagle, Prairie Falcon, Red-tailed Hawk, American Kestrel, and Sharp-shinned Hawk, particularly around Rotary Hill. Songbirds to watch and listen for are Gray Catbird, MacGillivray's Warbler, Warbling Vireo, Yellow Warbler, Yellow-breasted Chat, Northern Oriole, Rufous-sided Towhee, Swainson's Thrush, Brown Thrasher, Black-headed Grosbeak, and Western Tanager.

The **Chief Joseph Battlefield** loop road also offers interesting birding. The loop passes through grasslands, stock ponds, rocky buttes, riparian vegetation, and ponderosa pine. The loop starts in Chinook, twenty-one miles east of Havre on U.S. 2. Drive south on Secondary Road 240, which is paved all the way to Cleveland. About twelve miles south of the battlefield, take the dirt road west to Lloyd and head north out of Lloyd past Sayer Butte and the Bowles Oil Field. This dirt road eventually rejoins Road 240 about ten miles south of Chinook. Birds likely to be encountered along the loop include Sprague's Pipit, Baird's Sparrow, Bobolink, Burrowing Owl, McCown's Longspur, Chestnut-collared Longspur, Ferruginous Hawk, and the occasional flock of American White Pelican. A variety of raptors, waterfowl, and

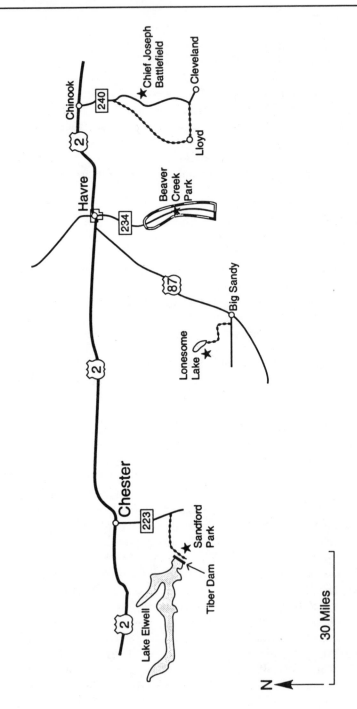

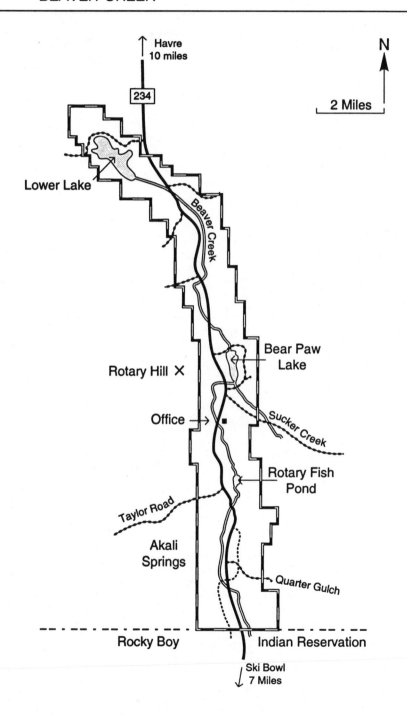

↑ Havre
10 miles

N

234

2 Miles

Lower Lake

Beaver Creek

Bear Paw
Lake

Rotary Hill ✕

Office →

Sucker Creek

Rotary Fish
Pond

Taylor Road

Akali
Springs

Quarter Gulch

Rocky Boy   Indian Reservation

↓ Ski Bowl
7 Miles

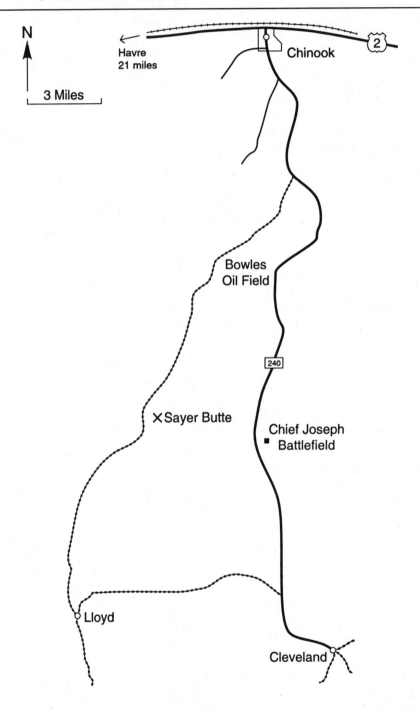

Beaver Creek Park.

shorebirds can be seen along the loop, particularly during migration.

Thirty miles southwest of Havre on U.S. 87, the road to **Lonesome Lake** offers good birding for Upland Sandpiper, Burrowing Owl, Short-eared Owl, Baird's Sparrow, and Grasshopper Sparrow. Inquire at Big Sandy for directions to Lonesome Lake (located eight miles northwest of town).

The **Lake Elwell Recreation Area** behind Tiber Dam lies sixty miles west of Havre on U.S. 2, about fifteen miles southwest of the town of Chester. Take paved road 223 south from Chester and follow the signs to Tiber Dam. Below the dam along the Marias River, Sandford Park offers delightful birding for Osprey, Prairie Falcon, Eastern Screech-Owl, Western Wood-Pewee, Mountain Bluebird, Gray Catbird, Brown Thrasher, Cedar Waxwing, Lazuli Bunting, McCown's Longspur, Chestnut-collared Longspur, and Northern Oriole. American White Pelican and various species of waterfowl frequent the reservoir during the summer, and Common Loon are regular visitors. Snow Goose and Tundra Swan are occasionally seen here during migration. Look for American Tree Sparrow and Bohemian Waxwing in Sandford Park during winter.

Helpful Information:
Elevation: Havre, 2,600 ft.
Habitat(s): Grasslands, sagebrush hills, riparian, lake.
Best Birding Season(s): Spring, summer.
Best Birding Month(s): April through June.

Montana Highway Map Location: 7-B.
Hazards: Mosquitoes, rattlesnakes, fair-weather roads.
Nearest Food, Gas, Lodging: Havre, Chinook, Chester.
Camping: Beaver Creek Park.
Land Ownership: Private, county, state, BLM.
Additional Information: Havre Chamber of Commerce, Box 308, Havre, MT 59501. Beaver Creek Park, Shambo Route, Box 368, Havre, MT 59501.
Recommended Length of Stay: 1 to 2 days.

17 PINE BUTTE SWAMP PRESERVE

General Information: *The 18,000-acre Pine Butte Swamp Preserve is the largest isolated wetland complex abutting the East Front of the Rocky Mountains in Montana. Owned and administered by The Nature Conservancy, the preserve safeguards crucial habitat for grizzly bears that venture out on to the plains. The area also is a haven for a rich array of native plant communities and associated birdlife. Access is limited to protect natural features, but good birding can be had from the roads. Before hiking cross-country on the preserve, please obtain permission from the Preserve Manager. The Nature Conservancy also runs guided birding tours and natural history workshops on the preserve.*

Birding Information: Five miles north of Choteau on U.S. Highway 89, take the **Teton River Road** west for about 17.5 miles. Watch for Red-tailed Hawk, Swainson's Hawk, and American Kestrel along the way. Turn left onto the gravel South Fork Road to enter the preserve.

The road crosses the **Teton River** in less than a half mile, providing a pleasant spot for a break. Park in the small pull-off on the left side of the road just before the bridge and scan the surrounding cottonwoods and limber pine for Black-capped Chickadee and Clark's Nutcracker.

Back on the road, cross the bridge and turn right onto the **South Fork Road** at the next junction (the Cutover road swings off to the left). As the South Fork Road meanders through the limber pine bordering the stream, watch for American Crow, Black-billed Magpie, and Mountain Bluebird. The vegetation changes dramatically from here to the Circle 8 Ranch, growing increasingly rugged with steep mountains slopes, cliffs, and exposed ridges. Species likely to be encountered along the way include Mourning Dove, Common Nighthawk, Western Wood-Pewee, Least Flycatcher, Dusky Flycatcher, Yellow Warbler, Rufous-sided Towhee, Common Grackle, Brown-headed Cowbird, and Northern Oriole.

Near **Circle 8 Ranch**, look for Cooper's Hawk, Northern Goshawk, Ruffed Grouse, Spotted Sandpiper, Rufous Hummingbird, Calliope Hummingbird, Dusky Flycatcher, Barn Swallow, Clark's Nutcracker, Common

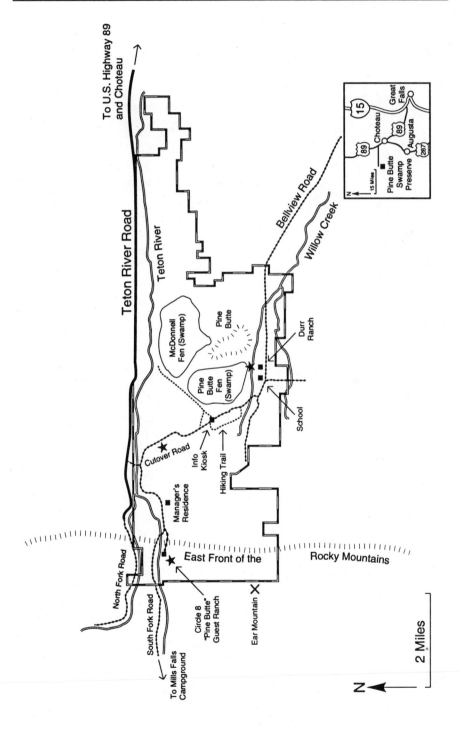

To U.S. Highway 89 and Choteau

Teton River Road

Teton River

Bellview Road

Willow Creek

15

Choteau

Great Falls

89

Augusta

89

287

Pine Butte Swamp Preserve

15 Miles

N

McDonnell Fen (Swamp)

Pine Butte

Pine Butte Fen (Swamp)

Durr Ranch

School

Cutover Road

Info Kiosk

Hiking Trail

Manager's Residence

North Fork Road

East Front of the

Rocky Mountains

Circle 8 "Pine Butte" Guest Ranch

South Fork Road

Ear Mountain

To Mills Falls Campground

2 Miles

N

Pine Butte Swamp Preserve.

Raven, Mountain Chickadee, Ruby-crowned Kinglet, Mountain Bluebird, Veery, Swainson's Thrush, Solitary Vireo, Warbling Vireo, Yellow-rumped Warbler, Ovenbird, MacGillivray's Warbler, Cedar Waxwing, Western Tanager, Lazuli Bunting, White-crowned Sparrow, Pine Siskin, American Goldfinch, and Dark-eyed Junco.

The road enters the Lewis and Clark National Forest just west of the ranch. On the ten-mile drive to the **South Fork trailhead** look for Prairie Falcon, Golden Eagle, Spotted Sandpiper, Belted Kingfisher, Gray Jay, Clark's Nutcracker, Red-breasted Nuthatch, American Dipper, Golden-crowned Kinglet, Ruby-crowned Kinglet, Townsend's Solitaire, Red-eyed Vireo, Ovenbird, Western Tanager, Lazuli Bunting, Chipping Sparrow, Cassin's Finch, Red Crossbill, and the occasional Townsend's Warbler.

Two hiking trails beckon beyond road's end, offering good birding for many of the species listed above. Trail 184 climbs earnestly for 4.5 miles to Our Lake, and Trail 165 follows a rushing mountain stream to 7,743-foot Headquarters Creek Pass and the boundary of the Bob Marshall Wilderness.

Heading back down the South Fork Road to the Cutover/South Fork junction, take the **Cutover Road** southeast toward Pine Butte. Amid limber pine and shortgrass prairie, the road provides spectacular views of Ear Mountain to the southwest and the Rocky Mountain Front to the west. Birds to watch for include Upland Sandpiper, Long-billed Curlew, Horned Lark, Sprague's Pipit, Vesper Sparrow, and Western Meadowlark.

Stop at the information kiosk for wonderful views of Pine Butte and the

Pine Butte Swamp, or hike up the short trail on the ridge west of the kiosk (no prior permission needed) for an even better panorama. Along the trail, watch for Clark's Nutcracker, Rock Wren, Mountain Bluebird, Rufous-sided Towhee, and Savannah Sparrow. Also from the kiosk, birders can hike the road northeast to the edge of the swamp to see Sharp-tailed Grouse, particularly in April. The swamp itself harbors a myriad of birds, including Ruffed Grouse, Sandhill Crane, Common Snipe, Willow Flycatcher, Red-naped Sapsucker, Veery, Warbling Vireo, Yellow Warbler, Northern Water-thrush, MacGillivray's Warbler, Common Yellowthroat, Clay-colored Sparrow, Savannah Sparrow, Song Sparrow, and Lincoln's Sparrow.

Just south of Pine Butte is the old **Durr Ranch** on the Bellview Road. With permission from the Preserve Manager, visitors can hike from the ranch to the top of **Pine Butte**. The view is wonderful, and Blue Grouse can be found here on occasion. From the Durr Ranch, return to Choteau by driving east on the Bellview Road for about twenty-four miles to the junction with U.S. 287, a half mile south of town.

Helpful Information:
Elevation: Ear Mountain, 8,580 ft; Choteau, 3,810 ft.
Habitat(s): Shortgrass prairie, limber pine, wetlands, willow, aspen, cotton-wood, conifers.
Best Birding Season(s): Spring, summer.
Best Birding Month(s): May, June, September.
Montana Highway Map Location: 3-C, 4-C.
Hazards: Bears, mosquitoes.
Nearest Food, Gas, Lodging: Choteau.
Camping: Mills Falls Campground (S. Fk. Teton River).
Land Ownership: The Nature Conservancy, USFS, private.
Additional Information: The Nature Conservancy, Pine Butte Swamp Preserve, Star Route 34B, Choteau, MT 59422 ph: (406) 466-5526.
Recommended Length of Stay: 1 to 2 days.

18 FREEZOUT LAKE

General Information: *Freezout Lake (also known as Greenfields Lake) received its name from a stagecoach station established here in 1885, which was the stopover point between Choteau and the Sun River. Travelers in the winter would spend the nights huddled close to the stove, playing a type of poker called "Freezout" as they tried to stay warm. According to legend, soldiers traveling from Fort Shaw on the Sun River were caught in a blizzard on a flat and called the area Freezout Flat. The original name has remained and could date back as early as the 1870s. Charles M. Russell (Montana's famed cowboy artist) and missionary Brother Van visited the Freezout stagecoach station. Brother Van, an early missionary to the Blackfeet Indians, recalled seeing bison herds drinking water from this alkali lake during his travels through the area. Freezout Lake and Priest Lake are natural sumps where water would accumulate from runoff. The lakes would dry up during drought years, leaving exposed alkali flats. But since the development of the Greenfield Irrigation Project, water has been diverted from mountain drainages leaving water at Freezout year-round.*

Birding Information: Freezout Lake (including Priest Lake) is one of the best birding areas in Montana. The lake is included in a 12,000-acre wildlife management area operated by the Montana Department of Fish, Wildlife and Parks. This large, prairie wetland just north of Fairfield is a key stopover for large numbers of migrant birds that travel along the East Front of the Rocky Mountains. Migratory and breeding waterfowl and gulls are especially numerous here due to the expanse of open water and the proximity to extensive grain fields. To reach Freezout, drive ten miles southeast from Choteau on U.S. 89. The highway bisects the north half of the area and passes the headquarters just east of Freezout Lake.

Spring is by far the best time to visit this wildlife management area, due to the sheer numbers of birds. Weather and timing play a key role when pursuing peak numbers of birds. Freezout Lake typically thaws out in March. Large numbers of birds are attracted to the area once the lake opens. Flocks of Northern Pintail move through early, and the rare Eurasian Wigeon can be found on occasion mixed in with flights of American Wigeon. The rare Trumpeter Swan passes through here, but they often go undetected since they migrate very early. Given ideal conditions, up to one million waterfowl can be found here during peak migration. Ideal conditions could mean that as many as 300,000 Snow Geese and 12,000 Tundra Swans can be seen in one day. Numbers are typically lower than this, but still can be very impressive. A window of time from mid-March through mid-April seems to be best, but peak migration dates vary from year to year depending on the weather. Other species worth noting at various times in the spring are Ross' Goose, Bald Eagle, Northern Harrier, Golden Eagle, Peregrine Falcon, Franklin Gull, Ring-billed Gull, California Gull, Bonaparte's Gull, Short-eared Owl, West-

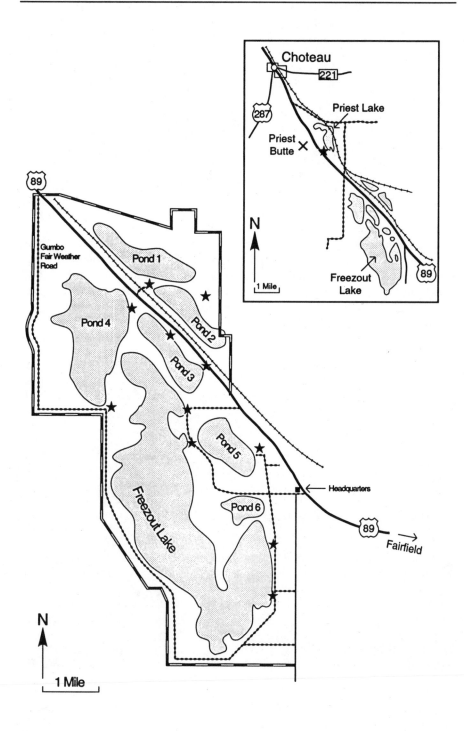

ern Meadowlark, and various species of shorebirds. Spring shorebird numbers peak during May.

Summer can also be an excellent time to bird Freezout. Mosquitoes are horrendous at times, so go prepared. Access is limited in the summer due to nesting birds. Species likely to be encountered during this period include Pied-billed Grebe, Eared Grebe, Western Grebe, Clark's Grebe, American White Pelican, Double-crested Cormorant, Black-crowned Night-Heron, White-faced Ibis, Canada Goose, Green-winged Teal, Blue-winged Teal, Cinnamon Teal, Mallard, Northern Pintail, Northern Shoveler, Gadwall, American Wigeon, Canvasback, Redhead, Lesser Scaup, Ruddy Duck, Northern Harrier, Gray Partridge, Ring-necked Pheasant, Sharp-tailed Grouse, Sora, American Coot, Killdeer, Black-necked Stilt, American Avocet, Willet, Long-billed Curlew, Marbled Godwit, Common Snipe, Wilson's Phalarope, Franklin's Gull, Ring-billed Gull, California Gull, Forster's Tern, Common Tern, Black Tern, Short-eared Owl, Common Nighthawk, Marsh Wren, Vesper Sparrow, Savannah Sparrow, and House Sparrow. In July and August, migrant shorebirds from the arctic start working their way south and pass through Freezout. As the summer progresses and more mudflats become exposed, the shorebird viewing becomes sensational. Black-bellied Plover, Semipalmated Plover, Greater Yellowlegs, Lesser Yellowlegs, Long-billed Dowitcher, and Red-necked Phalarope are other species likely to be encountered, as are Least Sandpiper, Baird's Sandpiper, Semipalmated Sandpiper, Western Sandpiper, Pectoral Sandpiper, Red Knot, Ruddy Turnstone, and

Freezout Lake.

Lesser Golden Plover.

Fall birdwatching at Freezout can be good, but migrant birds are usually more spread out and less approachable, and their movements are dictated by the weather. Also, hunting is allowed here in the fall, and birding may be impractical at times. Tundra Swan numbers can be impressive in late October and early November. Migrant Peregrine Falcon also venture through here in the fall and shorebirds seem to linger also. Once the lake freezes (typically in November), bird numbers are greatly reduced.

Throughout late fall and the entire winter, upland game birds such as Ring-necked Pheasant, Sharp-tailed Grouse, and Gray Partridge are more apparent than during other seasons. Migrant and wintering birds found here include Bald Eagle, Rough-legged Hawk, Golden Eagle, Northern Shrike, and American Tree Sparrow. Great Horned Owl are easier to see this time of year. The rare Gyrfalcon and Snowy Owl can be observed here, but typically show up when Canada is experiencing extremely harsh fall or winter weather conditions.

Helpful Information:
Elevation: Freezout Lake, 3,776 ft.
Habitat(s): Large lake, wetlands, shelterbelts, grasslands, grain fields.
Best Birding Season: Year-round (spring is best).
Best Birding Months: March through November.
Montana Highway Map Location: 4-C.
Hazards: Mosquitoes, gumbo roads, occasional rattlesnakes on west side.
Nearest Food, Gas, Lodging: Fairfield, Choteau.
Camping: Freezout Lake (near Pond 5), Choteau City Park.
Land Ownership: MDFWP.
Additional Information: Freezout Lake Wildlife Management Area, Montana Department of Fish, Wildlife and Parks, P.O. Box 6610, Great Falls, MT 59405 ph: (406) 454-3441 or 467-2646.
Recommended Length of Stay: 2 to 8 hours.

19 BENTON LAKE NATIONAL WILDLIFE REFUGE

General Information: *Benton Lake and Fort Benton were named in honor of Senator Thomas Benton of Missouri. The senator was instrumental in promoting western expansion and development during the late 1800s. In the 1860s, Lt. John Mullan established the first wagon road in the region. The Mullan Road stretched from Fort Benton on the Missouri River in Montana to Walla Walla on the Columbia River in Washington. The Mullan Road once passed through the Benton Lake area.*

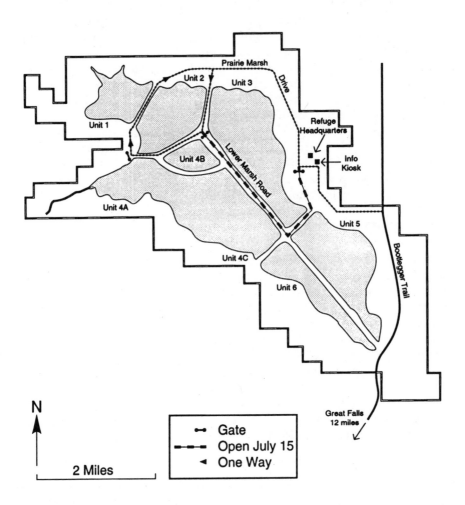

Birding Information: Benton Lake is an amazing wetland surrounded by gentle hills of shortgrass prairie, and acts as a magnet for birdlife. Because the marsh is a natural prairie pothole, water levels are dependent on meltwater from the winter snowpack. During most years, additional water is pumped to this area by way of the Greenfields Irrigation Project. Drought years can have a significant effect on bird populations here.

To reach **Benton Lake NWR** drive twelve miles north from Great Falls on Bootlegger Trail (Highway 225). Turn west onto the refuge entrance road, which leads through a grassland to the headquarters area. Be on the lookout for Horned Lark, Western Meadowlark, and the occasional Burrowing Owl. The first stop should either be at the information kiosk or the refuge headquarters area depending on the day and the hour you visit the refuge.

The shelterbelt area surrounding the **headquarters** compound can be productive for Swainson's Hawk, American Kestrel, Gray Partridge, Ring-necked Pheasant, Sharp-tailed Grouse, House Wren, and Tree Swallow. This little oasis out in the middle of a grassland is a migrant trap for passerines both spring and fall. Refuge personnel live at this compound, so please respect their privacy.

Slightly west of the headquarters and information kiosk is the junction of Lower Marsh Road and Prairie Marsh Drive. The **Lower Marsh Road** is one-way, and is open from July 15 through the end of September. The main reason for closing this road is to protect the high concentrations of nesting waterfowl. If the Lower Marsh Road is open, take a left—south—to eventually reach Prairie Marsh Drive. Lower Marsh Road can be good birding. Species likely to be encountered include Ring-billed Gull, California Gull, Franklin's Gull, and on occasion Black Tern, Common Tern, and Forster's Tern. Canada Goose, White-faced Ibis, Black-crowned Night-Heron, and sometimes American Bittern can be observed from this road. **Management Units 3 and 4C** (see map) are very shallow and are ideal for Northern Pintail, American Wigeon (spring-fall); Tundra Swan, Snow Goose (March-April and October-November); and shorebirds (especially mid July to September). The rare Eurasian Wigeon has been found here periodically, accompanying large flocks of American Wigeon primarily during migration. Fall waterfowl hunting is allowed on sections of Lower Marsh Road, so caution is advised.

If Lower Marsh Road is closed when you visit the refuge, the only choice is to take **Prairie Marsh Drive** to the west from the headquarters/information kiosk area. This road passes through native shortgrass prairie and is open from March 1 through November 30. Species likely to be encountered in this grassland include Upland Sandpiper, Burrowing Owl, Short-eared Owl, Horned Lark, Vesper Sparrow, Savannah Sparrow, Baird's Sparrow, Grasshopper Sparrow, Chestnut-collared Longspur, and Western Meadowlark. Marbled Godwit and Willet also nest in these grasslands, as do numerous species of waterfowl. On the corner, where Prairie Marsh Drive heads west, keep an eye open for Sharp-tailed Grouse (especially around Auto Tour stop 4). The refuge has set up a blind here that can be reserved for viewing or photographing courtship displaying Sharp-tailed Grouse on a dancing ground or lek.

Continuing west on Prairie Marsh Drive, stop at the junction in the road and look along the fenceline to the north for the rare Gyrfalcon, a visitor here from October through March. From this junction head left or south down the one-way road. Management Unit 2 is to the west, and Unit 3 is to the east. The one-way road continues southeast and waterfowl are abundant almost anywhere, including puddle ducks such as Mallard, Northern Pintail, Blue-winged Teal, Northern Shoveler, and Gadwall. Other species likely to be encountered include Northern Harrier, Killdeer, American Avocet, Wilson's Phalarope, Marsh Wren, Common Yellowthroat, Red-winged Blackbird, and Yellow-headed Blackbird. On the edge of the wetlands, pause at the ninety degree corner in the road and look due south to the fenceline. Prairie Falcon and the rare Peregrine Falcon can be observed during migration; the rare Gyrfalcon is found in this same area in winter.

The road continues north from this corner, eventually crossing more wetlands. **Management Unit 1** is to the west, while **Management Unit 2** is to the east, both holding deeper water than the other units. Here birders are more likely to observe Western Grebe and American White Pelican in summer, and Common Loon during migration. Diving ducks such as Lesser Scaup, Redhead, and Ruddy Duck are also found here. The one-way loop of Prairie Marsh Drive is completed at the next junction. Exit the refuge by heading east on Prairie Marsh Drive. Common Goldeneye, Bald Eagle, and on occasion Golden Eagle can be found on the refuge, particularly during spring and fall migration. Although the refuge is open year-round, winter snows usually close refuge roads and access is limited to hiking from the parking lot at headquarters.

Helpful Information:
Elevation: Benton Lake NWR, 3,600 ft.
Habitat(s): Lake, wetlands, shortgrass prairie.
Best Birding Season(s): Spring, summer.
Best Birding Month(s): May, June, September.
Montana Highway Map Location: 5-C.
Hazards: Mosquitoes, fair-weather roads, rattlesnakes.
Nearest Food, Gas, Lodging: Great Falls.
Camping: Private (Great Falls and vicinity).
Land Ownership: USFWS.
Additional Information: Benton Lake NWR, P.O. Box 450, Black Eagle, MT 59414 ph: (406) 727-7400.
Recommended Length of Stay: 1 day.

20 GREAT FALLS AND VICINITY

General Information: *The area around Great Falls was once inhabited by the Blackfeet Indian Nation and the Gros Ventres, or "big bellies." Lewis and Clark learned of the grand cascades on the Missouri from Indians further to the east. The Sioux Indians knew the Great Falls of the Missouri River as "Minni-Sose-Tanka-Kun-Ya."*

Captain Meriwether Lewis reached the Great Falls of the Missouri on June 13, 1805. The way upstream was blocked by a series of five cascades (Great Falls, Colter Falls, Crooked Falls, Beautiful or Rainbow Falls, and Black Eagle Falls), the downstream and highest falls (the "great falls") measuring more than eighty feet high. From June 21 to July 15, the Lewis and Clark Expedition undertook a remarkable human feat of portaging their boats eighteen miles overland around these formidable obstacles. Their accounts of local wildlife were incredible. Lewis was charged by a grizzly bear and had to retreat into the river. Standing above Black Eagle Falls, Lewis wrote, "in these plains and more particularly in the valley just below me, immense herds of buffaloe."

Four out of the five cascades are visible today; Colter Falls was inundated by the reservoir behind Rainbow Dam. Ryan Dam and the Giant Springs area are very impressive and are worth a visit. Great Falls is still called the "electric city" due to the number of hydroelectric dams on the river. It was also home of the famed Montana cowboy artist Charlie Russell. The C. M. Russell Museum in Great Falls is a must for those interested in Montana history.

Birding Information: Giant Springs State Park is a good place to start birding when in Great Falls. From 10th Ave south, follow River Road east and turn north on Giant Springs Road. The park-like lawns and tall trees bordering the south bank of the Missouri River act as a magnet for birdlife. Species likely to be found in the manicured park include American Kestrel, Great Horned Owl, Downy Woodpecker, Black-capped Chickadee, American Robin, House Wren, and Northern Oriole. Along the Missouri River look and listen for American White Pelican, Canada Goose, Mallard, Common Merganser, American Coot, California Gull, Belted Kingfisher, and Cliff Swallow. In the weedy fields search for Ring-necked Pheasant, Gray Partridge, American Goldfinch, and Mourning Dove. Vesper Sparrow can be found in the grasslands, Savannah Sparrow in the wetter areas, and Song Sparrow in the shrubbery along the river edges. Rough-legged Hawk, Bald Eagle, and Golden Eagle are easily found around the Great Falls area in winter.

The water coming out of Giant Springs is believed to originate in the Little Belt Mountains some thirty-eight miles to the south. Studies have found it takes years for the water to reach Giant Springs. Once this water bubbles up to the surface, it forms the shortest river in Montana and the world, the 201-foot Roe River.

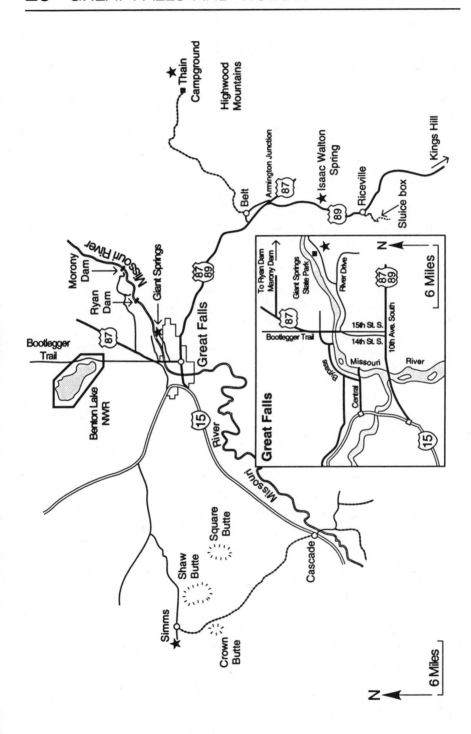

Ryan Dam area, Great Falls.

The **Ryan Dam** area northeast of Great Falls offers interesting birding. Because a large portion of the falls is still visible, visitors also get a wonderful impression of what the "great falls" of the Missouri must have been like.

From U.S. Highway 87 north of town, the eight-mile road is paved all the way to the dam, first passing through cultivated fields where Horned Lark and a variety of raptors can be found. Seven miles in, take a right at the fork in the road, and drive south to Ryan Dam. As the road descends through grasslands and past sandstone cliffs toward the river, watch for Vesper Sparrow, Rufous-sided Towhee, and Mourning Dove among the yucca, sumac, and juniper. Watch for a rough dirt road to the west, which leads to an overlook above the dam, a great place to scan the skyline for birds.

Return to the pavement and continue down the hill to the parking lot at road's end below the dam. The Montana Power Company owns this property and maintains several caretakers' homes here; please respect the resident's privacy. If you need to get to a private area, please ask permission.

The well-kept grounds feature tall trees and abundant shrubs that attract abundant birdlife during migration. If the foot bridge is open, walk across to the island and its stand of tall cottonwoods. Northern Oriole, Warbling Vireo, and Black-capped Chickadee are reliably found in the vicinity of Ryan Dam.

One mile back up the road from Ryan Dam, at the fork in the road, turn right (east) for five miles to reach **Morony Dam**. Although not as impressive as the Ryan Dam area, Morony offers fair birdwatching. Please respect the rights of these private land owners. House Wren, Barn Swallow, and Black-capped Chickadee are a few birds that can be found here.

An area east of Great Falls worth mentioning is the **Thain Campground** in the Highwood Mountains. The campground can be reached by driving east to Belt on U.S. highways 87/89, and driving fifteen miles on the slow, fair-weather Highwood Road to the northeast. Species likely to be encountered in this area include Red-tailed Hawk, American Kestrel, Gray Partridge, Ring-necked Pheasant, and Sharp-tailed Grouse.

Approximately twenty miles southeast of Great Falls is Armington Junction, where U.S. 89 forks south from U.S. 87. Head south of this junction seven miles on U.S. 89 until you get to **Isaac Walton Spring**. A stop here is worthwhile for woodland birds such as Black-headed Grosbeak, Western Wood-Pewee, Warbling Vireo, and Red-naped Sapsucker. Continue south about five miles on U.S. 89 to Riceville, which is easy to miss down in its little draw. Drive southwest on the road across Belt Creek and follow the dirt road for about one mile. Park at the historical mining area at **Sluice Box State Monument**. A trail leads from this area up Belt Creek and offers exciting birding for those interested in walking as they watch birds.

About forty miles south of Armington Junction on U.S. 89 stop at the **Kings Hill Campground** on the west side of the road. The campground is good for Hairy Woodpecker, Gray Jay, Clark's Nutcracker, Mountain Chickadee, Red-breasted Nuthatch, Pine Grosbeak, Cassin's Finch, Red Crossbill, and sometimes Steller's Jay. Directly across U.S. 89 from this campground, a gravel road leads to the 8,008-foot summit of **Kings Hill**. Although the road is slow, if the weather is right it can offer some wonderful vistas. Red-tailed Hawk, Golden Eagle, and the rare Great Gray Owl have been reported on this road. Gray Jay, Clark's Nutcracker, American Pipit, Pine Grosbeak, and Red Crossbill are also seen along this road.

Twenty-two miles southwest of Great Falls on I-15, the area around **Cascade** offers fun birding, particularly if you are interested in raptors. The dirt roads south of Cascade are especially good for Golden Eagle in the spring, especially mid-March. The **Missouri Canyon**, which stretches from Cascade thirty miles to Wolf Creek, offers exciting birding. For best results take the old highway known as Frontage Road. Species likely to be encountered include American White Pelican, Double-crested Cormorant, Great Blue Heron, Canada Goose, Green-winged Teal, Mallard, Common Merganser, Swainson's Hawk, Red-tailed Hawk, Golden Eagle, Belted Kingfisher, Tree Swallow, Cliff Swallow, Lazuli Bunting, Rufous-sided Towhee, Chipping Sparrow, Song Sparrow, and American Goldfinch, and on occasion Great Horned Owl, Lewis' Woodpecker, and Pinyon Jay. Common Loon and Tundra Swan are sometimes found along the river during migration. Bald Eagle and Golden Eagle are easily found here during winter, as are Rough-legged Hawk and American Tree Sparrow. The dirt road northwest of Cascade that goes to **Simms** is a rewarding road for viewing raptors in summer or during spring and fall migration.

Strong winds are common in the Great Falls area. The best birding is often found in the morning, before the wind builds.

Helpful Information:
Elevation: Great Falls, 3,312 ft.
Habitat(s): Riparian, cultivated fields.
Best Birding Season(s): Spring, summer.
Best Birding Month(s): May, June, September.
Montana Highway Map Location: 4-C, 4-D, 5-C, 5-D.
Hazards: Mosquitoes, fair-weather roads, rattlesnakes.
Nearest Food, Gas, Lodging: Great Falls.
Camping: Private (Great Falls and vicinity); Thain Campground (USFS).
Land Ownership: Private; city; state; USFS, USFWS.
Additional Information: Great Falls Visitors Bureau, P.O. Box 2127, Great Falls, MT 59403 ph: (406) 761-4434.
Recommended Length of Stay: 1 to 3 days.

21 HELENA AND VICINITY

General Information: *Helena (pronounced HEL-en-uh) is the capital of Montana. The town sprang up in 1864 when gold was discovered in Last Chance Gulch. Like other big towns in Montana, the birding in Helena is quite good. Three things are obvious when birding Helena: (1) the area is surrounded by mountains and broad vistas; (2) it does not take long to get away from the hustle and bustle of the city; and (3) there is good access to large bodies of water. The Last Chance Audubon Society has produced an excellent publication entitled* Birding in the Helena Valley, *available at Holton's of Helena, 1219 11th Avenue, or the Little Professor Bookstore, 331 N. Last Chance Gulch. The cost is $4.*

Birding Information: In and near the city of Helena there are three primary places to watch birds. **Grizzly Gulch**, southwest of Helena off of Park Avenue and West Main Street, is very accessible. Species to look for here include Ruffed Grouse, Calliope Hummingbird, White-breasted Nuthatch, Rock Wren, Swainson's Thrush, Hermit Thrush, Orange-crowned Warbler, and Lazuli Bunting. **Mount Helena City Park** is a good place to find Rufous-sided Towhee, Green-tailed Towhee, and Red Crossbill. Several hiking trails on Mount Helena begin from the parking lot at the end of Adams Street. (From the City-County Building on Park Avenue, take Clarke Street west one block to South Benton. Turn left on Benton and go two blocks then right—uphill—on Adams, which changes to gravel after crossing Howie Street. Continue on Adams a quarter mile to the Mount Helena parking lot.) Birders on foot should watch for Common Raven, Red-breasted Nuthatch, Ruby-crowned Kinglet, Mountain Bluebird, and Western Tanager.

    Spring Meadow Lake, west of town on Country Club Avenue, is good for species such as Cedar Waxwing, Yellow-rumped Warbler, and various

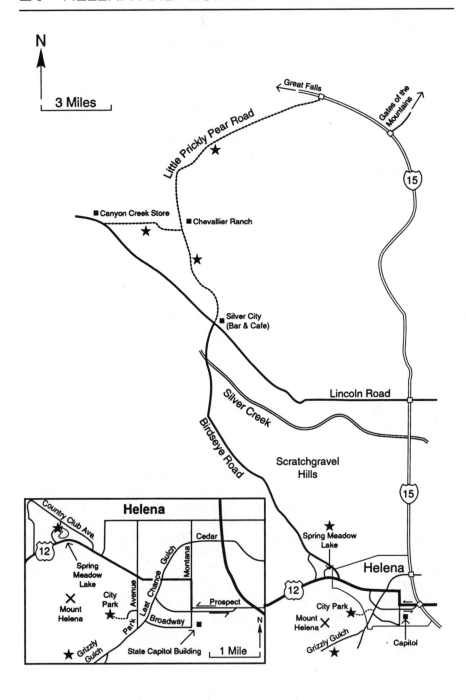

species of Swallows. Common Loons occasionally stop here during migration. Bohemian Waxwings can be found throughout the city of Helena in the winter. Follow U.S. 12 (Euclid Avenue) west to Joslyn and turn right. Veer left onto Country Club Ave and watch for the access road and parking lots on the left.

Drive 15.3 miles out Birdseye Road west of town to **Little Prickly Pear Creek Road** to see Sage Thrashers and Brewer's Sparrows in the sagebrush between Silver City and the Chevallier Ranch. Along Little Prickly Pear Creek Road, the riparian zone is good for Least and Willow Flycatcher, Warbling Vireo, American Redstart, Northern Waterthrush, and Northern Oriole. Look for Rock Wren, Rufous-sided Towhee, and Vesper Sparrow on the steep sideslopes of the small canyon. The back road between the Chevallier Ranch and the Canyon Creek Store crosses a wetland where Sandhill Cranes, Common Snipe, Savannah Sparrow, and Bobolink are found.

In summer, the two-hour **Gates of the Mountains** boat trip offers a close-up view of a wilderness reach of the Missouri River. The Gates were so named by Meriwether Lewis as he and William Clark passed between these awesome limestone cliffs in 1805. Prairie Falcon, Osprey, and Turkey Vulture are often seen during the tour. From Helena, drive seventeen miles north on I-15 to the Hilger Ranch interchange and follow the signs to the boat dock.

Eight miles north of Helena, **Lincoln Road** (secondary roads 279 and 453) is one of the better places to find Rough-legged Hawk and the rare Gyrfalcon in winter. The Blue Silo's area, about 2.5 miles east of I-15, is the only real access to **Lake Helena** if you are interested in seeing water and marsh birds. The road goes 150 yards down to the lake and is usually in poor condition; birders are better off walking. A Great Blue Heron rookery can be seen in the cottonwoods at the southwest corner of the lake. Drive east on Lincoln Road to the end of the pavement and turn left on the gravel road to **Hauser Dam** to see White-throated Swift, Violet-green Swallow, Pygmy Nuthatch, Rock Wren, Canyon Wren, and Rufous-sided Towhee. The Canyon Wrens are usually on the large cliffs downstream from the dam. A nice birding hike begins across the dam and around the buildings to the left. This two-mile hike along the river downstream from the dam is easy and offers fun birding.

The **Causeway** between Lake Helena and the Missouri is a popular fishing hole and often provides good birding anytime of the year. Look for Western Grebe, Eared Grebe, and Horned Grebe in summer, and Common Loon and Common Goldeneye during migration. Drive south on Lake Helena Drive to **Sid Martin's Overlook**—watch for the lone ponderosa pine on the west side of the road above Lake Helena. Northern Harrier, Sandhill Crane, and Savannah Sparrow frequent the fields below the overlook. With a spotting scope, a birder at Sid Martin's should see a good number of American White Pelican, Tundra Swan, Snow Goose, Canada Goose, and Northern Pintail especially in spring and fall. Bald Eagles come here in the winter and

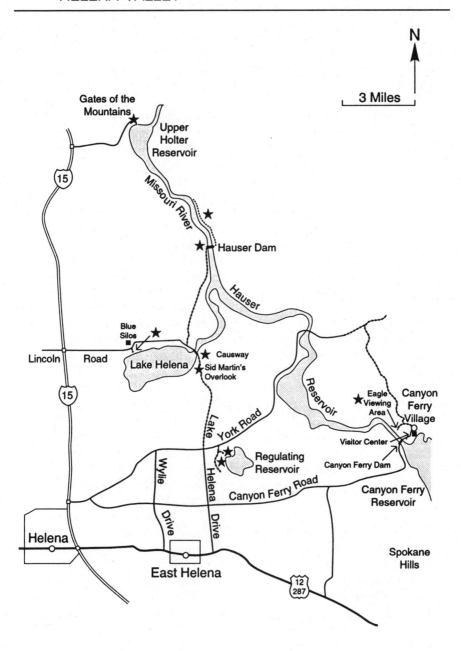

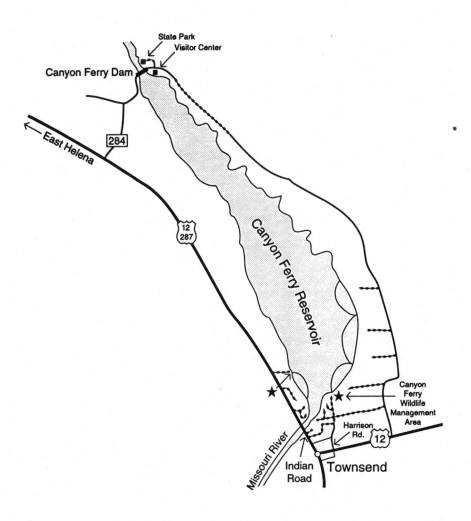

early spring to feed on winter-killed fish.

East of Helena on York Road, the **Regulating Reservoir** offers its best birding during spring and fall. Shorebirds and waterfowl are especially attracted to this area. Migrants such as Common Loons, Red-breasted Mergansers, and various species of Grebes are often found here. During summer, expect to find American White Pelican, Great Blue Heron, and Double-crested Cormorant.

In recent years the fall Bald Eagle concentration at **Canyon Ferry** has received national attention. The eagles are attracted to the area by spawning kokanee (a pacific landlocked relative of the sockeye salmon). Kokanee were introduced on this reach of the Missouri and appear to be doing well. The eagles gather between early November and mid-December, peaking in late November. Stop at the Community Hall (turned into a visitor center) in Canyon Ferry Village for updates on eagle numbers; the hall is a good place to warm up and talk to people about eagles. Bald Eagles are best seen from the **Eagle Viewing Area (Riverside Campground)** below Canyon Ferry Dam. The Montana Department of Fish, Wildlife and Parks charges a three dollar entrance fee here during the eagle-viewing season, and volunteers are available on site to answer questions. For those that have never seen large concentrations of Bald Eagles, this is well worth the visit.

The **Canyon Ferry Wildlife Management Area** (WMA), at the south end of Canyon Ferry Lake near Townsend, is also a good place to watch birds. Several gravel roads enter the west side of the WMA from U.S. 287 just north of Townsend. Or drive east through Townsend on U.S. 12, and turn north on Harrison Road to visit the east shore. A variety of dabbling and diving ducks and other waterfowl are found here. This is an important Canada Goose nesting area, and Tundra and Trumpeter Swans pass through here during migration. Common Loon are also present in fair numbers around this same time, but are typically found on the main lake. In summer, look for American White Pelican, Osprey, American Avocet, and Caspian Tern. Bald Eagle, Rough-legged Hawk, and Northern Shrike are found here in the winter. The area is closed to boats during the nesting season and hunting is allowed in the fall. Check with MDFWP (406) 444-2535 if you have any questions about this wildlife management area.

Helpful Information:
Elevation: Helena, 4,157 ft.; Mount Helena, 5,460 ft.
Habitat(s): Conifers, deciduous shrubs, riparian, lakes, ponds, grasslands, cliffs.
Best Birding Season: Spring.
Best Birding Month(s): May, June.
Montana Highway Map Location: 4-E, 5-E.
Hazards: Mosquitoes in wetland areas.
Nearest Food, Gas, Lodging: Helena, Townsend.
Camping: MDFWP Canyon Ferry (multiple sites); USFS Tenmile (fifteen miles west of Helena), and MacDonald Pass; Helena KOA.
Land Ownership: MDFWP, USFS, Bureau of Reclamation, municipal,

and private.

Additional Information: Montana Department of Fish, Wildlife and Parks, 1420 East Sixth Avenue, Helena, MT ph: (406) 444-2535; or Last Chance Audubon Society, P.O. Box 924, Helena, MT 59624.

Recommended Length of Stay: 2 to 3 days.

22 LEWISTOWN AND VICINITY

General Information: *Lewistown is named not in honor of Meriwether Lewis, but after the 7th Calvary Major William Lewis who established Fort Lewis here in 1874, where Frank Day Park is found today. Lewistown is the geographical center of Montana. The headquarters for the C. M. Russell National Wildlife Refuge is located in Lewistown, though the refuge lies about fifty miles to the northeast.*

Birding Information: This beautiful little town nestled on the banks of Big Spring Creek is a pleasant place to visit and watch birds. During the heat of summer, Lewistown is an oasis on the plains with its numerous shade trees and lush vegetation.

Start birding with a visit to the **Big Springs State Fish Hatchery** eight miles south of town off of Highway 238. Take 1st Avenue south along Big Spring Creek and follow signs to the Fish Hatchery. The birdlife here is diverse, ranging from Common Merganser, Belted Kingfisher, and Song Sparrow to House Wren, Veery, and Common Yellowthroat. Wood Duck are periodically seen here. For best results, try birding the picnic area and the Big Springs source itself.

Across the road west of the Fish Hatchery a dirt road follows **Castle Creek** through hay fields; stands of aspen, ponderosa pine, and spruce; and riparian brush, with fun birding along the way. Watch for Sharp-shinned Hawk, Cooper's Hawk, Northern Goshawk, American Kestrel, and Golden Eagle. Other likely sightings here include Mourning Dove, Western Wood-Pewee, Least Flycatcher, Veery, Gray Catbird, Rufous-sided Towhee, Song Sparrow, and American Goldfinch, .

Frank Day Park, on 5th Avenue South in Lewistown, also offers good birding in a manicured park environment. Six miles north of Lewistown on U.S. Highway 191, the **Carter Ponds** on the east side of the highway harbor waterfowl, and marsh and waterbirds. Upper Carter Pond is the better of the two ponds for birdwatching, though fishing pressure here sometimes diminishes the birding opportunities. The birding is best early in the morning, preferably the first two hours after sunrise.

For perhaps the greatest diversity of birdlife in the Lewistown area, take the thirty-mile drive from town to **Crystal Lake** in the Big Snowy Moun-

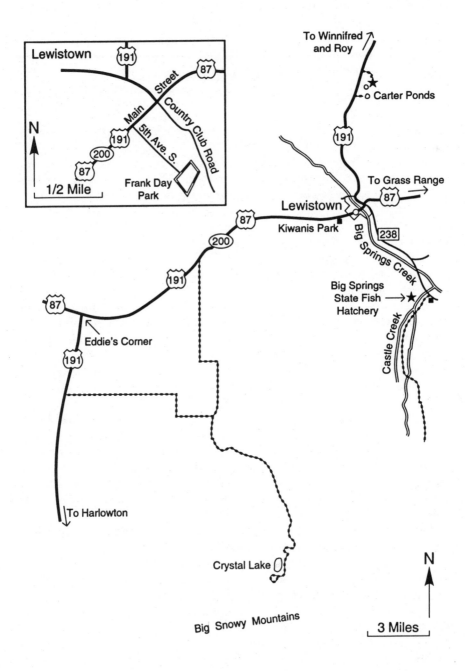

To Winnifred
and Roy

Carter Ponds

191

Lewistown

191

87

Main Street

Country Club Road

5th Ave. S.

200

87

N

1/2 Mile

Frank Day
Park

To Grass Range

87

Lewistown

87

Kiwanis Park

200

238

191

Big Springs Creek

Big Springs
State Fish
Hatchery

87

Castle Creek

Eddie's Corner

191

To Harlowton

Crystal Lake

Big Snowy Mountains

N

3 Miles

Castle Creek area, on the north side of the Big Snowy Range.

tains. Go eight miles west of town on U.S. 191 and turn south on a gravel road. The first ten to twelve miles pass through cultivated fields and stands of willow and aspen, good habitat for passerines and upland birds. Watch for Gray Partridge, Red-naped Sapsucker, Yellow Warbler, Song Sparrow, and American Goldfinch. At the National Forest boundary, the road is paved again and continues through open forest of Douglas fir and spruce to the lake. Mountain residents include Spotted Sandpiper, Williamson's Sapsucker, Hairy Woodpecker, Three-toed Woodpecker, Clark's Nutcracker, Common Raven, Mountain Chickadee, Red-breasted Nuthatch, Ruby-crowned Kinglet, Veery, Hermit Thrush, Ovenbird, Western Tanager, Dark-eyed Junco, Pine Grosbeak, Red Crossbill, and Pine Siskin. Birding is good to excellent at the campground, picnic area, and boat ramp. Also try the National Recreation Trail circling Crystal Lake, and Trail 409, which climbs three miles from the end of the road to the crest of the Big Snowies. Crystal Lake is a popular recreation area, and is especially crowded on holiday weekends through the summer; plan accordingly.

Helpful Information:
Elevation: Lewistown, 3,963 ft; Crystal Lake, 6,080 ft.
Habitat(s): Cropland, grassland, riparian, mixed conifers/deciduous, coniferous forest.
Best Birding Season(s): Spring, summer.
Best Birding Month(s): May through July.

Montana Highway Map Location: 7-D.

Hazards: Mosquitoes, horse flies.

Nearest Food, Gas, Lodging: Lewistown.

Camping: Kiwanis Park (Lewistown); Crystal Lake (Big Snowy Mountains).

Land Ownership: Private, city, state, BLM, USFS.

Additional Information: Lewistown Chamber of Commerce, P.O. Box 818, Lewistown, MT 59457 ph: (406) 538-5436.

Recommended Length of Stay: 1 to 2 days.

A Great Gray Owl primary feather. The silent flight of an owl, which enables it to surprise prey, is the result of structured adaptations of feathers. The barbs on the leading edge of the feather are long and curved to reduce air turbulence, resulting in little if any sound.

NORTHEAST MONTANA

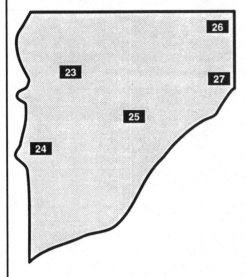

23. Bowdoin National Wildlife Refuge
24. Charles M. Russell National Wildlife Refuge-West Side
25. Charles M. Russell National Wildlife Refuge-East Side And Fort Peck Area
26. Medicine Lake National Wildlife Refuge
27. Fort Union National Historic Site

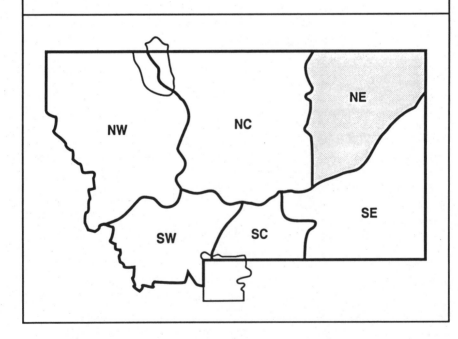

23 BOWDOIN NATIONAL WILDLIFE REFUGE

General Information: *Bowdoin is situated on the Montana "Hi Line," where the twin ribbons of the Great Northern Railroad and U.S. Highway 2 run straight across the plains of northern Montana from Poplar to Glacier National Park. Malta is supposedly named for the island in the Mediterranean.*

Geologists claim that Lake Bowdoin was once an ancient pre-glacial oxbow of the Missouri River. Historically this lake basin was filled by spring runoff, leaving warm, shallow, stagnant water by summer's end. The refuge was established by the U.S. Fish and Wildlife Service in 1936, and a system of dikes and ditches was built to divert additional water from the Milk River.

Birding Information: Bowdoin National Wildlife Refuge is situated seven miles east of Malta on Old Highway 2. Bowdoin's 15,500 acres provide excellent habitat for waterfowl, colonial nesting birds, and shortgrass prairie birdlife. More than 236 species of birds have been seen here. Look for Wood Duck on a canal just two miles west of the refuge on Old Highway 2. Turn right onto the refuge and stop at **headquarters**, where a diversity of trees and shrubs make this ideal habitat for American Goldfinch and Northern Saw-whet Owl. Immediately south of headquarters, a short trail leads to **Strater Pond** for some of the best birding in the middle of the day due to the diversity of vegetation here.

Driving east from headquarters, an **auto tour loop** heads clockwise along the north shore of Lake Bowdoin. The auto loop is open year-round unless weather makes the roads impassable. A careful inspection of the grasslands from the headquarters to **Long Island** will usually yield Sprague's Pipit and, on occasion, Baird's Sparrow. Long Island is an excellent place to see shorebirds; Ring-billed Gull and California Gull nest here.

Stop at site 4 on the auto tour and walk to the top of the hill to see ancient tipi rings and a good view of the refuge beyond. Further south, the **Pelican Islands Overlook** is a good spot to view American White Pelican. Bowdoin is also noted for other colonial nesting birds, including Eared Grebe, Double-crested Cormorant, Great Blue Heron, Black-crowned Night-Heron, White-faced Ibis, and Franklin's Gull.

All three species of teal (Green-winged, Cinnamon, Blue-winged) can be found in the **Teal Ponds** area, as can Pied-billed Grebe, American Coot, Marsh Wren, and Song Sparrow. A short stretch of grasslands following Teal Ponds is another fine place to see Sprague's Pipit. White-faced Ibis seem to be most prevalent near the southeast and southwest arms of Lake Bowdoin.

Here the road turns west and parallels the railroad tracks. At the next junction go straight ahead for a half mile (do not cross the railroad tracks) and watch for a weedy grassland on the south end of **Big Island** where Baird's Sparrow and Sprague's Pipit are reliably found. Further up Big Island, look for Western Meadowlark, McCown's Longspur, Horned Lark, American

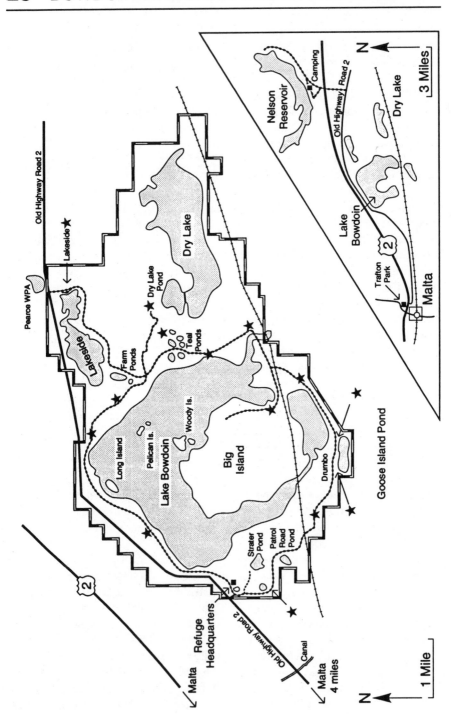

Bowdoin National Wildlife Refuge.

Kestrel, and Swainson's Hawk. Surprisingly, a fair number of waterfowl nest in this grassland.

Returning from Big Island to the auto tour route, cross the railroad tracks and continue west toward **Goose Island Pond**. Look for Brown Thrasher and Loggerhead Shrike in the Russian olive trees near the road. At Goose Island Pond look for Northern Harrier, Virginia Rail, Sora, Spotted Sandpiper, and Common Yellowthroat. This is also an excellent shorebird area, especially during migration, when Long-billed Dowitcher are abundant. Near the second railroad crossing as the road wends north, look for Loggerhead Shrike in summer and Northern Shrike in winter. Back in the vicinity of **refuge headquarters**, the road passes a small creek lined with willows where American Goldfinch, Gray Catbird, and Brown Thrasher can be found.

For additional birding on the refuge, drive east on Old Highway 2 for 6.5 miles from headquarters. Take the gravel road south for less than a half mile to **Lakeside**, a good birding area with abundant waterfowl and songbirds. This road continues along the south shore of Lakeside and eventually parallels a dike near the **Farm Ponds** where Ring-necked Pheasant and Gray Partridge are present year-round. Turn east at the next crossroads and drive about one mile to a grouse dancing ground, or lek, marked with a wooden fence post. Sharp-tailed Grouse perform their courtship display on this shortgrass prairie in April and May.

Other species likely to be encountered at Bowdoin in the summer include

Snowy Egret, Northern Shoveler, Gadwall, Redhead, Lesser Scaup, Ruddy Duck, Upland Sandpiper, and Great Horned Owl. From mid-September through October, as many as 10,000 Sandhill Cranes have been known to gather at the refuge. Tundra Swan and sometimes Snow Goose are seen in late October-early November. Peregrine Falcon migrate through here during spring and fall, and the rare Snowy Owl and Gyrfalcon have been sighted here in winter.

North of the refuge, directly across Old Highway 2 from Lakeside, the **Pearce Waterfowl Production Area** harbors many of the same species found on Bowdoin.

Four miles north and east of the refuge, on the north side of U.S. 2, **Nelson Reservoir** provides good birding for American White Pelican, Double-crested Cormorant, Killdeer, Ring-billed Gull, California Gull, Caspian Tern, Common Tern, Black Tern, and the rare Piping Plover. Common Loon and White-winged Scoter are seen here during migration, and Common Loon is occasionally seen here in summer. Nelson Reservoir typically freezes up later than Lake Bowdoin.

Helpful Information:
Elevation: Malta, 2,250 ft.
Habitat(s): Wetlands, shortgrass prairie, riparian, cultivated trees, and shrubs.
Best Birding Season(s): Spring.
Best Birding Month(s): Mid-May through June.
Montana Highway Map Location: 8-B.
Hazards: Mosquitoes, heat prostration, fair-weather roads.
Nearest Food, Gas, Lodging: Malta.
Camping: Trafton Park (Malta), Nelson Reservoir.
Land Ownership: USFWS, private.
Additional Information: Bowdoin National Wildlife Refuge, P.O. Box J, Malta, MT 59538 ph: (406) 654-2863.
Recommended Length of Stay: 1 day.

24 CHARLES M. RUSSELL NWR—WEST SIDE

General Information: *The CMR Wildlife Refuge was named for the famous Montana cowboy artist Charlie Russell, who captured on canvas the beauty and drama of the Montana plains, western tradition, early inhabitants, and Montana wildlife. Before Russell, the explorers Lewis and Clark traveled through this country, as did James Kipp, who set up the first trading post within the Blackfeet Nation. The Missouri River remained a major travel corridor through Montana until the advent of the railroads.*

The lay of the land here is an intriguing maze of high buttes and benches, deep draws and jutting headlands, all splashed by colorful sunrises and sunsets. In the heavy heat of summer, powerful thunderstorms sweep these plains, filling the sky and turning the roads to gumbo. The west end of the refuge, a remote corridor along the Missouri River sixty miles northeast of Lewistown, best exemplifies the rough, highly eroded cliffs and gullies known as the "Missouri Breaks." Here the refuge preserves some of the most extensive ungrazed stands of riparian vegetation found anywhere in Montana.

Birding Information: When visiting this remote refuge, birders should stop at the Sand Creek headquarters at the south entrance on U.S. 191 for additional information about the refuge. North on U.S. Highway 191 from Sand Creek, the highway makes a long straight descent to the Missouri River and Fred Robinson Bridge, with outstanding views of the rugged breaks.

Immediately south of the Fred Robinson Bridge, turn east to enter the **James Kipp Recreation Area**, operated by the BLM. Large cottonwood groves with dense underbrush border the Missouri here, offering excellent birding. Resident species include American Kestrel, Northern Flicker, Western Wood-Pewee, Eastern Kingbird, Tree Swallow, Cliff Swallow, Black-capped Chickadee, Gray Catbird, Yellow Warbler, Common Grackle, and American Goldfinch. Most impressive is the number of Brown Thrashers milling around in the understory. Common Nighthawk abound here, easily recognized by their swift, dodging flight and nasal "peent" call. During courtship displays, the males swoop toward the ground, making a hollow booming sound with their wings.

Drive north of Fred Robinson Bridge less than one mile to a C. M. Russell National Wildlife Refuge information kiosk on the east side of U.S. 191. The kiosk is occasionally stocked with bird lists and refuge brochures, but it is advisable to write for this information prior to your trip (see Helpful Information for address). The **Wildlife Tour Route** begins and ends at this kiosk. To follow the thirty-mile loop, drive north on U.S. 191 for eleven miles and turn east down a well-traveled gravel road. This road crosses extensive grasslands, descends through stands of ponderosa pine and juniper, and eventually parallels a large riparian area by the Missouri River. The road

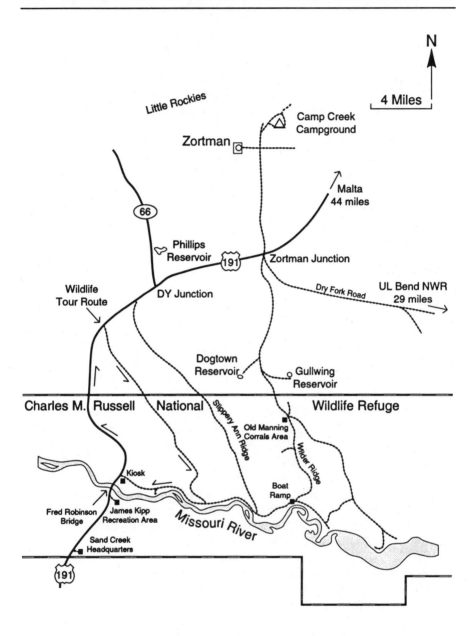

eventually climbs again through ponderosa pine and juniper and returns to the informational kiosk. Birds likely to be encountered on the Wildlife Tour Route include Northern Harrier, Red-tailed Hawk, American Kestrel, Sage Grouse, Sharp-tailed Grouse, Poorwill, Mountain Bluebird, Sage Thrasher, Clay-colored Sparrow, Vesper Sparrow, Western Meadowlark, and Red Crossbill.

Continuing north on U.S. 191, turn south at mile marker 109, just opposite the Zortman Road. This dirt road leads eight miles to the **Old Manning Corrals Area** within the CMR Refuge. The corrals no longer exist, but black-tailed prairie dogs are incredibly abundant on this shortgrass bench. At Manning Corrals, look for Northern Harrier, Red-tailed Hawk, Ferruginous Hawk, Golden Eagle, American Kestrel, Killdeer, Mourning Dove, Burrowing Owl, Say's Phoebe, Horned Lark, Black-billed Magpie, Mountain Bluebird, Loggerhead Shrike, Western Meadowlark, and Mountain Plover. Mountain Plover are hard to see because they are quite small and blend perfectly with this environment. Look in the actively grazed portion of the prairie dog town where insects are more abundant. The pause-and-dash motion of the Mountain Plover can be detected by stopping and scoping the area from the road.

For a distinctive change of scenery and a refreshing spot to camp, relax, and watch birds, return to U.S. 191 and drive north about six miles on the gravel road to Zortman. Go straight through the crossroads and continue 1.5 miles to Camp Creek Campground at the foot of the **Little Rockies**. This small, isolated mountain range harbors vegetation similar to that found in the major mountain ranges much farther to the west. The campground boasts exciting birding, nestled in a beautiful riparian zone dominated by aspen and surrounded by conifers. Species likely to be seen here include Cooper's Hawk, Red-breasted Nuthatch, Cedar Waxwing, Warbling Vireo, Yellow Warbler, Western Tanager, Pine Siskin, and Red Crossbill. Camp Creek is one of the most pleasant birding and camping areas east of the continental divide.

UL Bend National Wildlife Refuge is located on the "Great Bend of the Missouri River." This is a very remote wildlife refuge at the end of a fair-weather road. Birding this territory requires a lot of time and luck with the weather. The refuge is thirty-nine miles by dirt road from Zortman Junction. A short loop drive (counter-clockwise on roads 201-319-416-201) passes Hawley Flat where Burrowing Owl frequent the prairie dog towns. Also found in the area are American Kestrel, Ferruginous Hawk, Golden Eagle, Swainson's Hawk, and Horned Lark. Look for Sage Grouse in the Valentine Creek/Dry Lake area, especially in the spring.

Helpful Information:
Elevation: Missouri Breaks, 2,350 ft.
Habitat(s): Badlands, riparian, pine/juniper.
Best Birding Season(s): Spring.
Best Birding Month(s): April, May, June.

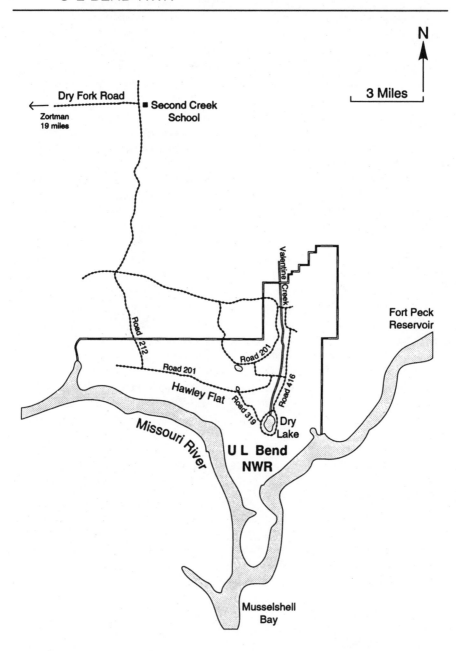

Montana Highway Map Location: 8-C.
Hazards: Mosquitoes, rattlesnakes, fair-weather roads, thunderstorms.
Nearest Food, Gas, Lodging: Zortman.
Camping: James Kipp Recreation Area, Camp Creek.
Land Ownership: USFWS, BLM.
Additional Information: Charles M. Russell National Wildlife Refuge, P.O.
Box 110, Lewistown, MT 59457 ph: (406) 538-8707.
Recommended Length of Stay: 2 to 3 days.

25 CHARLES M. RUSSELL NWR—EAST SIDE AND FORT PECK AREA

General Information: *Fort Peck, named after Campbell Kennedy Peck, was established as a fur trading post in the 1860s. The original site of the fort was destroyed by the undercutting force of the Missouri River long before the area was inundated by the waters of Fort Peck Reservoir. Fort Peck Dam is not only the largest dam in Montana, but is the largest hydraulic-filled, earth-filled dam in the world. Large numbers of dinosaur remains, fossils, and bison skulls have been recovered in the vicinity of Fort Peck. First-time visitors to Fort Peck will notice two striking qualities of the place: how well-organized it is, and the abundance of trees, shrubs, and water, which together act as a magnet for both humans and birdlife.*

Birding Information: Fort Peck is an excellent place to watch birds, especially from late April through May, and from November through early January. Habitats vary from the wide open water of Fort Peck Reservoir and its immense shoreline, to the flowing waters of the massive Missouri River and its associated riparian vegetation. Nearby, the manicured parks and lawns of the town of Fort Peck give way to badlands—locally called "breaks"—to the east and south, and cultivated fields to the north and west.

A variety of songbirds are found throughout the **Fort Peck** townsite, but most notable is the Chimney Swift. The easiest place to find Field Sparrow and Clay-colored Sparrow is in the shrubbery between town and the dam on the south side of the Power Plant Road and west of the campground. The **Old Tree Nursery Area** and the **Kiwanis Park Campground** (especially the nature trail just east of the campground) are two superb birding areas and are a must for serious birders. Songbird species likely to be seen include Red-headed Woodpecker, Northern Flicker (Red-shafted Race, Yellow-shafted Race, Red and Yellow Intergrades), Western Kingbird, Eastern Kingbird, Gray Catbird, Brown Thrasher, Yellow-breasted Chat, Yellow Warbler, Black-headed Grosbeak, Orchard Oriole, and Northern Oriole (Bullock's Race, Baltimore

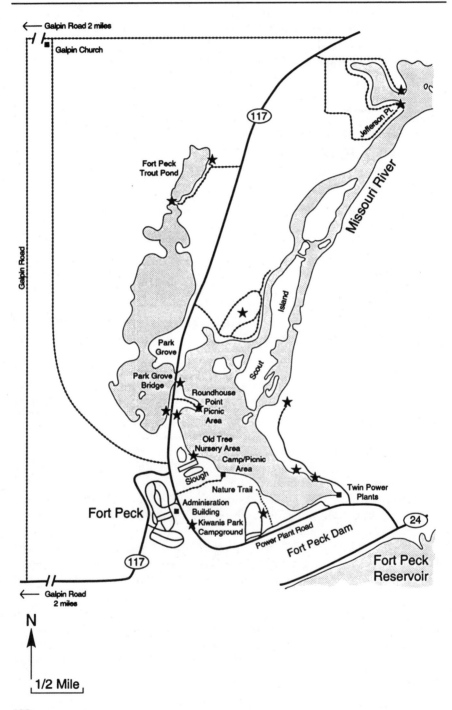

← Galpin Road 2 miles

Galpin Church

117

Jefferson Pt.

Missouri River

Fort Peck
Trout Pond

Galpin Road

Island

Scout

Park
Grove

Park Grove
Bridge

Roundhouse
Point
Picnic
Area

Old Tree
Nursery Area

Camp/Picnic
Area

Slough

Nature Trail

Twin Power
Plants

Administration
Building

Fort Peck

Kiwanis Park
Campground

Power Plant Road

Fort Peck Dam

24

117

← Galpin Road
2 miles

Fort Peck
Reservoir

N

1/2 Mile

Race). A small population of Eastern Bluebirds nest in the riparian cottonwoods downstream from Fort Peck.

For those especially interested in Larids (gulls and related allies), the area below the dam is the best bet. Areas worth visiting include the **Power Plants, Picnic Area Point, Park Grove Bridge**, and, north of town on Highway 117, **Jefferson Point** (see map). Numerous species of Larids have been found here, including Franklin's Gull, Bonaparte's Gull, Mew Gull, Ring-billed Gull, California Gull, Thayer's Gull, Glaucous-winged Gull, Glaucous Gull, Great Black-backed Gull, Ivory Gull, and Blacklegged Kittiwake. The best time to see some of the rare and unusual Larids is from November to early January. In summer, the edge of **Fort Peck Reservoir** is a good place to view Ring-billed Gull, California Gull, Caspian Tern, Common Tern, and with some luck, the Least Tern.

Also along the shoreline of the reservoir, look for American White Pelican, Double-crested Cormorant, and the rare Piping Plover and Least Tern in summer. Waterfowl are easy to find in summer, but their numbers do not appear to be sizeable because the flocks are spread out. During migration and throughout the winter, waterfowl numbers are much more concentrated, thus luring in large numbers of Bald Eagles. Common Loon are especially noticeable during spring and fall, and are best observed on Fort Peck Reservoir from the dam. The **Fort Peck Trout Pond** is also a good place to look for migrant Lesser Scaup, Common Loon, and occasionally White-winged Scoter.

The **Power Plants** area offers excellent birding in winter, as does **Galpin Road**. Northern Shrike, Bald Eagle, Lapland Longspur, Snow Bunting, the rare Gyrfalcon (White Morph, Gray Morph), and Snowy Owl can be spotted along Galpin Road in winter. Other areas worth visiting but requiring much more time are the **Pines Recreation Area** (thirty-one miles southwest of Fort Peck), which is especially good for raptors, and the break country south of Fort Peck along Highway 24, which is good for Field Sparrow, Clay-colored Sparrow, Lark Sparrow, and Rufous-sided Towhee.

Helpful Information:
Elevation: Fort Peck, 2,000 to 2,200 ft.
Habitat(s): Manicured parks and lawns, open water, shoreline, riparian, badlands.
Best Birding Season(s): Spring, late fall through early winter.
Best Birding Month(s): April, May, November, December, January.
Montana Highway Map Location: 10-B, 10-C.
Hazards: Mosquitoes, rattlesnakes, fair-weather roads, thunderstorms.
Nearest Food, Gas, Lodging: Fort Peck, Glasgow.
Camping: Kiwanis Park Campground in Fort Peck.
Land Ownership: U.S. Army Corps of Engineers, USFWS, private.
Additional Information: Charles M. Russell National Wildlife Refuge, P.O. Box 110, Lewistown, MT 59457 ph: (406) 538-8707.
Recommended Length of Stay: 1 to 3 days.

26 MEDICINE LAKE
NATIONAL WILDLIFE REFUGE

General Information: *Medicine Lake received its name for its abundance of plants, water, and wildlife, evidence to the Indians that this oasis had spiritual powers. Bison once roamed here in large numbers. The rolling topography, soil structure, lakes, and potholes in this section of Montana are the result of ice age glaciation.*

Birding Information: Medicine Lake National Wildlife Refuge is off the beaten track, but the birding is superb. The surrounding landscape harbors a unique combination of tallgrass prairie characteristic of North Dakota and the shortgrass prairie typical of central Montana. This varied habitat attracts many migrant birds, particularly waterfowl and shorebirds. Migrants that pause to rest here include Whooping Crane, Sandhill Crane, and Tundra Swan. Songbirds, especially Wood Warbler, also pass through briefly during migration. Fed entirely from natural runoff, these wetlands shrink dramatically during dry years, with a corresponding decline in birding opportunities.

Other species likely to be found here in summer include Black-crowned Night-Heron, American Avocet, Willet, Upland Sandpiper, Long-billed Curlew, Short-eared Owl, Northern Rough-winged Swallow, Sedge Wren, Clay-colored Sparrow, Baird's Sparrow, Grasshopper Sparrow, and Sharp-tailed Sparrow can also be seen in this area. Fall migration brings notable numbers of raptors, including Peregrine Falcon, Gyrfalcon, Merlin, and Swainson's Hawk. Winter birding is slow, with occasional sightings of Snowy Owl, Northern Shrike, Bohemian Waxwing, Snow Bunting, and Common Redpoll.

The refuge is located two miles south of the town of Medicine Lake on Highway 16, about twenty-three miles north of Culbertson. A **picnic area** and kiosk on the east side of Highway 16 is the best place to get acquainted with the 31,457-acre refuge and its birdlife. The islands north of the picnic area and east of the main highway are good places to observe California Gull, Ring-billed Gull, and Great Blue Heron. Look west of the highway to see Western Grebe.

Excellent birding begins on the refuge entrance road off Highway 16. Western Meadowlark, Chestnut-collared Longspur, and Baird's Sparrow are common in the grasslands along this two-mile stretch to the **refuge headquarters.**

The trees and shrubs that surround headquarters are an oasis for songbirds, especially during migration. Chestnut-collared Longspur, American White Pelican, Common Tern, and Forster's Tern can be seen from a cattleguard that overlooks **Gopher Point**. Continue 1.5 miles down the road to a Sharp-tailed

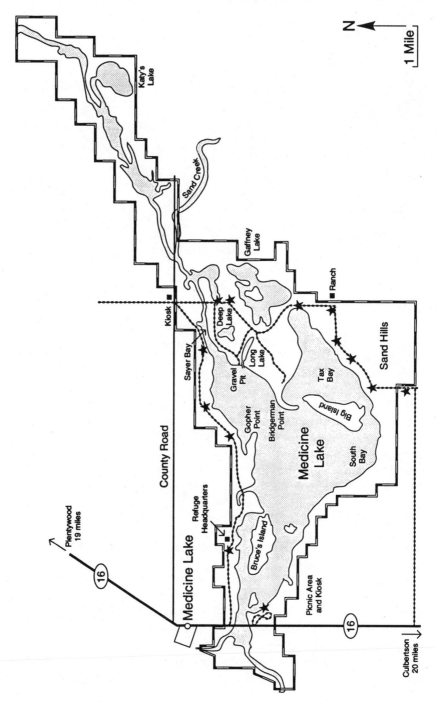

View from the Culbertson Bridge, south of Culbertson, Montana, looking east down the Missouri River.

Grouse lek, usually active in April. Shorebirds and waterfowl gather in **Sayer Bay**, particularly during migration. The road parallel to Sayer Bay is lined with shrubs where Song Sparrow, Eastern Kingbird, and American Goldfinch are likely to be found. This section of road ends at the kiosk by the county road.

From the kiosk, head due south for about a half mile to a small bridge. American Bittern, Black Tern, Barn Swallow, Marsh Wren, Common Yellowthroat, Chipping Sparrow, and Song Sparrow are often found here. Lucky birders might glimpse the secretive Sharp-tailed Sparrow hidden in the bulrush and weeds. This is the only reliable place in Montana to find this species. Past the bridge, a turn to the west and north of Deep Lake leads to a view of **North Bay** where shorebirds, terns, and waterfowl congregate. The **Gravel Pit** area is an excellent birding spot due to the mix of cottonwoods, shrubs, shoreline, and open water. Piping Plover are seen here, as are House Wren, Eastern Kingbird, and Western Kingbird. Migrants that pause here include Veery, Orange-crowned Warbler, and Black-and-white Warbler. Drive out to **Bridgerman Point** for good views of Great Blue Heron and Double-crested Cormorant. Scope along the Medicine Lake shoreline around **Tax Bay** to see Piping Plover in summer, and Bald Eagle in fall, winter, and spring. A variety of birds also frequent **Gaffney Lake**.

The road passes a ranch house where songbirds gather. Please ask permission at the ranch before birding on this private property. Loggerhead Shrike (in summer) and Northern Shrike (in winter) can be seen from the road here. The road then veers to the west between the **Sand Hills** and **Big**

Island. Chestnut-collared Longspur and Lark Bunting are plentiful in the grasslands and Sand Hills, and American White Pelican are common near Big Island. Passenger cars are not suited for driving along the Sand Hills due to the deep, soft sand, but Lark Bunting and Sharp-tailed Grouse are common along this road. From here, it's best to return along the same route to the kiosk, then take the paved county road to the town of Medicine Lake.

The town of **Westby**, forty-four miles northeast of Medicine Lake on Highway 5, was once the most westerly town in North Dakota. But Westby gradually relocated across the state line to Montana, following the railroad west during construction in the early 1900s. Birding in the Westby town park is especially good for warblers in May and September.

Helpful Information:
Elevation: Medicine Lake, 1,990 ft.
Habitat(s): Lake, wetlands, marshes, grasslands.
Best Birding Season(s): Spring, fall.
Best Birding Month(s): May, September.
Montana Highway Map Location: 12-B.
Hazards: Gnats, ticks.
Nearest Food, Gas, Lodging: Culbertson, Plentywood.
Camping: Culbertson, Plentywood.
Land Ownership: USFWS, private.
Additional Information: Medicine Lake National Wildlife Refuge, HC 51, Box 2, Medicine Lake, MT 59247 ph: (406) 789-2305.
Recommended Length of Stay: 1 day.

27 FORT UNION NATIONAL HISTORIC SITE

General Information: *Although the actual location of old Fort Union is in present-day North Dakota 500 feet east of the Montana line, it was once a part of the original Montana Territory and played a significant role in the exploration of Montana. Lewis and Clark passed by here in 1805 and 1806, well before the fort was established in 1829. Fort Union, built near the banks of the Missouri River and close to the confluence of the Yellowstone River, was an important frontier trading post for beaver furs and bison hides until 1866. Indians, trappers, traders, artists, priests, explorers, and scientists visited Fort Union. Such famous people as George Catlin, Prince Maximilian, Karl Bodmer, Father DeSmet, Jim Bridger, Jedediah Smith, and John James Audubon visited the fort. Today's Fort Union National Historic Site is a partial reconstruction on the original site, and is a fascinating place to visit, where a walk over the state line from the parking lot to the fort will put you in a different time zone (Mountain Standard Time-Central Standard Time).*

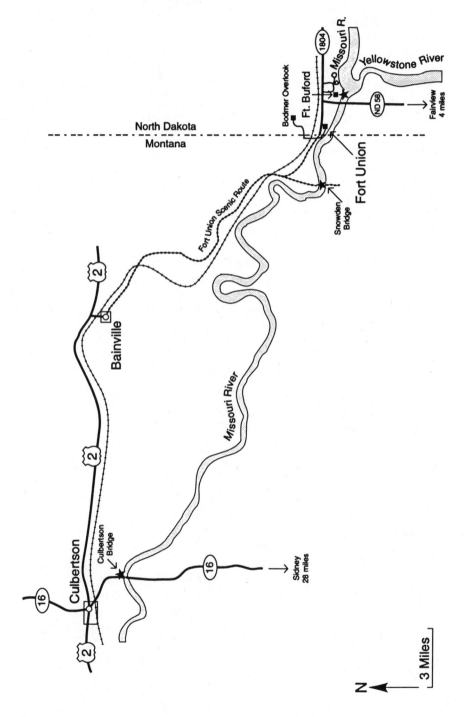

Birding Information: To reach Fort Union, drive fifteen miles east from Culbertson on U.S. 2 and turn south onto Secondary Road 327 at Bainville. Follow this gravel road, locally known as the **Fort Union Scenic Route**, eleven miles to the North Dakota state line and the **Fort Union National Historic Site**. Clay-colored Sparrows can be seen along this drive. The parking lot lies adjacent to the riparian zone of the Missouri River where the birding is quite good. Species likely to appear are American White Pelican, Spotted Sandpiper, Least Tern, Willow Flycatcher, Eastern Kingbird, Black-billed Magpie, American Crow, House Wren, Eastern Bluebird, Gray Catbird, Cedar Waxwing, Lazuli Bunting, Yellow-breasted Chat, Song Sparrow, and American Goldfinch. Directly north of the Fort Union access road, a two-mile drive to the **Bodmer Overlook** provides opportunities to see Golden Eagle, Red-tailed Hawk, Western Meadowlark, Rufous-sided Towhee, and Clay-colored Sparrow.

Other good birding spots near Fort Union include the **Culbertson Bridge** about three miles south of Culbertson on Highway 16, the **Snowden Bridge** some four miles west of Fort Union on a gravel spur from the Scenic Route, and **Fort Buford**. Least Terns are sometimes seen at the Culbertson and Snowden bridges. Fort Buford, four miles east of Fort Union on North Dakota 1804, overlooks the confluence of the Yellowstone and Missouri rivers; look here for an occasional Least Tern.

Helpful Information:
Elevation: Fort Union, 1,873 ft.
Habitat(s): Riparian, grassland.
Best Birding Season(s): Spring.
Best Birding Month(s): May to early June.
Montana Highway Map Location: 12-B.
Hazards: Gnats, mosquitoes.
Nearest Food, Gas, Lodging: Culbertson and Fairview, Montana; Williston, North Dakota.
Camping: Centennial Park (Culbertson), Fort Buford.
Land Ownership: NPS, private, State of North Dakota.
Additional Information: Fort Union Trading Post National Historic Site, Buford Route, Williston, ND 58801 ph: (701) 572-9083.
Recommended Length of Stay: 3 to 8 hours.

SOUTHEAST MONTANA

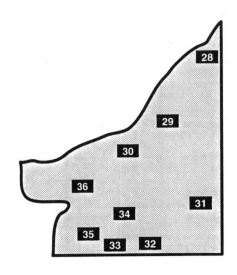

28. Elk Island and Fox Lake
29. Makoshika State Park
30. Miles City and Vicinity
31. Ekalaka and Vicinity
32. Youngs Creek and
    Tongue River Reservoir
33. Bighorn Canyon National
    Recreation Area
34. Little Bighorn Battlefield
    National Monument
35. Pryor Mountains
36. Billings and Vicinity

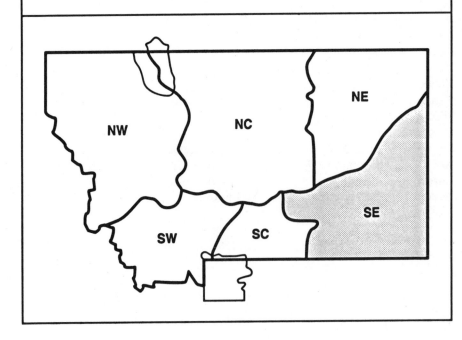

28 ELK ISLAND AND FOX LAKE

General Information: *Elk and bison were once abundant on the Great Plains as evidenced in the journals of Lewis and Clark in 1804-1806 and in the writings of Prince Paul of Wurttemberg, who explored the West in 1830. Prince Paul was the first in a long list of nobility—and also the first person with exceptional scientific background--to visit Montana. If Prince Paul's unpublished journals had survived the bombing of Germany during World War II, they would probably have ranked with those of Lewis and Clark, Maximilian, Audubon, and others instrumental in the exploration of North America.*

Elk are no longer found naturally along the Yellowstone River in eastern Montana, but old bison skulls and elk antlers are occasionally discovered. Elk are being reintroduced into sections of eastern Montana today by the Montana Department of Fish, Wildlife and Parks.

Birding Information: Elk Island Recreation and Wildlife Area lies one mile north of Savage and nineteen miles south of Sidney at mile marker 32 on Highway 16. Habitats here include large cottonwoods with a variety of understory shrubs, backwater sloughs, oxbows, islands of riparian vegetation, and an active braided reach of the Yellowstone River. Species likely to be sighted here include American White Pelican, Great Blue Heron, Turkey Vulture, American Kestrel, Wild Turkey, Mourning Dove, Eastern Screech Owl, Belted Kingfisher, Northern Flicker, Barn Swallow, Blue Jay, Eastern Bluebird, House Wren, Red-eyed Vireo, and Northern Oriole.

Fox Lake is a 1,534-acre Wildlife Management Area, twenty-one miles west of Sidney on Highway 200. At mile marker 50 turn into the town of Lambert and drive straight through town. A little more than a mile south of Lambert, turn right or west at the next junction for 2.2 miles. The entrance to Fox Lake is on the right. The entrance road may be impassible when wet. During drought years, birding here can be difficult. Fox Lake is mostly marsh surrounded by shortgrass prairie and upland habitat with rolling hills. The grasslands support Ferruginous Hawk, Burrowing Owl, Horned Lark, Sprague's Pipit, McCown's Longspur, Chestnut-collared Longspur, and Lark Sparrow. Look for Sharp-tailed Grouse and Upland Sandpiper in the rolling hills.

Marsh residents include American White Pelican, Green-winged Teal, Mallard, Northern Pintail, Blue-winged Teal, Northern Shoveler, Gadwall, Redhead, Gray Partridge, Ring-necked Pheasant, Virginia Rail, Sora, American Avocet, Willet, Marbled Godwit, Wilson's Phalarope, Marsh Wren, Red-winged Blackbird, and Yellow-headed Blackbird. Migrants to watch for are Tundra Swan, Sandhill Crane, and a variety of shorebirds.

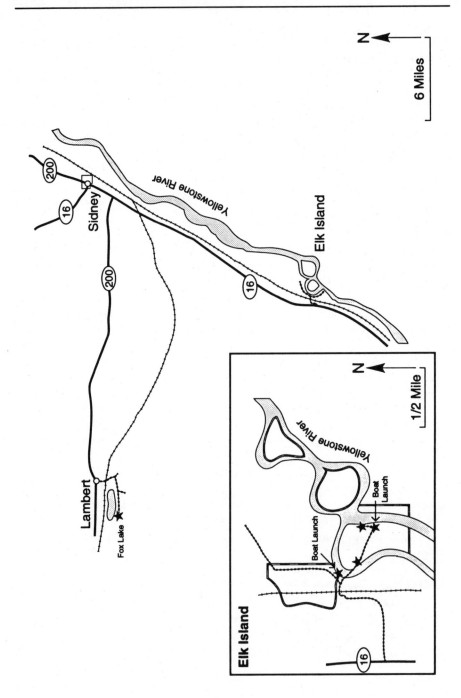

Helpful Information:
Elevation: Elk Island, 2,000 ft; Fox Lake, 2,300 ft to 2,500 ft.
Habitat(s): Elk Island: riparian; Fox Lake: marsh, shortgrass prairie, uplands.
Best Birding Season(s): Spring, summer.
Best Birding Month(s): April, May, June, October.
Montana Highway Map Location: 12-C.
Hazards: Elk Island: mosquitoes; Fox Lake: rattlesnakes, gumbo roads.
Nearest Food, Gas, Lodging: Sidney.
Camping: Elk Island.
Land Ownership: Elk Island: BLM, MDFWP; Fox Lake: MDFWP.
Additional Information: Montana Department of Fish, Wildlife and Parks, Route 1, Box 2004, Miles City, MT 59301 and Bureau of Land Management, P.O. Box 940, Miles City, MT 59301.
Recommended Length of Stay: 1 day.

29 MAKOSHIKA STATE PARK

General Information: *Makoshika (pronounced Ma-KOH-shi-kuh) is a Sioux Indian word meaning "bad earth" or "badlands." The area was set aside as a state park in 1953 to preserve these unique geological features. The exposed rock here is older than in the badlands of the Dakotas, and a large diversity of fossilized dinosaur remains have been uncovered at this site. The "Gate City" of Glendive welcomes travelers entering Montana from the east. Many tourists (including Teddy Roosevelt) lured by the promotions of the railroads came through Glendive en route to Yellowstone Park. Glendive is also the gateway to Makoshika State Park.*

Birding Information: Makoshika State Park is located 1.5 miles southeast of Glendive, about three miles from Interstate 94. Take the exit for Highway 16 and drive south for two-thirds of a mile. Then turn east on Highway 10 for three-quarters of a mile to Merrill Avenue. Follow a quick series of zig-zags: right on Merrill, left on Barry, right on Taylor, and finally, left on Cains Coulee Drive. A visitor center marks the entrance to this 8,123-acre park, the largest in the state park system.

Erosion played a key role in shaping these badlands, leaving remnants of upland prairie, coulees, and finger-like ridges and mesas of ponderosa pine. This harsh, arid landscape may seem barren at first, but the patient observer will soon discover an abundance of wildlife. South-facing slopes are typically dry and sun-baked, with little vegetation, but shadier, cooler north-facing slopes retain moisture better and can support dense stands of trees and shrubs. Cottonwood and willow thrive in the bottoms of coulees, and higher

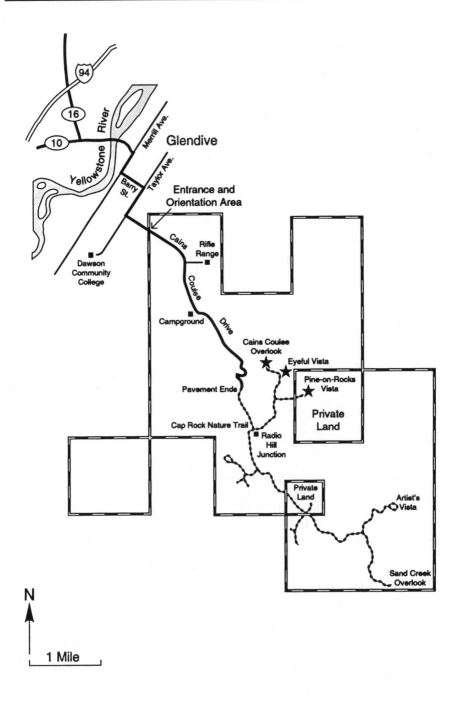

94

16

10

River

Yellowstone

Merrill Ave.

Glendive

Taylor Ave.

Barry St.

Entrance and
Orientation Area

Cains

Rifle
Range

■ Dawson
Community
College

Coulee

Drive

■ Campground

Cains Coulee
Overlook ★

Eyeful Vista ★

Pine-on-Rocks
★ Vista

Pavement Ends

Private
Land

Cap Rock Nature Trail

■ Radio
Hill
Junction

Private
Land

Artist's
○ Vista

Sand Creek
Overlook

N

1 Mile

elevations are home to Rocky Mountain juniper and ponderosa pine mixed with rabbitbrush, sagebrush-grassland, and yucca.

Birding is good at each of several stops along **Cains Coulee Drive**, including Cains Coulee, Cap Rock Nature Trail, Radio Hill Junction, Pine-On-Rocks Vista, Eyeful Vista, and Cains Coulee Overlook. Species commonly sighted include Turkey Vulture, Red-tailed Hawk, Golden Eagle, American Kestrel, Prairie Falcon, Horned Lark, Mountain Bluebird, Rock Wren, Yellow-rumped Warbler, Chipping Sparrow, Brewer's Sparrow, Vesper Sparrow, Lark Sparrow, Western Meadowlark, and American Goldfinch. Look for Red Crossbill on the higher ridges in the groves of ponderosa pine. Turkey Vulture are best seen in the middle of the day above the ridges, taking advantage of the thermal air currents. Rock Wren can be found near almost every tall rock outcrop.

Those traveling through Makoshika with trailers or large motor homes should camp at the Cains Coulee Campground. One-and-a-half miles beyond the campground the road negotiates a tight set of switchbacks on a fifteen percent grade—fearsome going for RVs and towing units. The road also turns to gravel above the switchbacks. Primitive camping is allowed at the Pine-On-Rocks Vista, but no drinking water is available at this site or at any of the higher elevations within the park.

Two nearby areas deserve mention. To reach Montana's most accessible viewing site for Least Tern, take the Fallon Exit off Interstate 94 between Glendive and Miles City. Head two miles north on Frontage Road along the east side of I-94. After crossing the Yellowstone River, turn right to a boat ramp on the river bank. Least Tern are periodically seen here.

The **Terry Badlands** also lie between Glendive and Miles City north of the interstate. Take the Terry Exit off I-94 and head north two miles on Highway 253. Turn west on a fair-weather road that leads through the Terry Badlands. The area is managed by the BLM and contains a unique example of badland country. Continue down this narrow dirt road six miles to a scenic overlook. The badlands are interspersed with shortgrass prairie, juniper, and ponderosa pine. Birds to watch for include Turkey Vulture, Golden Eagle, American Kestrel, Prairie Falcon, Upland Sandpiper, Long-billed Curlew, Great Horned Owl, Horned Lark, Pinyon Jay, Western Tanager, and Sprague's Pipit.

Helpful Information:
Elevation: Glendive, 2,131 ft.
Habitat(s): Cottonwood, willow, sagebrush-grassland, juniper, ponderosa pine.
Best Birding Season(s): Spring, early summer.
Best Birding Month(s): April, May, June.
Montana Highway Map Location: 12-D.
Hazards: Rattlesnakes, heat prostration.
Nearest Food, Gas, Lodging: Glendive.
Camping: Makoshika State Park: RVs, trailers, tents (Cains Coulee); primi-

tive camping, tents (Pine-On-Rocks Vista).
Land Ownership: MDFWP.
Additional Information: Makoshika State Park, Manager, P.O. Box 1242, Glendive, MT 59330 ph: (406) 365-8596.
Recommended Length of Stay: 4 hours to 1 day.

30 MILES CITY AND VICINITY

General Information: *Miles City, originally called Milestown, was named for General Nelson Miles who accepted Chief Joseph's surrender in the Bearpaw Mountains. General Miles later took command of Fort Keogh, at one time the largest army post in Montana. Fort Keogh, built after the Battle of Little Bighorn, continued providing horses for the U.S. Calvary until 1908. The Miles City area became an important stop-over point for the long cattle drives from Texas, and was one of the first areas where sheep were introduced into Montana.*

Birding Information: Birds common to the Miles City area include Wood Duck, Great Horned Owl, Chimney Swift, Red-headed Woodpecker, Downy Woodpecker, Hairy Woodpecker, White-breasted Nuthatch, Brown Thrasher, Yellow Warbler, Yellow-rumped Warbler, Vesper Sparrow, Lark Sparrow, Lark Bunting, and Northern Oriole (Bullock's Race). Blue Jay, Orchard Oriole, and Eastern Screech-Owl are also found in Miles City.

There are six birding areas easily accessible to the public near Miles City. **Spotted Eagle Recreation Area**, located off Garryowen Road near the fairgrounds, is an excellent birding area. Spotted Eagle Lake, in the middle of the RA, gets a fair amount of recreational use, but the vegetation and the trails surrounding the lake are where the birding is best. Habitats in the vicinity of Spotted Eagle RA include cottonwood groves, hardwood draws, and a mixture of wetland and sagebrush-grasslands. Look for Sage Thrasher and Marsh Wren.

Branum Lake, located on Business 94 on the west side of Miles City, offers excellent viewing for waterfowl and shorebirds in the spring. **Scanton Lake** is a popular swimming hole in the middle of town, and **Cook Lake** is on the north side of Main Street. When they are filled with water they can be good for Wood Ducks. Between the west exit on I-94 and the Highway 59 exit, several sloughs along the Tongue River line the south side of the interstate (at mile marker 137). This is an excellent place to see Wood Duck. This land is private property; please do not trespass.

Drive southeast of Miles City on Highway 12 toward Baker to look for Prairie Falcon and Rock Wren, especially near **Strawberry Hill**. Ten miles east of town on Highway 12 at mile marker 16, turn into the ponderosa pine hills of **Woodruff Park** for Common Nighthawk, Red-breasted Nuthatch,

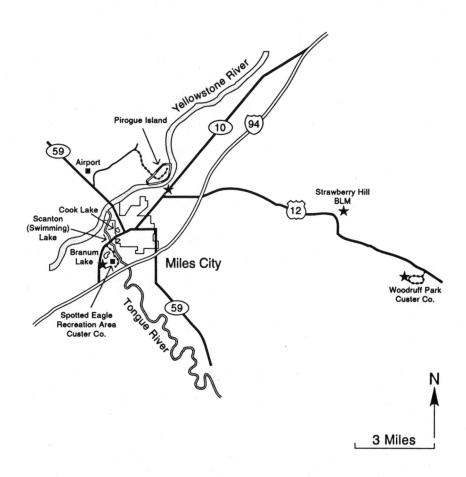

White-breasted Nuthatch, Mountain Bluebird, Chipping Sparrow, and Red Crossbill.

North of Miles City, **Pirogue Island** provides excellent habitat for birds using the Yellowstone River corridor. Drive two miles north on Highway 59 and head northeast on Secondary Road 489 (toward Kinsey) for roughly two miles. Turn right on the dirt road down to Pirogue Island. Groves of large cottonwoods mixed with open meadows and sloughs on the edge of the mighty Yellowstone River give cover for American White Pelican, Double-crested Cormorant, Great Blue Heron, Red-tailed Hawk, Spotted Sandpiper, Belted Kingfisher, Red-headed Woodpecker, Brown Thrasher, and various species of waterfowl in summer. Bald Eagle fish here, especially in fall and winter.

Helpful Information:
Elevation: Miles City, 2,371 ft.
Habitat(s): Primarily riparian; sagebrush-grassland, ponderosa pine.
Best Birding Season(s): Spring, early summer.
Best Birding Month(s:): May.
Montana Highway Map Location: 11-E.
Hazards: Mosquitoes, thunderstorms, heat prostration.
Nearest Food, Gas, Lodging: Miles City.
Camping: KOA Miles City.
Land Ownership: BLM; MDFWP; private; Custer County.
Additional Information: Rosebud Audubon Society, P.O. Box 361, Miles City, MT 59301.
Recommended Length of Stay: 1 to 2 days.

---

31 EKALAKA AND VICINITY

General Information: *Alzada, located in the extreme southwest corner of Montana, was once called Stoneville. Lou Stone originally operated a saloon at this settlement. In 1885 the town was named Alzada, after a pioneer rancher's wife by the name of Mrs. Alzada Sheldon. Ekalaka was named after an Indian girl, born on the Powder River and daughter of Eagle Man (an Oglala Sioux). She was the niece of Red Cloud and distant relative of Sitting Bull, and married the first white man to settle in this area.*

Birding Information: Birding in the southeast corner of Montana can be exciting. However, travelers should bear in mind that the region is sparsely populated and there are few paved roads. Highway 7 south from Baker to Ekalaka is paved, as are the first fifteen miles of Highway 323 south of Ekalaka, but most of the remaining routes here are rough gravel or fair-weather dirt roads.

The town of Baker, at the crossroads of U.S. 12 and Highway 7, offers good birding for various species of waterfowl at **Baker Lake**. The lake is on the east side of Highway 7 about a quarter mile south of town.

Drive south of Baker on Highway 7 to mile marker 11 and **Medicine Rocks State Park**. Legend has it that the Medicine Rocks area possessed magical spirits that gave "Big Medicine" or good luck to Indian hunting parties. In the late 1800s Teddy Roosevelt camped here and inscribed his name into the sandstone pillars only to have it worn away by erosion. Today, this 220-acre park provides good birding in the grasslands, rolling ponderosa pine hills, and around the sandstone pillars and escarpments. Raptors are especially noticeable here and include Northern Harrier, Red-tailed Hawk, Ferruginous Hawk, Golden Eagle, American Kestrel, Merlin, Prairie Falcon,

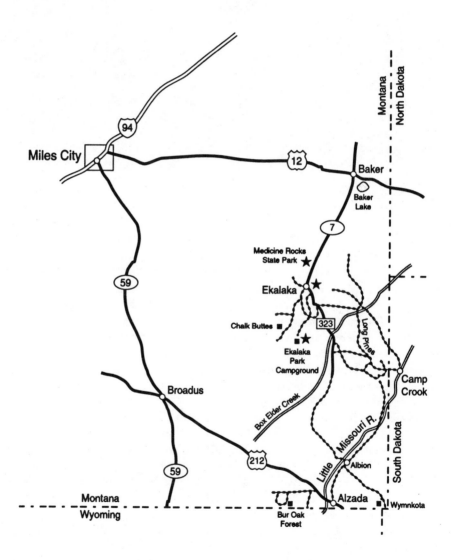

View from the Ekalaka Hills.

and Great Horned Owl. Sharp-tailed Grouse, Cliff Swallow, Red-breasted Nuthatch, Mountain Bluebird, Rufous-sided Towhee, and Western Meadowlark are other species likely to be encountered here. The Medicine Rocks area is also a good place to camp, and the drinking water here is fantastic.

Thirty-five miles south of Baker on Highway 7 is the small, quiet, quaint town of **Ekalaka**. Western Wood-Pewee, Yellow Warbler, and House Sparrow are easily found in the middle of town. South of town, nestled among several isolated segments of the Custer National Forest, **Chalk Buttes** can be approached by heading west at the county courthouse in Ekalaka for 1.5 miles, then south. The buttes are essentially inaccessible because they are surrounded by private land.

To bird on the Custer National Forest and the Ekalaka Hills, drive five miles southeast of Ekalaka on Highway 323 and look for the county road heading west. This route leads to **Ekalaka Park Campground**, five miles west of Highway 323, where the birding is very good. Ekalaka Park is a delightful oasis in a hardwood draw surrounded by hills of ponderosa pine, with patches of aspen and deciduous shrubs. Two other roads may tempt the more adventurous birder (with time to spare and a high-clearance vehicle) into the Ekalaka Hills. From the junction just east of Ekalaka Park Campground, go north on the **Joseph Smith Road**, which winds through ponderosa pines back to Ekalaka. Or go south from the same junction on the narrow, rutted road that loops south through rimrock country and past **Camp Needmore**. Shortly after passing Camp Needmore, this road rejoins

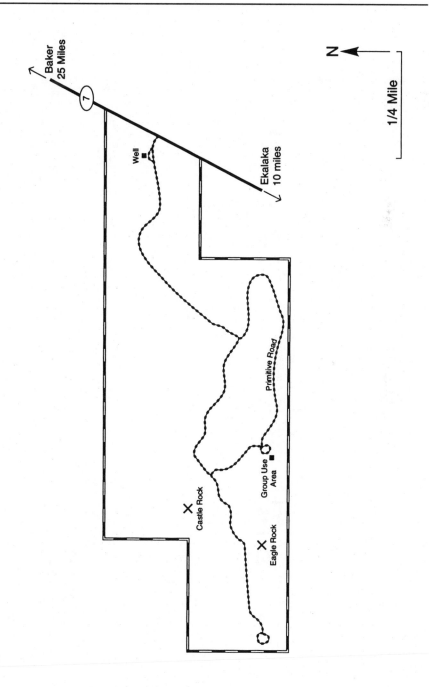

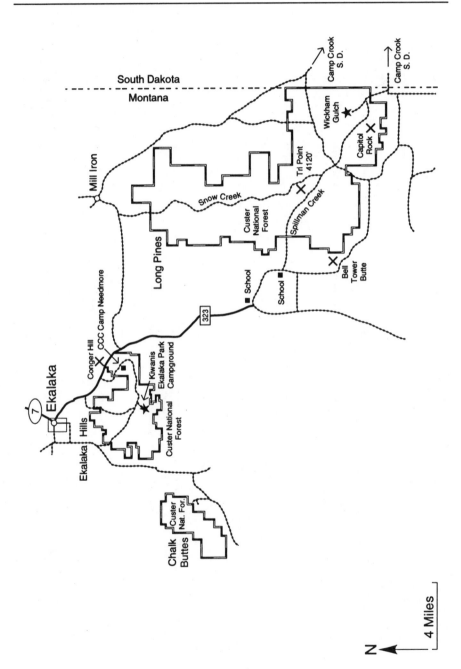

South Dakota
Montana

Camp Crook S. D.

Camp Crook S. D.

Wickham Gulch

Capitol Rock

Mill Iron

Tri Point 4120'

Snow Creek

Spillman Creek

Custer National Forest

Long Pines

CCC Camp Needmore

Bell Tower Butte

School

School

323

Conger Hill

Kiwanis

Ekalaka Park Campground

Ekalaka

7

Ekalaka Hills

Custer National Forest

Chalk Buttes

Custer Nat. For.

N

4 Miles

the county road a few miles west of Highway 323. This loop road offers spectacular views of this unique country. Vegetation found here—and in **Long Pines** to the southwest—is similar to the vegetation in the Black Hills of South Dakota.

The **Snow Creek Road**, running for twenty miles south on the crest of the Long Pines, takes a fair amount of time to drive but is often worthwhile for birding. To reach the Snow Creek Road, drive seven miles south from Ekalaka on Highway 323, past Cougar Hill, and turn onto the gravel road heading due east toward Mill Iron. Go ten miles to the Snow Creek Road on the right and follow this road along the crest of the Long Pines to **Spillman Creek**—also known as Speelman Creek. From here, the Spillman Creek Road leads west eleven miles back to Highway 323.

Other birding options in the southern sector of Long Pines include **Capitol Rock** and **Bell Tower Butte**, both fair sites for Golden Eagle. **Wickham Gulch**, in the southeast corner of Long Pines, is another beautiful oasis in the pines worth birding and camping. Just 2.5 miles from the South Dakota state line, Wickham Gulch is best approached on the dirt road from Camp Creek, South Dakota (see map). Though many of the large trees in the Long Pines area were lost to a recent wildfire, the birding is still good.

Some species likely to be discovered in the Ekalaka Hills-Long Pines area include Sharp-shinned Hawk, Red-tailed Hawk, Golden Eagle, American Kestrel, Merlin, Prairie Falcon, Wild Turkey, Lewis' Woodpecker, Downy Woodpecker, Hairy Woodpecker, Northern Flicker, Mountain Chickadee, White-breasted Nuthatch, Ovenbird, Western Tanager, Chipping Sparrow, Dark-eyed Junco (White-winged race), and Pine Siskin.

The narrow riparian corridors of **Box Elder Creek** and the **Little Missouri River**, which are surrounded by grasslands, are the best places in Montana to see large numbers of Western Kingbird. (The rare Cassin's Kingbird is found 100 miles to the west on U.S. 212 in the juniper and ponderosa hills and riparian habitat near Ashland.) About fifteen miles south of Ekalaka, Highway 323 changes from pavement to dirt and parallels Box Elder Creek for more than ten miles. The Little Missouri River rises in Wyoming, then intersects U.S. 212 just west of **Alzada**, an extremely small town just three miles from the Wyoming border. From Alzada, birders can follow the Little Missouri as it heads northeast toward South Dakota. Drive fourteen miles north on Highway 323 to an intersection and continue northeast toward Wickham Gulch and Camp Creek, South Dakota. The riparian area offers good birding free from the intrusions of other people, even other birders.

Just west and south of Alzada is the only bur oak forest in all of Montana. The tiny forest lies on BLM and private land; ask for directions at the bar in Alzada. Look for Blue Jays in the bur oak. East of Alzada, "Wymnkota" is the rarely visited corner of Montana that touches South Dakota and Wyoming.

Helpful Information:
Elevation: Ekalaka, 3,430 ft; Long Pines, 4,120 ft.
Habitat(s): Ponderosa pine, deciduous trees, grassland, cliff escarpments, riparian.
Best Birding Season(s): Spring, early summer.
Best Birding Month(s): April, May, June.
Montana Highway Map Location: 12-F, 12-G.
Hazards: Rattlesnakes, thunderstorms, heat prostration, flat tires.
Nearest Food, Gas, Lodging: Baker, Ekalaka.
Camping: Medicine Rocks, Ekalaka Park, Wickham Gulch.
Land Ownership: primarily USFS, some BLM and private.
Additional Information: Custer National Forest, P.O. Box 2556, Billings, MT 9103 ph: (406) 657-6361; or Camp Crook, SD ph: (605) 797-4432.
Recommended Length of Stay: 2 to 3 days.

32 YOUNGS CREEK AND TONGUE RIVER RESERVOIR

General Information: *The name of the Tongue River has a few possible origins from Native Americans. One theory on the origin of the name holds that the meandering of this river was crooked like a white man's tongue. Another derivation centers around a tongue-shaped formation of trees and rocks on a hillside at the headwaters of the Little Tongue and Tongue Rivers. But still another account is that the Indians called it "talking river," and the whites translated this as Tongue River. Regardless, it is a beautifully long, meandering river that flows north from the Bighorn Mountains and empties into the Yellowstone River at Miles City.*

Birding Information: The **Tongue River** country of Montana is a beautiful blend of rolling plains, tree-lined streams, sandstone outcroppings, and ponderosa pine clad foothills and mountains. The area is rich in coal deposits and coal mines interrupt the lines of this landscape, but the birding is nevertheless quite good.

The area is best approached by taking Wyoming Highway 339 north from Sheridan, Wyoming. Approximately fifteen miles north of town, Highway 339 crosses the Montana/Wyoming line and becomes Montana Highway 314. Three miles north of the state line is the small town of Decker, and five miles north of the line is the intersection of Highway 314 and the Otter Creek Road. Go east a half mile down Otter Creek Road to the **Tongue River bridge**, which is a fairly good place to stop and watch birds in the riparian zone. Turkey Vulture are easily seen in this area. Return to **Highway 314** and

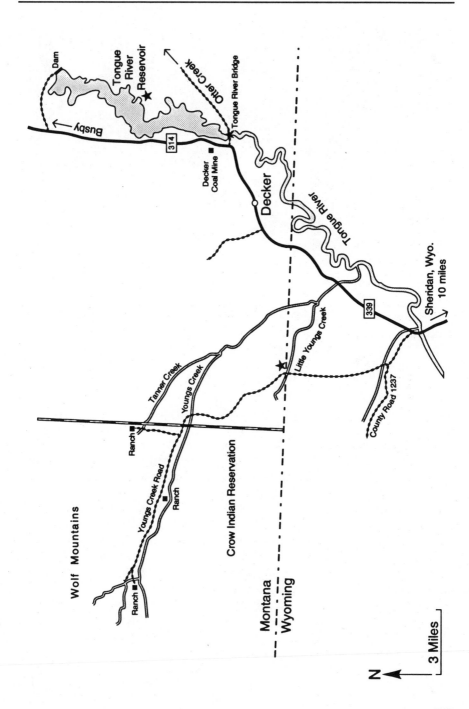

Youngs Creek.

continue north for a half mile to a dirt road and abandoned homestead to the east. Birding in this area can produce Mallard, Spotted Sandpiper, Belted Kingfisher, Western Wood-Pewee, Yellow Warbler, Northern Oriole, and American Goldfinch.

Driving another mile north on Highway 314 provides excellent views of **Tongue River Reservoir** and species such as Great Blue Heron, American White Pelican, Double-crested Cormorant, American Kestrel, and Turkey Vulture. The mudflats of the Tongue River delta are quite good for shorebirds during migration. Birding below the Tongue River Dam is good for birds in the riparian habitat. The dam can easily be reached by driving about nine miles north of Decker on Highway 314 and turning east on the three-mile dirt access road to the dam.

Another excellent birding area—**Youngs Creek**—awaits to the west of Decker, and is also best reached from Wyoming Highway 339 north of Sheridan. About half a mile north of the Highway 339 bridge over the Tongue River in Wyoming, look for a red gravel road on the west side of the highway. This is the **Ash Creek Road** or County Road 1237. Follow the Ash Creek Road northwest for slightly more than a mile, and turn north at the next junction toward Youngs Creek. Three miles up this road, watch for an open pit coal mine to the west and then the riparian zone of **Little Youngs Creek**. Keep an eye open along this route for Golden Eagle, Red-tailed Hawk, American Kestrel, and possibly Prairie Falcon. Black-tailed prairie dogs can also be found along this road.

Once across Little Youngs Creek, the road passes through a gap in a sandstone outcrop and enters Montana. About 4.5 miles north of the Montana line the road crosses **Youngs Creek**. Follow the left fork of the road west along the riparian zone. Birding along this creek can be absolutely fantastic for Mourning Dove, Black-billed Cuckoo, Downy Woodpecker, Northern Flicker (red-shafted race), Western Wood-Pewee, American Crow, Black-capped Chickadee, House Wren, Gray Catbird, Brown Thrasher, Red-eyed Vireo, Black-headed Grosbeak, Rufous-sided Towhee, American Red-start, Common Yellowthroat, Yellow-breasted Chat, Lark Sparrow, Northern Oriole, and American Goldfinch.

In the sagebrush-grasslands look for Upland Sandpiper, Sage Grouse, Sharp-tailed Grouse, Horned Lark, Sage Thrasher, Brewer's Sparrow, Vesper Sparrow, Lark Bunting, Grasshopper Sparrow, and Western Meadowlark. In the ponderosa pine watch for Poorwill, Western Wood-Peewee, Say's Phoebe, Eastern Kingbird, Mountain Bluebird, White-breasted Nuthatch, Rock Wren, Solitary Vireo, Yellow-rumped Warbler (Myrtle Race) Western Tanager, and Chipping Sparrow. Also be alert for Golden Eagle, Sharp-tailed Grouse, Great Horned Owl, Long-eared Owl, Lewis' Woodpecker, Mountain Chickadee, Red Crossbill, and on occasion Northern Saw-whet Owl.

The road forks at the end of Youngs Creek near a ranch. To bird the **Wolf Mountains** to the west, first ask permission from the landowner. The Wolf Mountains are very beautiful. Species that can be encountered here include Northern Goshawk, Swainson's Hawk, Ovenbird, Green-tailed Towhee, and Rufous-sided Towhee.

Helpful Information:
Elevation: 3,450 ft to 4,717 ft.
Habitat(s): Riparian, sagebrush-grassland, ponderosa pine.
Best Birding Season(s): Late spring, summer.
Best Birding Month(s): May, June.
Montana Highway Map Location: 9-G, 10-G.
Hazards: Mosquitoes, rattlesnakes.
Nearest Food, Gas, Lodging: Sheridan, Wyoming.
Camping: Tongue River Reservoir State Park; Along county road, only if you keep a clean camp.
Land Ownership: Private.
Additional Information: Ask landowner permission if birding away from road.
Recommended Length of Stay: 1 to 2 days.

33 BIGHORN CANYON NATIONAL RECREATION AREA

General Information: *French fur trader Francois Laroque was probably the first white European explorer to float through Bighorn Canyon in 1805. Famed mountainman Jim Bridger claimed to have rafted through the dangerous rapids of Bighorn Canyon during the 1825 Ashley fur trading expedition.*

Birding Information: Bighorn Canyon National Recreation Area consists of three components: the seventy-one-mile reservoir created when Yellow-tail Dam was constructed at Fort Smith, Montana, in 1964; the canyon; and the rough terrain that surrounds the canyon and lake. Bighorn Lake is named, as are the canyon and river, for the bighorn sheep that inhabit the region. The canyon is a geologic marvel that was formed as the Bighorn River carved a natural meander through limestone layers over thousands of years. Reminiscent of the Grand Canyon and Canyonlands country, though smaller in scale, Bighorn Canyon has steep-walled cliffs reaching more than 1,000 feet above the lake surface.

Bighorn Canyon NRA is divided into a north and a south district, with the park headquarters, north district offices, and a small visitor center at Fort Smith, Montana. The south district offices and the main park visitor center are in Lovell, Wyoming. The two areas are quite different in topography and vegetation. The southern half of Bighorn Canyon is unique to the northern Rocky Mountain region and similar to the red rock canyon country of the American Southwest. Traveling north, across the Montana/Wyoming state line, the terrain grows more rugged, featuring steep mountain slopes forested with mountain mahogany, juniper, and limber pines, with scattered pockets of cottonwood, boxelder, ponderosa pine, and Douglas fir.

The **South District** of Bighorn Canyon National Recreation Area is one of the most overlooked birding areas in Montana. The setting is reminiscent of Utah, Arizona, or New Mexico. It represents a one-of-a-kind environment in Montana. Start at Lovell, Wyoming, and get oriented with a quick stop at the solar-powered visitor center at the junction of U.S. 14A and U.S. 310. Then head three miles east on U.S. 14A, and turn north on Highway 37 to the NRA boundary nine miles north. Dust off the binoculars and watch for Wyoming birds where Crooked Creek crosses the highway. The **Montana/ Wyoming line** is a good place to see Violet-green Swallow, Pinyon Jay, White-throated Swift, and bighorn sheep and wild horses.

The **Devil Canyon Overlook** offers a wonderful, close view of the canyon country. The turn-off to the overlook is about nine miles from the NRA boundary and is well marked. Species likely to be encountered include Green-tailed Towhee, Rock Wren, Rock Dove, Pinyon Jay, American Kestrel, Red-tailed Hawk, Prairie Falcon, and Golden Eagle. Canyon Wren and

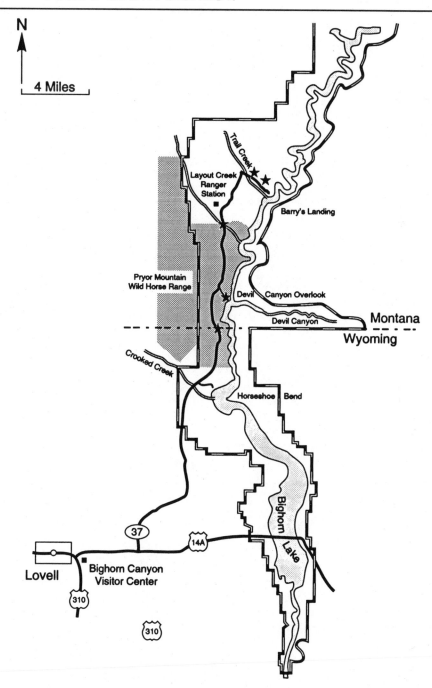

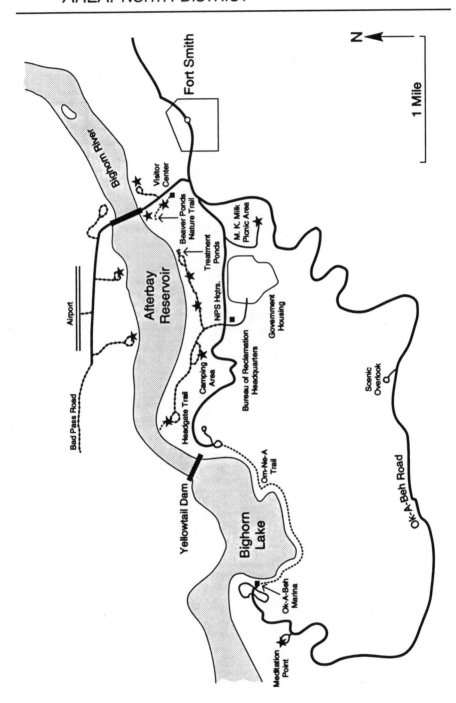

N

1 Mile

Fort Smith

Bighorn River

Visitor Center

Beaver Ponds Nature Trail

Treatment Ponds

M. K. Milk Picnic Area

Afterbay Reservoir

Airport

NPS Hqtrs.

Government Housing

Bad Pass Road

Camping Area

Headgate Trail

Bureau of Reclamation Headquarters

Scenic Overlook

Yellowtail Dam

Om-Ne-A Trail

Bighorn Lake

Ok-A-Beh Road

Ok-A-Beh Marina

Meditation Point

Bighorn Canyon.

Peregrine Falcon can be found at the Devil Canyon Overlook on occasion. American White Pelican are occasionally seen flying in coordinated flocks from one end of the reservoir to the other.

A beautiful cottonwood draw, **Layout Creek**, crosses the road about 4.5 miles north of Devil Canyon Overlook. Birding is excellent along the creek and up the gravel side road toward the Ranger Station. Species likely to be encountered on Layout Creek include Common Nighthawk, Poorwill, Downy Woodpecker, Western Wood-Pewee, Eastern Kingbird, Tree Swallow, Barn Swallow, House Wren, Townsend's Solitaire, Yellow Warbler, Yellow-breasted Chat, Lazuli Bunting, Chipping Sparrow, Lark Sparrow, Lincoln's Sparrow, Pine Siskin, American Goldfinch, and Western Tanager. The cottonwoods and deciduous understory along **Trail Creek** also offer good places to bird and camp. Tent campers are advised to use the upper portion of the creek, and RV campers are better off at the lower end near Barry's Landing.

The **North District** of Bighorn Canyon National Recreation Area is also often neglected by birders, yet the birding is quite good. Stop at the visitor center in Fort Smith, about forty-one miles south of Hardin on Highway 313, to get oriented to the area. The **Beaver Ponds Nature Trail**, which leaves from the parking lot of the visitor center, is a good place to bird and stretch your legs.

From the visitor center drive north toward the airport for good views of the **Afterbay Reservoir** below Yellowtail Dam, a hot spot for birding.

Search the Afterbay Reservoir for waterfowl, California Gull, and Pied-billed Grebe. During spring and fall migration, Herring Gull can be found here, as can Bald Eagle and an occasional rarity such as the Glaucous Gull. During winter, open water below the dam attracts large numbers of gulls, waterfowl, and Bald Eagles.

On the south side of Afterbay Reservoir, the roads to the **treatment ponds and the Headgate Trailhead** offer especially good birding, thanks to a wide diversity of deciduous trees and shrubs ranging from wild plum and buffaloberry to boxelder and cottonwood. Species likely to be encountered include Black-billed Cuckoo, Western Wood-Pewee, Eastern Kingbird, Gray Catbird, Cedar Waxwing, Yellow Warbler, MacGillivray's Warbler, Yellow-breasted Chat, Lazuli Bunting, Green-tailed Towhee, Lark Sparrow, and American Goldfinch.

The scenic **Ok-A-Beh Road** climbs the foothills of the Bighorn Mountains before spiraling down to the water's edge at Ok-A-Beh Marina, 5.5 miles south of Fort Smith. Wildflowers here are sensational throughout early summer. Habitats change along the route from deciduous draws, yucca's, and grasslands to mountain mahogany, ponderosa pine, and steep-walled canyons. Blue Grouse can be found at times near Meditation Point. Look for Rock Wren near rock outcrops and the occasional Canyon Wren, most often near tall canyon walls.

Helpful Information:

Elevation: Lovell, 3,910 ft, Fort Smith, 3,281 ft.
Habitat(s): Juniper, riparian, open water, steep canyon walls, cliffs.
Best Birding Season(s): Spring, early summer.
Best Birding Month(s): April, May, June.
Montana Highway Map Location: 8-G.
Hazards: Rattlesnakes, heat prostration, poison ivy (N. District)
Nearest Food, Gas, Lodging: Lovell, Fort Smith, Hardin.
Camping: Bighorn: NRA Trail Creek/Barry's Landing; Fort Smith: Afterbay.
Land Ownership: NPS.
Additional Information: Bighorn Canyon National Recreation Area, Headquarters (& North District), P.O. Box 458, Fort Smith, MT 59035 ph: (406) 666-2412. Bighorn Canyon NRA, South District, 20 Highway 14A East, Lovell, WY 82431 ph: (307) 548-2251.
Recommended Length of Stay: Bighorn Canyon: 4 hours to 2 days. Fort Smith: 4 to 8 hours.

34 LITTLE BIGHORN BATTLEFIELD NATIONAL MONUMENT

General Information: *Formerly called Custer Battlefield, the name of this national monument has been rightfully changed to recognize the Indians who also fought in this famous battle on the hills above the Little Bighorn River. This 1876 battle marked the last major victory for the Northern Plains Indians, including Sitting Bull and Crazy Horse, to preserve their traditional way of life.*

The Crow people are also called Absarokee, which means "children of the large-beaked bird." In frontier times, the tribe was known for its sign language, which relied on much flapping of the arms, thus suggesting the association with ravens and crows.

Birding Information: The Little Bighorn Battlefield lies on the Crow Indian Reservation, just east of I-90 near the town of Crow Agency. Take the U.S. 212 exit about two miles south of Crow Agency and turn south on Battlefield Road. Watch for songbirds near the **visitor center** and particularly in the **National Cemetery**, especially during migration (May and September). Other fine birding spots along Battlefield Road are **Custer Hill, Calhoun Hill, Deep Coulee, Medicine Tail Coulee, Weir Point**, and **Reno-Benteen Battlefield**. For best results, start birding when the battlefield opens at 8 a.m. Later in the day, the sheer number of people reduces the numbers of birds that can be observed. Species to look for on the Little Bighorn Battlefield include Red-tailed Hawk, Mourning Dove, Common Nighthawk, Horned Lark, Cliff Swallow, Black-billed Magpie, Vesper Sparrow, and Western Meadowlark.

Helpful Information:
Elevation: Crow Agency, 3,050 ft.
Habitat(s): Sagebrush-grassland, riparian, manicured parkland.
Best Birding Season(s): Late spring, early summer.
Best Birding Month(s): May.
Montana Highway Map Location: 9-G.
Hazards: Rattlesnakes, heat prostration.
Nearest Food, Gas, Lodging: Sheridan, Wyoming; Crow Agency and Hardin, Montana.
Camping: Fort Smith (Bighorn Canyon National Recreational Area).
Land Ownership: NPS, Crow Indian Reservation.
Additional Information: Superintendent, Little Bighorn Battlefield, P.O. Box 39, Crow Agency, MT 59022.
Recommended Length of Stay: 2 to 4 hours.

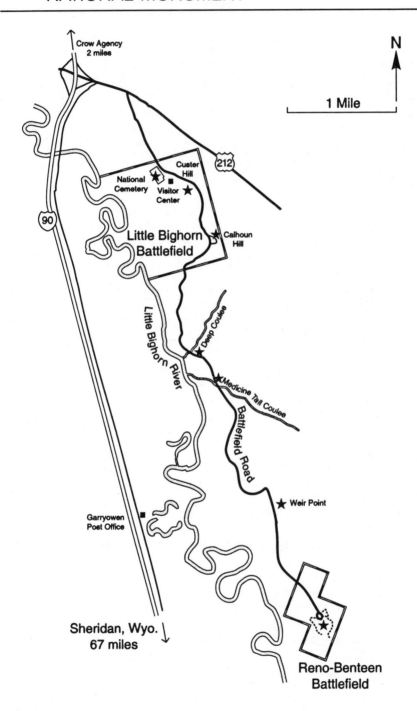

35 PRYOR MOUNTAINS

General Information: *The Pryor Mountains and Pryor Creek were named by Lewis and Clark for Nathaniel Pryor, a member of the expedition. Wild horses roam the range on the south and east edges of the Pryor Mountains. Lowland valleys surrounding the Pryors receive less rainfall than almost any other region of Montana. Incoming moisture is stripped from the sky by the high mountains of the Beartooth Plateau. The Chief Plenty Coups Memorial State Monument, in the town of Pryor, is worth visiting.*

Birding Information: The Pryor Mountains are best approached up the Sage Creek Road from Warren to Sage Creek Junction or by way of Bridger through Bowler Flats to Sage Creek Junction. The **Sage Creek Road** (Forest Service Road 3085) is not heavily traveled, and birders should wait for favorable weather. Watch for Golden Eagle, Prairie Falcon, Sage Thrasher, and Loggerhead Shrike. The road from Bridger to Sage Creek Junction is more heavily traveled. Species likely to be encountered include Golden Eagle, Loggerhead Shrike, Mourning Dove, and Mountain Bluebird.

Birding from Sage Creek Junction into the Custer National Forest and along Sage Creek can be rewarding. Likely sightings include Common Yellowthroat, American Crow, Yellow-breasted Chat, Lazuli Bunting, Gray Catbird, Chipping Sparrow, Green-tailed Towhee, Yellow Warbler, Cedar Waxwing, Eastern Kingbird, Willow Flycatcher, Song Sparrow, Cliff Swallow, Warbling Vireo, and American Goldfinch.

Sage Creek Campground is worth a stop to rest and watch for Calliope Hummingbird, Rufous Hummingbird, and Green-tailed Towhee. Mountain Bluebird and Green-tailed Towhee are common in the sagebrush meadows around the Crooked Creek turnoff. The bumpy road down Crooked Creek is not recommended for driving, but it makes a good birding hike.

Continue on this road to the **Big Ice Cave** in the Pryor Mountains, scanning the stands of Douglas fir for Ruby-crowned Kinglet, Pine Siskin, Cassin's Finch, Western Tanager, Red Crossbill, and Blue Grouse. A short walk to Big Ice Cave is a refreshing treat in summer. Be alert for the occasional Cordilleran Flycatcher here. The road ends at the **Dry Head Overlook**, with exceptional views of the Bighorn Canyon country. The overlook is also a good spot to watch for Golden Eagle, Turkey Vulture, Prairie Falcon, and other raptors.

Helpful Information:
Elevation: Bridger, 3,720 ft; Pryor Mountains, 8,875 ft.
Habitat(s): Sagebrush-grassland, riparian, coniferous forests.
Best Birding Season(s): Late spring, early summer.
Best Birding Month(s): May, June.
Montana Highway Map Location: 8-G.

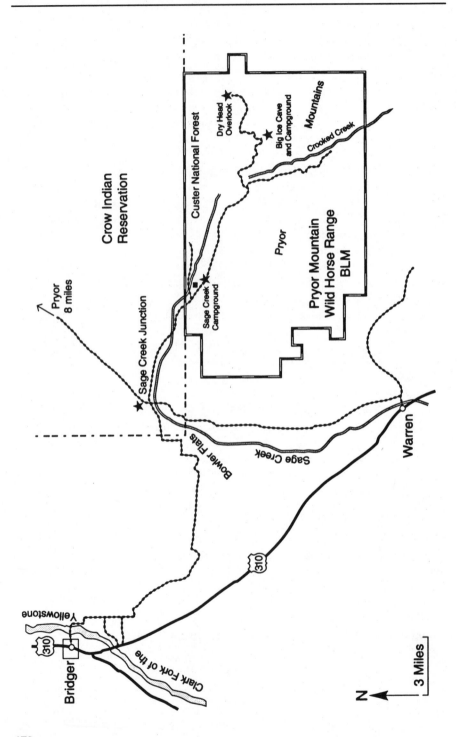

Hazards: Rattlesnakes, mosquitoes, thunderstorms.
Nearest Food, Gas, Lodging: Bridger.
Camping: Custer National Forest.
Land Ownership: BLM, USFS, Crow Indian Reservation, private.
Additional Information: Custer National Forest, 2602 First Avenue North P.O. Box 2556, Billings, MT 59103 ph: (406) 657-6361.
Recommended Length of Stay: 1 to 2 days.

36 BILLINGS AND VICINITY

General Information: *Billings is called the "Magic City" because of its phenomenal human and economic growth since it was founded in 1882. Today it is the largest city in Montana. The city was named in honor of Frederick Billings, a local businessman and stockholder of the Northern Pacific Railroad.*

Birding Information: The Billings area abounds with Indian history, beautiful scenery, good fishing, and excellent birding opportunities. Perhaps the best birding area in Billings is **Two Moon County Park** on the northeast side of town. Take Main Street north a half mile past the Metra arena and turn right on Bench Boulevard. Turn right again and descend the hill to the entrance of the 150-acre park near the parking lot. The best birding is had from a series of trails through riparian vegetation along the Yellowstone River. Two Moon Park is an excellent area to observe warblers (including Orange-crowned, Tennessee, Nashville, Yellow, and Yellow-rumped), American Redstart, and Yellow-breasted Chat, particularly during spring migration. Wood Duck and Song Sparrow are found here, as is the rare Eastern Screech-Owl. Look for White-throated Sparrow during spring and fall.

Also north of town, follow Lake Elmo Drive 2.5 miles from Main Street to **Lake Elmo State Park**. Take a stroll on the Lake Elmo hiking trail for likely sightings of California Gull, Ring-billed Gull, Franklin's Gull, Pied-billed Grebe, Eared Grebe, Killdeer, Mallard, Redhead, and Canvasback. During migration, watch for Common Loon and the occasional Glaucous Gull.

South of town, **Sacrifice Cliff** offers excellent views of the Billings skyline and wonderful sunsets. Take the Coburn Road south of Billings to Pictograph Caves. One mile from the interstate, a short dirt road to the west leads to the edge of Sacrifice Cliff, a sandstone outcrop sprinkled with ponderosa pines. Rock Wren are common here, and Poorwill are occasional visitors.

Continue south from the Sacrifice Cliff turnoff on Coburn Road and turn west on the gravel road to **Pictograph Caves State Monument**. While driving, watch for Pinyon Jay in the ponderosa pine/juniper and Rufous-sided Towhee, Yellow-breasted Chat, Northern Oriole, and House Wren in

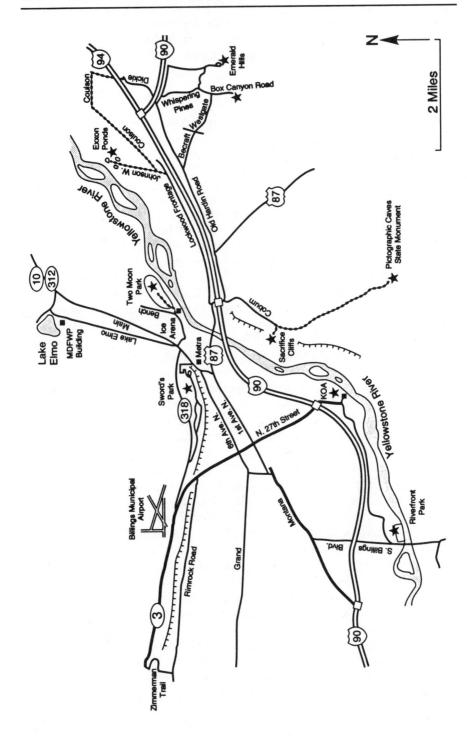

the narrow cottonwood-lined draw. The picnic area at the caves is a wonderful place to relax and watch Mountain Bluebird, Rock Wren, Cliff Swallow, White-throated Swift, and even Prairie Falcon and Canyon Wren. Don't forget to hike up to see the pictographs. This day-use area is currently open only during the summer due to funding constraints and to protect the pictographs from vandalism.

East of Billings there are five areas worth birding, though all are primarily private property. Please respect the rights of these property owners and stay on the county roads. **Box Canyon** and the **Emerald Hills** can both be reached by taking the Lockwood exit off of I-90 and following the Old Hardin Road on the south side of the interstate for 2.5 miles to Becraft Road. Drive two miles southeast on Becraft and turn right onto Box Canyon Road. In the Box Canyon area look for Solitary Vireo and Pinyon Jay in the ponderosa pine. Turn around and drive north on Box Canyon Road, eventually winding east to the Emerald Hills. Summers here are usually cooler than in Billings and local birds are typical of a more mountainous environment. In summer, look for Hammond's Flycatcher, Dusky Flycatcher, Least Flycatcher, Pygmy Nuthatch, Red-breasted Nuthatch, and White-breasted Nuthatch. Thanks to numerous bird feeders close to a ponderosa pine forest, winter residents include Red Crossbill, Pine Siskin, Cassin's Finch, and Wild Turkey.

Return north to the Old Hardin Road and pass under I-90 to Dickie Road. Follow Dickie north to **Coulson Road**, which bends west and south, to see American Kestrel and Western Meadowlark during summer and Sharp-tailed Grouse and Red-tailed Hawk during winter. At the instersection of Coulson and Johnson Lane, turn north on Johnson for one mile to the **Exxon Ponds**. These ponds form an interesting wetland complex of cattails and brush, and offer excellent views of waterfowl, Northern Harrier, and Loggerhead Shrike in summer and Northern Shrike in winter.

Twenty miles east of Billings, between I-94 and the Yellowstone River, **Pompey's Pillar** boasts a variety of birdlife and an interesting history. On July 25, 1806, William Clark of the Lewis and Clark Expedition carved his name on this 200-foot sandstone tower next to ancient Indian pictographs. The signature is still legible and today the site is a Registered National Historic Landmark. Look for Rock Wren and Northern Oriole around the pillar and Yellow Warbler in the cottonwoods.

The **KOA Campground** south of Billings on Garden Avenue is a good place to camp and watch birds. A variety of songbirds frequent the campground and the banks of the Yellowstone River, with especially good birding during migration. Southwest of town on the north bank of the Yellowstone River, **Riverfront Park** is laced with trails that skirt ponds and side channels bordered by large cottonwood groves. This fine birding park harbors Great Blue Heron, Belted Kingfisher, Downy Woodpecker, Northern Flicker, Warbling Vireo, Yellow Warbler, Dark-eyed Junco, Yellow-headed Blackbird, Northern Oriole, and the occasional Merlin, Great Horned Owl, and Eastern Screech-Owl. In winter, watch for Bohemian Waxwing feeding on the bright orange berries of mountain ash trees.

Swords Park, on the rimrocks just north of town, is another good area for birdwatching, viewing the busy town below, and enjoying spectacular sunsets. Black Otter Trail goes right through Swords Park. The area is characterized by ponderosa pine, juniper, yucca, skunkbrush, greasewood, and high sandstone cliffs. Rufous-sided Towhee, Rock Wren, Mountain Bluebird, and Black-billed Magpie are often found here. Stop one-quarter mile west of Yellowstone Kelly's gravesite on Black Otter Trail, and overlooking the rimrock, to see Violet-green Swallow, White-throated Swift, and on occasion Canyon Wren. Red Crossbill and Common Redpoll can be found in this same general area in the winter. Along the top of the rimrocks, Vesper Sparrow and Lark Sparrow can be found.

From Sword's Park, drive west past the airport on Highway 3 to a small gravel parking lot just west of Zimmerman Trail. Several rough trails lead west for two miles atop the rims, providing good birding among ponderosa pine and juniper for Common Raven, Northern Flicker, and the occasional Prairie Falcon, Great Horned Owl, and Canyon Wren.

Zimmerman Trail drops through a gap in the rims to Rimrock Road. Turn right and drive a half mile west on Rimrock Road, then turn right on Laredo to the end of the road below the rims. Canyon Wren are sometimes found here.

Head ten miles west of Billings on Grand Avenue (then 88th Street and Lipp Road) to a road junction with a historic marker for the Canyon Creek Battlefield. On Sept. 13, 1877, Chief Joseph and his small band of warriors, elders, and children out-maneuvered and out-shot Colonel Sturgis and his force of 400 men at this site. From the Canyon Creek Monument, travel northwest on a gravel road known as the Buffalo Trail. After one mile turn left or west up **Canyon Creek** and watch for a variety of birds over the next mile. The small, brushy creek meanders through stands of ponderosa pine and sandstone cliffs, good habitat for Red-tailed Hawk, Golden Eagle, Prairie Falcon, Great Horned Owl, Say's Phoebe, Eastern Kingbird, Horned Lark, Cliff Swallow, Pinyon Jay, Common Raven, Canyon Wren, Vesper Sparrow, Lark Sparrow, Savannah Sparrow, and Red Crossbill. Return to the Buffalo Trail and head northwest passed cultivated fields to the paved **Molt Road (County 302)**. Turn left toward Molt, and watch for Chestnut-collared Longspur along the way, particularly one to two miles east of Molt.

Take the fair-weather **Eastlick Road** just before (southeast of) Molt and head west. Two miles down the Eastlick Road, turn north on another fair-weather road. Within 100 yards, look on the west side of the road for a prairie dog town where Burrowing Owl are often found. These small owls are diurnal and midday is a good time to see them. Check the Corral Ponds (on the east side of the road) for shorebirds and waterfowl, especially during migration. In the shortgrass prairie to the west of the road, look for Sprague's Pipit, McCown's Longspur, and Chestnut-collared Longspur. Other birds to look for in this general area include Golden Eagle, Long-billed Curlew, Upland Sandpiper, Mourning Dove, Horned Lark, Western Meadowlark, Brewer's Sparrow, and Lark Sparrow. Once at the junction of the Molt-

Rapelje Road and the Corral Pond road, head north three- quarters of a mile to a windrow or shelterbelt on the east side of the road. The shelterbelt attracts Swainson's Hawk, Gray Partridge, Sharp-tailed Grouse, Mourning Dove, Great Horned Owl, Western Wood-Pewee, Say's Phoebe, and Yellow Warbler. A variety of spring and fall migrants also pause here.

Continue north and west on the Molt-Rapelje Road to the abandoned town of **Wheat Basin**, a lonesome crossroads with a church and grain elevator. Look in the weedy fields just south of the church or east of town for the elusive Baird's Sparrow. From Wheat Basin, drive south to Big Lake, watching for Upland Sandpiper and Short-eared Owl along the way.

Birding at **Big Lake** can be great if enough water is present. Drought years find the lake bed completely dry and birds scarce, but during wet years, exceptional numbers of birds congregate here. If there is water, this is a great place to look for rare birds during spring and fall migration. Nearby Hailstone and Halfbreed National Wildlife Refuges are also at the mercy of the drought cycle, and the area around Molt offers better birding possibilities than these small satellite refuges.

Laurel, sixteen miles west of Billings, offers interesting birding opportunities right off I-90. Check out the ponds by **Exit 433**. Pull off the west on-ramp and park well off the pavement beyond the end of the guardrail. The east pond often holds Common Loon during migration, and the west pond is excellent for migratory shorebirds and waterfowl. South of Laurel on U.S. 212, stop at Riverside Park on the south bank of the Yellowstone River. This is a good place to camp and watch birds in riparian habitat. A side trip along Thiel Road on the south side of the Yellowstone River leads 5.5 miles to a dirt road along **Duck Creek**. Travel south along Duck Creek and scan the riparian vegetation for Red-tailed Hawk, Yellow-breasted Chat, Rufous-sided Towhee, and the occasional Eastern Screech-Owl. Look for Common Merganser at the Duck Creek bridge over the Yellowstone River.

Helpful Information:
Elevation: Billings, 3,117 ft.
Habitat(s): Riparian, rimrock, ponderosa pine, cultivated fields, wetlands.
Best Birding Season(s): All seasons.
Best Birding Month(s): May, June, September (songbirds), August through September (shorebirds).
Montana Highway Map Location: 8-F, 8-G.
Hazards: Rattlesnakes, ticks, mosquitoes.
Nearest Food, Gas, Lodging: Billings, Laurel.
Camping: KOA (Billings); Riverside Park (Laurel).
Land Ownership: Private, city, county, state.
Additional Information: Yellowstone Valley Audubon Society, P.O. Box 1075, Billings, MT 59103-1075.
Recommended Length of Stay: 2 to 4 days.

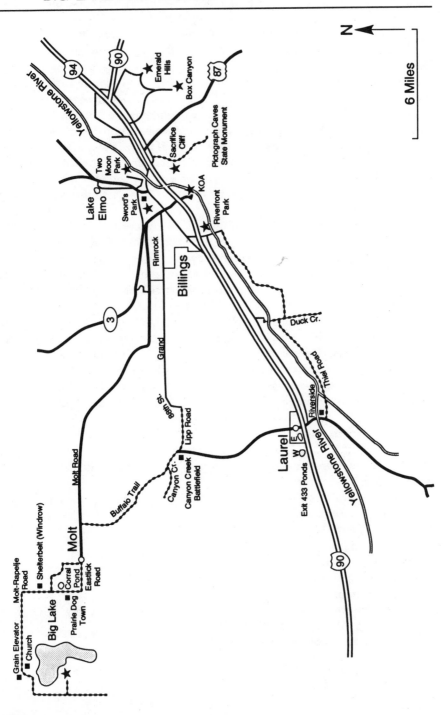

SOUTHCENTRAL MONTANA

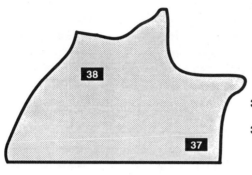

37. Beartooth Highway
    (Cooke City to Red Lodge)
38. Livingston and Vicinity

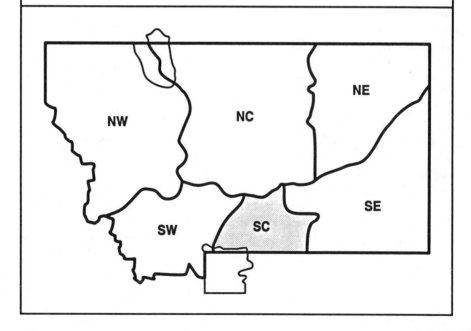

37 BEARTOOTH HIGHWAY
COOKE CITY TO RED LODGE

General Information: *The Beartooth Highway (U.S. 212), from Cooke City to Red Lodge, traverses from Montana into Wyoming and back into Montana, crossing some of the highest and most spectacular country in the Big Sky state. Television commentator Charles Kuralt calls the route over the Beartooth Plateau "the most scenic drive in America." The name "Beartooth" is derived from a rock formation in this mountain range resembling a bear's tooth. Granite Peak, the highest point in Montana at 12,799 feet, rises west of the highway in the Beartooth Mountain Range, home to some of the oldest rocks on earth.*

Birding Information: The highway over Beartooth Pass is maintained by Yellowstone National Park but is closed in winter due to severe weather. The road typically opens on Memorial Day weekend and closes around Halloween, but the actual dates depend on the weather. For Beartooth Pass road conditions contact Yellowstone National Park.

    Silver Gate and Cooke City are located near the northeast entrance to Yellowstone National Park. In the vicinity of Cooke City/Silver Gate look for Steller's Jay, Mountain Chickadee, Golden-crowned Kinglet, Lincoln's Sparrow, and Dark-eyed Junco (pink-sided race). In the winter, Northern Saw-whet Owl and the rare Boreal Owl are found here.

    Immediately east of Cooke City on U.S. Highway 212, a steep, rough jeep trail leads to **Daisy and Lulu passes**, both just under 10,000 feet. A four-wheel-drive vehicle with high clearance is recommended for this climb. Clark's Nutcracker are found at high elevations, as are Blue Grouse, Golden Eagle, and American Pipit. Roughly three miles east from Cooke City on U.S. 212, 8,000-foot **Colter Pass** (also called Cooke Pass) is worth a stop, as is the nearby **Chief Joseph Campground** on the south side of the highway. Look for Red Crossbills and Pine Grosbeak. Also stop at any aspen grove along the route for reliable sightings of Red-naped Sapsucker, Dusky Flycatcher, Mountain Bluebird, House Wren, and Warbling Vireo.

    The Pilot Peak Vista on U.S. 212 in Wyoming, about 7.5 miles east of the junction with Highway 296, is worth a stop to photograph the Matterhorn-like crag to the west known as Pilot Peak. One mile east from the vista pull-out, turn left up a jeep road to **Clay Butte** for glimpses of the same species found on Daisy and Lulu passes. Stop at the bog just below Clay Butte to see Lincoln's Sparrow.

    Continue east on U.S. 212, skirting three high-elevation lakes in the next 8.5 miles. **Beartooth, Island, and Long lakes** are each worth a visit for breathtaking scenery and relaxing birding. Look for Spotted Sandpiper along the shores of these lakes in summer, and Solitary Sandpiper and other shorebirds during fall migration. As U.S. 212 climbs toward 10,947 feet,

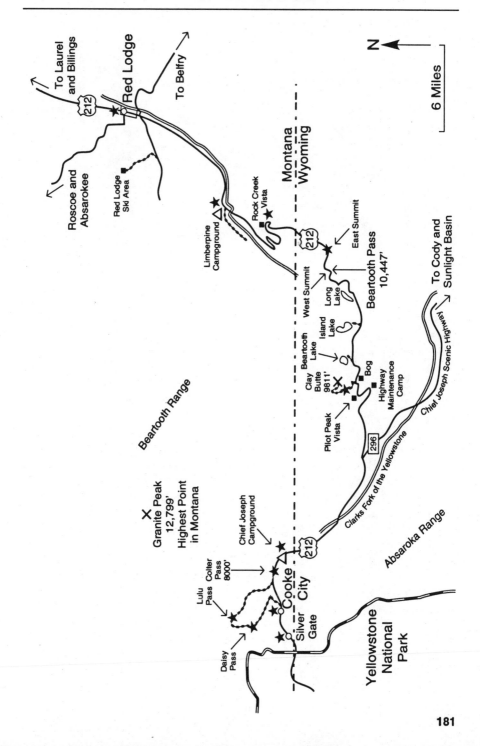

N

6 Miles

To Laurel and Billings

Red Lodge

To Belfry

Roscoe and Absarokee

Red Lodge Ski Area

212

Limberpine Campground

Rock Creek Vista

Montana
Wyoming

212

East Summit

Beartooth Pass 10,447'

West Summit

Long Lake

Island Lake

Beartooth Lake

Clay Butte 9811'

Bog

Highway Maintenance Camp

Pilot Peak Vista

Beartooth Range

296

To Cody and Sunlight Basin

Chief Joseph Scenic Highway

Clarks Fork of the Yellowstone

X Granite Peak 12,799' Highest Point in Montana

Chief Joseph Campground

Colter Pass 8000'

Lulu Pass

Cooke City

212

Silver Gate

Daisy Pass

Absaroka Range

Yellowstone National Park

181

Beartooth Plateau.

make frequent stops at the west and east summits of **Beartooth Pass** and the Montana state line. These are the best places on the Beartooth Plateau to observe Rosy Finch (black race), and American Pipit in summer. Also look for Golden Eagle, Prairie Falcon, Red-tailed Hawk, Common Raven, Clark's Nutcracker, and White-crowned Sparrow in summer, and a variety of raptors during fall migration. Wildflower colors can be incredible on this plateau, if the timing is right. Be on the lookout for red fox and mountain goat.

Continue north on U.S. 212, dropping quickly into the Rock Creek drainage in Montana. Three miles from the state line, stop at the **Rock Creek Vista** for Clark's Nutcracker, Ruby-crowned Kinglet, and Yellow-rumped Warbler. The same species frequent **Limberpine Campground**, roughly 2.5 miles down the road from the last big switchback as the highway descends from the plateau. Beyond the campground, the gravel road up **Rock Creek** deteriorates as it climbs toward the plateau on the west side of the creek, but the lower section cuts through willows and conifers, with good views of Ruby-crowned Kinglet, Swainson's Thrush, American Robin, Warbling Vireo, MacGillivray's Warbler, Wilson's Warbler, Chipping Sparrow, and Pine Siskin. Common Merganser and American Dipper are often found along Rock Creek. Harlequin Duck have been reported here, but only very rarely.

From Rock Creek, drive north fifteen miles to the small town of **Red Lodge,** named for the red-clay shelters once built here by local Indian tribes. The city park on the south side of town is a nice place to relax and watch birds. American Dipper are often found on the creek bordering the small park, as

Beartooth Plateau.

are a variety of passerines that frequent the cottonwoods. The road to the Red Lodge Ski Area is worth a visit to find Green-tailed Towhee and excellent views of the Pryor Mountains to the east.

Helpful Information:
Elevation: Silver Gate, 7,389 ft; Beartooth Pass, 10,947 ft; Red Lodge, 5,254 ft.
Habitat(s): Coniferous forests; subalpine and alpine lakes; alpine; rivers; aspen; willow; sagebrush.
Best Birding Season(s): Summer.
Best Birding Month(s): June, July, August.
Montana Highway Map Location: 6-H, 7-H.
Hazards: Mosquitoes; thunderstorms; snow.
Nearest Food, Gas, Lodging: Red Lodge; Cooke City/Silver Gate.
Camping: Numerous USFS Campgrounds.
Land Ownership: USFS, private.
Additional Information: Yellowstone National Park, P.O. Box 168, Yellowstone National Park, WY 82190 ph: (307) 344-7381; Beartooth Ranger District, Box 4300, Red Lodge, MT 59068 ph: (406) 446-2102.
Recommended Length of Stay: 1 to 2 days.

General Information: *Livingston is one of the windiest places in Montana. It was originally known as Clark City, after Captain William Clark of the 1804 Corps of Discovery, then renamed in honor of Crawford Livingston, a former director of the Northern Pacific Railroad. The Paradise Valley south of Livingston is aptly named, graced by the cottonwood-lined Yellowstone River and surrounded by the rugged peaks of the Gallatin and Absaroka mountains. The valley serves as the northern gateway to Yellowstone National Park. Like Livingston, the Paradise Valley is noted for its strong winds, but here they predominately come from the south. The Yellowstone, the longest free-flowing river in the lower Forty-eight, is a floater's delight, with broad flatwater sections, shallow riffles around small islands, and a short stretch of wild rapids through Yankee Jim Canyon.*

Birding Information: Notorious for windy skies, the **Livingston area** is also noted for its eagles. Golden Eagle are found here year-round, and Bald Eagle are primarily found in winter and during migration. Traveling south from Livingston to the north entrance of Yellowstone National Park on U.S. 89, look for Golden Eagle year-round. The **Paradise Valley** and the **Corwin, Gardiner, and Jardine areas** are reliable places to observe this species. Most impressive is the winter concentration of Bald Eagle, especially along the Yellowstone River from Livingston to Gardiner. All different age classes of Bald Eagle can be observed feeding on carrion, big-game gut piles discarded by hunters, or fish. October through March is the best time for observing eagles here.

Thanks to the riparian habitat along the Yellowstone River, the Livingston area also offers good viewing for waterfowl. **Sacajawea Park**, in the center of town at the south end of Livingston Street, is a good place to observe Canada Goose, Mallard, and occasionally Wood Duck throughout the year.

Five miles south of Livingston is private land known as the **Call of the Wild Ranch**. Carefully pull off in the space beside the guardrail on the east side of U.S. 89 to view birds in the ponds here. Please respect the landowner's privacy, and remain in your car. Make sure your vehicle is parked well off the highway. The traffic here can be extremely dangerous. Birders have a good chance of seeing Trumpeter Swan and the occasional Mute Swan. The trumpeters found here are the result of a cooperative effort by this landowner, private individuals, a private corporation, and Yellowstone National Park. The ranch originally started off with two Mute Swans and ended up with the population peaking at 120. Concern over these Mute Swans expanding their range and possibly getting into Yellowstone resulted in a project that gradually replaced the Mute Swans with Trumpeter Swans. Mute Swans are native to Eurasia, and are extremely territorial and prolific breeders. This project was funded with private monies. Today the ranch is occupied by permanently pinioned and free-flying swans. The ponds also

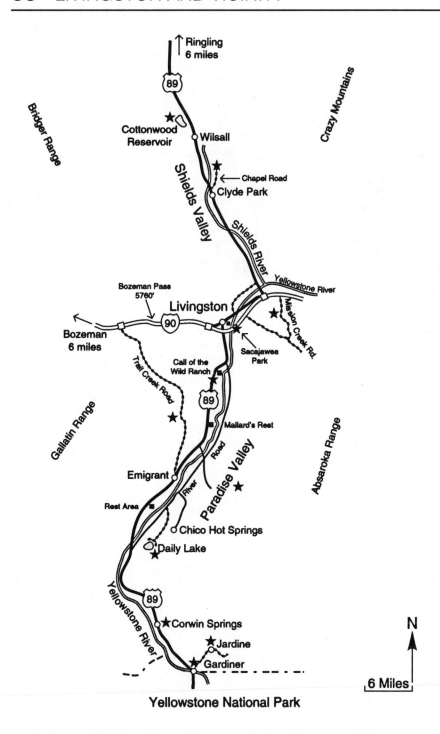

Yellowstone National Park

Cottonwood Reservoir, Shields River Valley.

lure waterfowl and raptors year-round.

Halfway between Livingston and Gardiner on U.S. 89 is the small town of Emigrant, home of the famous Paradise Valley landmark, the Old Saloon. Head east out of Emigrant off U.S. 89 by crossing the Yellowstone River, and drive south on the River Road to the gravel road and sign for **Dailey Lake**. Turn left and drive 6.5 miles to the lake. In the summer this is a popular spot for anglers and sailboarders, so it can be crowded. During spring and fall bird migration some interesting species end up here, including Common Loon, Eared Grebe, Horned Grebe, Red-necked Grebe, Snow Goose, Tundra Swan, and even Trumpeter Swan.

Just north of Emigrant, **Trail Creek Road** leaves the west side of the highway and eventually ends up on I-90 eight miles east of Bozeman. This gravel road is a particularly good road to observe large numbers of Mountain Bluebirds due to the many bluebird nest boxes found along the fencelines.

Ten miles east of Livingston and south of I-90 is a fair-weather road that parallels **Mission Creek**. The area is primarily private property, but a diversity of birds can be observed from the road. Species likely to be encountered include Turkey Vulture, American Kestrel, Prairie Falcon, Dusky Flycatcher, Willow Flycatcher, Gray Catbird, Rufous-sided Towhee, Lazuli Bunting, Cassin's Finch, American Goldfinch, and Black-headed Grosbeak.

The **Shields Valley** runs north of Livingston along U.S. 89. The river and valley is named in honor of Private John Shields, a scout for the Lewis and

Clark Expedition. Just north of Clyde Park on U.S. 89, **Chapel Road** branches north. One-half mile up this fair-weather road, look for Bank Swallow, Northern Rough-winged Swallow, Lazuli Bunting, and Golden Eagle. The road is maintained by the county, but the land is private. Please respect the privacy of these landowners.

Continuing on U.S. 89, watch for **Cottonwood Reservoir** roughly four miles north of Wilsall on the west side of the road. As small as this area seems, it attracts a diverse array of birdlife. In summer Brewer's Sparrow, Vesper Sparrow, and Lark Bunting are often found in the sagebrush. On and around the pond summer visitors range from Common Nighthawk and Eared Grebe to Franklin's Gull, Blue-winged Teal, and American Wigeon. During spring and fall migration, this place can be exciting. Species likely to be encountered during migration include Western Grebe, Tundra Swan, Sandhill Crane, Greater Yellowlegs, Lesser Yellowlegs, Pectoral Sandpiper, and on occasion Trumpeter Swan and Common Loon.

From **Clyde Park to Ringling** an impressive number of raptors can be seen in the summer, including Red-tailed Hawk, Ferruginous Hawk, Northern Harrier, American Kestrel, and Golden Eagle. Most impressive is the eagle migration that occurs in this area in the spring. Mid to late March seems to be the best time to observe large numbers of migrating Golden and Bald Eagles. The locals call this area around Ringling "the valley of the eagles" and rightfully so. Given ideal migrating conditions, the area holds true to its name. Say's Phoebe can be reliably found around old buildings in Ringling in the summer.

Helpful Information:
Elevation: Livingston, 4,487 ft; Bozeman Pass, 5,760 ft.
Habitat(s): Streams, rivers, ponds, sagebrush flats.
Best Birding Season(s): Spring, summer, fall.
Best Birding Month(s): May, June, September.
Montana Highway Map Location: 6-G,6-H.
Hazards: Mosquitoes, some rattlesnakes, fair-weather roads.
Nearest Food, Gas, Lodging: Livingston, Gardiner, Clyde Park.
Camping: Mallard's Rest, Pine Creek, private.
Land Ownership: private; state; BLM; USFS.
Additional Information: Gallatin National Forest, P.O. Box 130, Federal Building, Bozeman, MT 59771 ph: (406) 587-6701.
Recommended Length of Stay: 1 to 2 days.

YELLOWSTONE
NATIONAL PARK

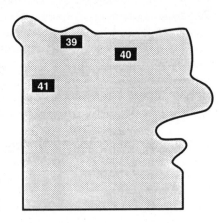

39. Gardiner to Mammoth Hot Springs
40. Mammoth Hot Springs to Cooke City
41. Mammoth Hot Springs to West
   Yellowstone

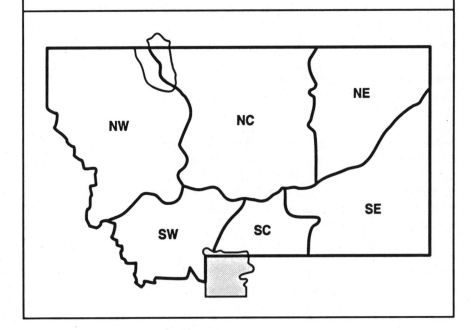

YELLOWSTONE NATIONAL PARK

Although only eight percent of Yellowstone National Park actually lies in Montana, the people of Montana have always considered Yellowstone as theirs and rightfully so. For it was energetic and enterprising citizens of the Montana Territory that laid the framework for the series of expeditions that led to the discovery of the Yellowstone River and the development of the national park idea.

The Sioux Indians once called this land "Mi tsi a-da-zi," meaning Rock Yellow River. French fur trappers referred to the river as "Roche Jaune," meaning Yellow Rock—hence the name Yellowstone. The area has a rich and colorful history of Native Americans, trappers, hunters, prospectors, and mountain men. Although Native Americans used this traditional area for hundreds of years, the first European man to lay eyes on this region was John Colter, followed by Jim Bridger.

The Yellowstone area is noted for many things: its pristine geologic features; the largest concentrations of large mammals and associated predators in the lower forty-eight states; one of the largest intact ecosystems in the temperate zone; and one of the largest caldera's in the world.

Declared a national park on March 1, 1872, Yellowstone was the first national park in America. The Gardiner, Montana, entrance or North Entrance is the oldest entrance into the park. Today there are five entrances to Yellowstone of which three of these originate in Montana—the West Entrance (West Yellowstone), the North Entrance (Gardiner), and the Northeast Entrance (Silver Gate/Cooke City).

Rather than providing detailed birding information on the entire park, this section is broken down into three parts as they relate to the three Montana park entrances of Yellowstone: **Gardiner, Montana, to Mammoth Hot Springs, Wyoming; Mammoth Hot Springs, Wyoming to Cooke City, Montana**, via Tower Junction, Wyoming; and **Mammoth Hot Springs, Wyoming, to West Yellowstone, Montana**, via Norris and Madison junctions. (Note: the road from Gardiner to Cooke City is the only road through Yellowstone open year-round for automobiles.) For more detailed information on Yellowstone's birds consult the *Birds of Yellowstone* by Terry McEneaney, published in 1988 by Roberts Rinehard of Boulder, Colorado. The 171-page book gives specific details of where to find birds in Yellowstone National Park and also is filled with details about habitat and ecology.

The birdlife of Yellowstone is highly underrated. Although bird concentrations are not extraordinary, the quality of birdlife is. An updated list of birds found in the park is usually available at all Yellowstone visitor centers.

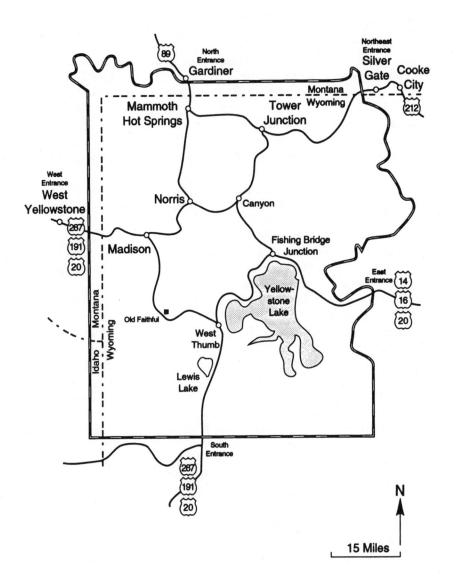

15 Miles

N

Looking north from Mammoth toward Gardiner, Montana.

39 GARDINER, MONTANA, TO MAMMOTH HOT SPRINGS, WYOMING

General Information: *A trip through Gardiner is not complete unless one drives through the stone archway known as the Roosevelt Memorial Arch. This unique basaltic structure was dedicated in 1903 by Teddy Roosevelt, commemorating the birth of the park. But before traveling through the arch, take a rewarding side trip on the Stevens Creek Road. This route gives access to a less traveled part of the park, quality birding, and expansive vistas.*

Birding Information: To get to the Stevens Creek Road turn west past the football field in Gardiner. The gravel road crosses into the park at Reese Creek, four miles from Gardiner, and offers excellent views of Electric Peak (10,992'). In the grasslands and shrub draws, Red-tailed Hawk, Golden Eagle, American Kestrel, Common Raven, Horned Lark, Mountain Bluebird, Western Meadowlark are often encountered, and on occasion American Crow, Sage Thrasher, and Cedar Waxwing.

Starting back at Gardiner begin the drive into the park by passing through the **Roosevelt Arch** and head south to Mammoth Hot Springs. This portion of the drive often results in seeing Horned Lark and Mountain Bluebird in the

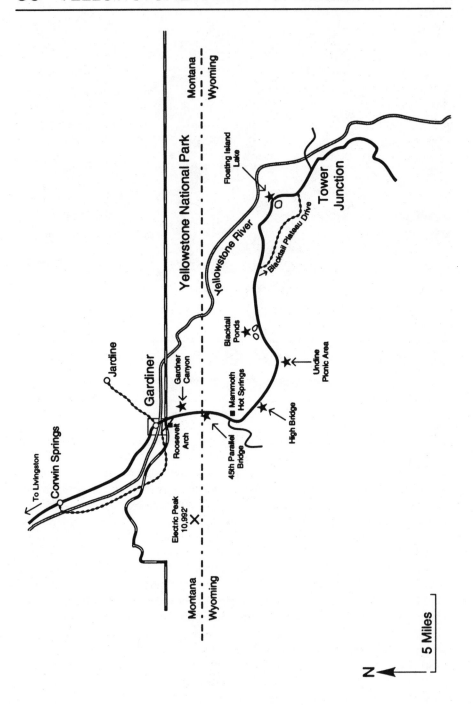

grasslands, especially during migration. After the first half mile, the road traverses for the next 2.5 miles through **Gardner Canyon** and very close to the Gardner River. Look for such species as Red-tailed Hawk, American Kestrel, White-throated Swift, Belted Kingfisher, Clark's Nutcracker, American Dipper, and Townsend's Solitaire. Osprey, Golden Eagle, and Prairie Falcon also can be seen here periodically.

At the **45th Parallel Bridge**, three miles from Gardiner, look for Barn Swallow, American Dipper, and Lazuli Bunting. From here to the Mammoth Campground (1.5 miles further south), Bohemian Waxwing and Rosy Finch are often encountered. In winter, look for Black, Gray-crowned, and Hepburn's races. A side trip through the **Mammoth Campground** can result in finding Hairy Woodpecker, Clark's Nutcracker, Black-billed Magpie, Red-breasted Nuthatch, Mountain Bluebird, and Townsend's Solitaire. Another 0.6 mile south of the campground is the area formerly called Fort Yellowstone and now is named **Mammoth Hot Springs**.

Be sure to stop at the **Albright Visitor Center** at Mammoth Hot Springs to get out of your vehicle, stretch, and obtain birding information. But before entering the visitor center look around for Red-napped Sapsucker, Ruby-crowned Kinglet, Warbling Virea, Brewer's Blackbird, and the elusive Great Horned Owl. Birding information is available at the Albright Visitor's Center as well as other visitor centers in the park. Once inside the visitor's center take some extra time to view the incredible watercolor paintings of Yellowstone by the famous artist Thomas Moran and go upstairs to look at a small wildlife exhibit that offers an opportunity to see Yellowstone birds up close.

From the visitor center either head east to Tower Junction and Cooke City, Montana, or south to Norris Junction, Madison Junction, and west to West Yellowstone, Montana. The turnoff for these two roads is 100 yards south of the visitor center.

40 MAMMOTH HOT SPRINGS, WYOMING, TO COOKE CITY, MONTANA VIA TOWER JUNCTION

Birding Infomation: The tall expansion bridge known as the High Bridge, approximately 0.6 mile east of Mammoth (following mileage readings taken from Mammoth Junction), is a good place to look for Golden Eagle, Prairie Falcon, Common Raven, Vesper Sparrow, and Western Meadowlark. At 4.6 miles, the Undine Picnic Area look for American Dipper feeding in the fast moving water of Lava Creek and Ruby-crowned Kinglet in the tops of conifers. The Northern Pygmy-Owl is sometimes found in this area in the winter. Heading further east to the 6.4 mile mark, watch for a series of ponds on the north side of the road known as Blacktail Pond. Species often found here include Green-winged Teal, Mallard, Cinnamon Teal, Gadwall, Ringed-neck Duck, Lesser Scaup, Barrow's Goldeneye, Ruddy Duck, Wilson's Phalarope, Red-winged Blackbird, and Yellow-headed Blackbird. For the

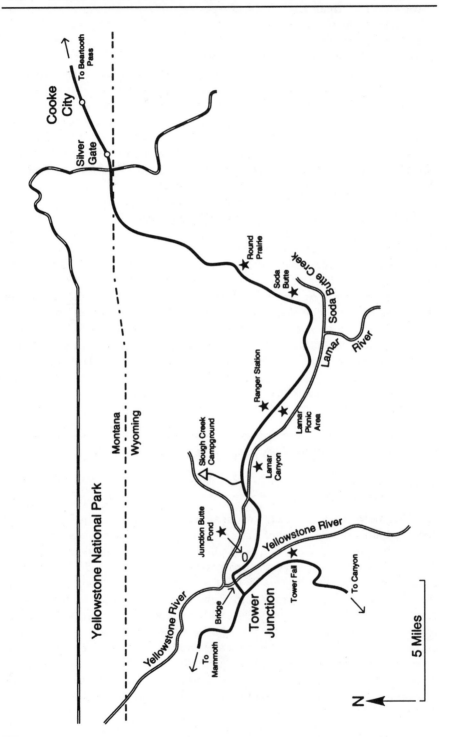

next three miles east of these ponds check out the skies for Red-tailed Hawk and Prairie Falcon, and in the sagebrush for Brewer's Sparrow and Vesper Sparrow.

At mile mark 9.8, a one-way dirt road known as the Blacktail Plateau Drive heads south. This road offers good birding as long as there are only a few vehicles on it. It is not uncommon anymore for this road to get a lot of traffic, between the dust and the disturbance it takes the fun away from birding here. Birds found along this dirt road can include Blue Grouse, Williamson's Sapsucker, Red-naped Sapsucker, Three-toed Woodpecker, Northern Flicker, Tree Swallow, Brown Creeper, Mountain Bluebird, Warbling Vireo, and Yellow-rumped Warbler to name a few.

A stop at Floating Island Lake, 15.5 miles from Mammoth along the main road, can result in finding Pied-billed Grebe, Barrow's Goldeneye, Ruddy Duck, American Coot, Red-winged Blackbird and Yellow-headed Blackbird. Look for American Kestrel, Red-tailed Hawk, Ruffed Grouse, Hairy Woodpecker, and Mountain Bluebird between this point and Tower Junction at 18.9 miles. From Tower Junction either head south to Tower Fall and Canyon or east to Cooke City. A three mile trip south to Tower Fall will often result in finding White-throated Swift and Voilet-green Swallow for starters.

From Tower Junction at mile mark 18.9 head east 0.6 mile to the Yellowstone River Bridge. Canada Goose, Barrow's Goldeneye, Common Merganser, Belted Kingfisher, Western Tanager can be found here most of the time, and on occasion Harlequin Duck. At a pond on the north side of the road known as the Geology Exhibit or Junction Butte Pond at mile mark twenty-one look at the variety of waterfowl—ranging from Cinnamon Teal to Lesser Scaup—and search the skies for raptors such as Red-tailed Hawk, Golden Eagle, and Prairie Falcon. Farther east, a dirt road appears on the north side of the road at mile mark 25.1 that leads to the Slough Creek Campground only three miles away. From the main road to the campground, one can view Pied-billed Grebe, Cinnamon Teal, Lesser Scaup, Bufflehead, Bald Eagle, Golden Eagle, Warbling Vireo, Western Tanager, and on occasion Trumpeter Swan. At the campground look for Spotted Sandpiper, Dusky Flycatcher, Hammond's Flycatcher, and on occasion Red Crossbill.

Returning to the main road at mile mark 25.1 continue east and go through Lamar Canyon at mile mark 26.7, where Common Merganser and American Dipper are often found. American Kestrel and Cliff Swallow are seen quite often in the vicinity of the Buffalo Ranch also known as Lamar Ranger Station at mile mark 29.9. The Lamar Picnic Area at 32.9 miles is a pleasant place to take a break. Be on the lookout for Barrow's Goldeneye, Peregrine Falcon, Spotted Sandpiper, Northern Flicker, Barn Swallow, European Starling, and Brown-headed Cowbird to name a few species. After a series of curves in the road a dazzling array of mountains in the background to the east-northeast is displayed. This is known as the Soda Butte area.

Soda Butte at 35.3 miles and Round Prairie at 38.7 miles are the last of the large areas of open country. From the Round Prairie to Silver Gate/Cooke City, the road passes primarily through conifers. Species found along this forested corridor to Silver Gate, Montana, include Northern Saw-whet Owl, Steller's Jay, Brown Creeper, American Dipper, Golden-crowned Kinglet, Yellow-rumpled Warbler, Pine Grosbeak, and Red Crossbill. For information on Silver Gate-Cooke City-Beartooth Pass, consult the section on the Beartooth Highway.

41 MAMMOTH HOT SPRINGS, WYOMING TO WEST YELLOWSTONE, MONTANA
VIA NORRIS AND MADISON

Birding Information: Heading up the hill from the junction, the first major stop is the **Upper Terraces**, 2.1 miles south of Mammoth Junction (the following mileage readings taken from Mammoth Junction). Take the short, one-way **Upper Terrace Loop Drive** to see the gigantic or mammoth hot springs complex and some excellent scenic views. Killdeer are often found on the geothermal runoff channels, and Great Horned Owl frequent this same area. In the limber pine/juniper habitat look for Mountain Bluebird, Townsend's Solitaire, and sometimes even Red Crosbill pass over the area. After returning to the entrance of the loop drive, continue heading south on the main road. From here to the Hoodoo's look for Red-naped Sapsucker, Williamson's Sapsucker, MacGillivray's Warbler, Green-tailed Towhee, and sometimes Orange-crowned Warbler. At the jumbled rock area known as the **Hoodoo's**, mile mark 3.8, look for the elusive Rock Wren.

Traveling further south go past majestic Rustic Falls, and on the east side of the main road is a dirt road called the **Bunsen Peak Road**, mile mark 4.9. This road is closed during inclement weather, but when open it offers views of Osprey, Mountain Bluebird, White-throated Swift, and Violet-green Swallow. The narrow one-way road eventually ends up approximately one mile south of Mammoth.

Continuing on the main road from the Bunsen Peak Road entrance, a stop at **Swan Lake Flats** at 5.8 miles can result in seeing Cinnamon Teal, Sandhill Crane, Vesper Sparrow, Savannah Sparrow, and occasionally Trumpeter Swan. The **Indian Creek Campground** (8.8 miles) is a place to see Three-toed Woodpecker and American Dipper. In the fall, Great Gray Owl have been known to show up in this area. Besides seeing moose at the Moose Exhibit or **Willow Park** (10.4 miles), look in the willows for Common Snipe, Wilson's Warbler, and Common Yellowthroat. The geothermally heated Nymph Lake at 11.9 miles almost always has waterfowl (Canada Goose, Barrow's Goldeneye), and on occasion Trumpeter Swan. **Norris Meadow** at mile mark 20.8 typically is blessed with Canada Goose, Killdeer, Common Raven, and on occasion Great Blue Heron.

At Norris Junction (21.7 miles) either head east to Canyon and south to

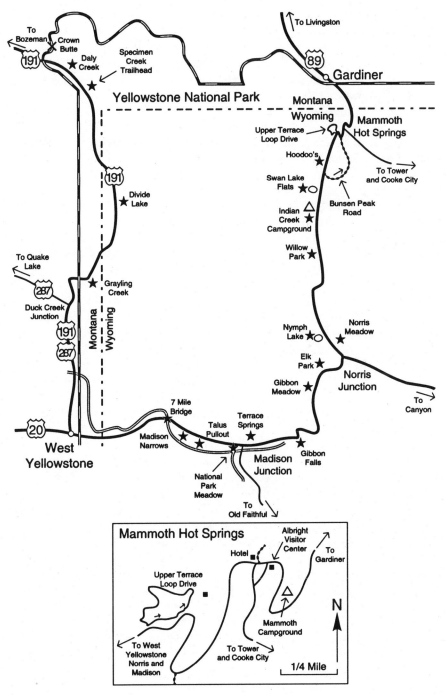

Hayden Valley, continue south to Madison and then west to West Yellowstone, or continue further south to Old Faithful. Going toward Madison Junction and just 1.5 miles south of Norris Junction is an open meadow area known as **Elk Park** (23.2 miles). In this meadow expect to find Canada Goose, Mountain Bluebird, and on occasion Sandhill Crane in the summer and Trumpeter Swan in the winter. **Gibbon Meadow** at 25.6 miles is located south of Elk Park and has a similar complement of bird species. While taking in the breathtaking views of **Gibbon Falls** (30.5 miles), look around for Clark's Nutcracker in the trees, and American Dipper in the fast moving water. Mountain Bluebird and American Robin are often found around the **Terrace Springs** area at 34.9 miles.

At Madison Junction (35.4 miles) either head south to Old Faithful or west to West Yellowstone.

Driving west of Madison Junction to West Yellowstone, the first large meadow encountered is **National Park Meadow** at mile marks 35.6-38.0. The rock cliffs surrounding this area are truly spectacular. Bald Eagle can be found in this meadow and along the Madison River year-round, but Trumpeter Swan congregate here in large numbers primarily in the winter. **Talus Pullout** at 39.8 miles and the **Madison Narrows** at 40.2 miles are good places to find Trumpeter Swan in the winter. But the **7 Mile Bridge** area, forty-two miles from Mammoth and seven miles east of West Yellowstone, is the most reliable place to find Trumpeter Swan year-round.

A side trip north on U.S. Highway 191 from Duck Creek Junction offers a less heavily traveled and often overlooked portion of Yellowstone. Eight miles north of West Yellowstone is the junction of highways 191 and 287, which is commonly referred to as Duck Creek Junction. *Mileage readings for this side trip begin from the junction.*

Continue north on U.S. 191 for three miles to where the highway enters the park at **Grayling Creek**. In the willows search for Yellow Warbler, Common Yellowthroat, and Lincoln's Sparrow, and look for American Dipper along the creek and Sparrow and Vesper Sparrow, Steller's Jay in the tall spruce.

The highway enters Wyoming at mile seven and remains in that state for the next six miles. A stop at mile mark nine further up the road can possibly result in finding Red Crossbill. At approximately twelve miles and on the east side of the road is **Divide Lake**. This is a good place to find migrant waterfowl, and in the summer look for Mallard on the lake. Search the meadows at dawn and dusk for the always spectacular Great Horned Owl.

U.S. 191 crosses back into Montana one mile north of Divide Lake. Continue five miles north of the Montana line until you come to **Specimen Creek Trailhead** at mile mark twenty-three on the east side of the road. Birds such as Gray Jay, Steller's Jay, Clark's Nutcracker, Red-breasted Nuthatch, and Red Crossbill can be found here. Savannah Sparrow can be found almost anywhere in the open wet meadows that parallel the highway.

In the open country near **Daly Creek** at mile mark twenty-seven look for an assortment of birds ranging from Red-tailed Hawk, Golden Eagle,

American Kestrel, to Prairie Falcon, Brewer's Blackbird, and, occasionally, Peregrine Falcon.

U.S. 191 passes out of the park in the vicinity of Crown Butte at mile mark twenty-eight. It is approximately twenty-four miles to the Big Sky Resort and sixty miles to Bozeman from the north park boundary on U.S. 191.

SOUTHWEST MONTANA

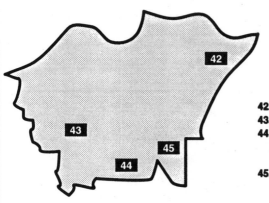

42. Bozeman and Vicinity
43. West Yellowstone and Vicinity
44. Red Rock Lakes National
    Wildlife Refuge and the
    Centennial Valley
45. Dillon and the Big Hole Valley

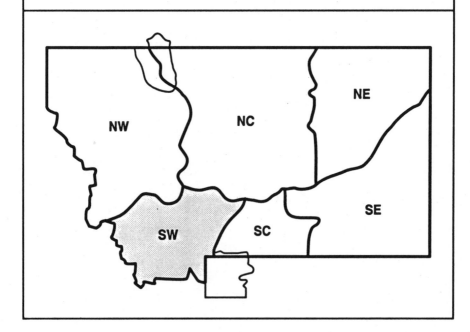

42 BOZEMAN AND VICINITY

General Information: *The city of Bozeman is named after John Bozeman, the famous trail blazer and pioneer guide who in the 1860s established a wagon trail from Wyoming to the Gallatin Valley. The Bozeman Trail split from the Oregon Trail about 100 miles northwest of Laramie, Wyoming, and paralleled present-day Interstate 25 north to Billings and Interstate 90 west to Three Forks. In April of 1867, John Bozeman met his fate when he was killed by Indians in the Gallatin Valley. Jim Bridger was a popular explorer, mountain man, and guide of the region during this same era. He is believed to be the second white man—after John Colter—to explore the Yellowstone country, and once boasted that he had seen "petrified trees a-growing with petrified birds on them a-singing petrified songs." Many local landmarks today are named in Bridger's honor.*

Lewis and Clark visited the present-day Three Forks area on July 27, 1805. At the current site of the Missouri Headwaters State Park, they were unable to determine which of these three forks was the main stem of the Missouri River. Consequently, they named the river to the west for President Thomas Jefferson, the river to the south for Secretary of State James Madison, and the river to the east for Secretary of Treasury Albert Gallatin.

Birding Information: The rivers, forests, foothills, mountains, and rolling grasslands around Bozeman offer an array of birdwatching opportunities. A nominal entrance fee is charged at the **East Gallatin Recreation Area**, but birding can be good here, especially in the early spring. From downtown Bozeman, drive north on North 7th Avenue over I-90 and turn right on Griffin Drive, then go north on Manley Road for one mile. The main feature of the site is a small pond surrounded by grassy fields. Common Loon have been recorded here, along with various species of waterfowl. In the summer, look for Black-billed Cuckoo, Gray Catbird, and Lazuli Bunting in the deciduous shrubs northeast of the pond. The pond also serves as a popular watering hole for Bozeman's windsurfers and sun bathers, and often the best birding is had by hiking to the opposite side of the pond or northeast to the East Gallatin River.

The **U.S. Fish Cultural Development Center** (a fish hatchery) is nestled on Bridger Creek about five miles northeast of Bozeman on Bridger Canyon Road (Highway 86). The birding here is excellent thanks to lush riparian habitat and the mixture of aspen, cottonwood, and Douglas-fir. Common summer residents include Belted Kingfisher, Red-naped Sapsucker, Downy Woodpecker, Northern Flicker, Tree Swallow, Violet-green Swallow, Veery, Swainson's Thrush, Ruby-crowned Kinglet, Warbling Vireo, Yellow Warbler, Yellow-rumped Warbler, MacGillivray's Warbler, Black-headed Grosbeak, and Song Sparrow. For best results, take the short wildlife observation trail loop. American Dipper are often seen along the creek.

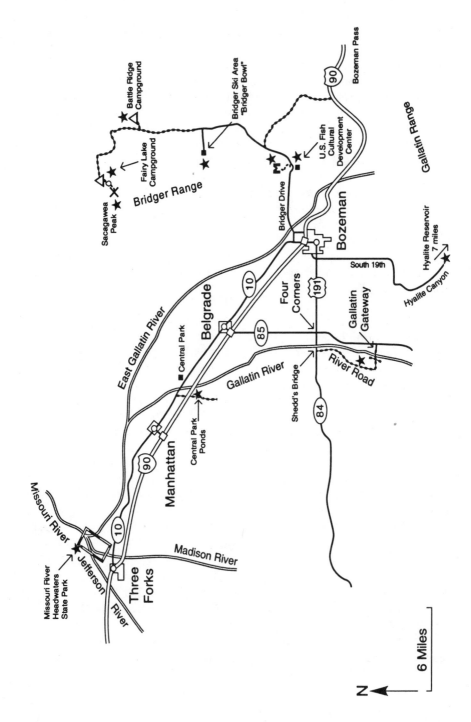

Bozeman Pass

90

Gallatin Range

Battle Ridge
Campground

Bridger Ski Area
"Bridger Bowl"

Fairy Lake
Campground

U.S. Fish
Cultural
Development
Center

Bridger Range

Bridger Drive

Sacagawea
Peak

Bozeman

Hyalite Reservoir
7 miles

South 19th

Hyalite Canyon

East Gallatin River

Belgrade

10

Four
Corners

191

Gallatin
Gateway

Central Park

85

River Road

Gallatin River

Shedd's Bridge

84

Central Park
Ponds

90

Manhattan

10

Missouri River

Madison River

Jefferson River

Three
Forks

10

Missouri River
Headwaters
State Park

N

6 Miles

Just across the road from the fish hatchery is the **"M" Picnic Ground**. A steep hike up the trail (follow the route that switchbacks up to the left of the "M") will likely yield Brown-headed Cowbird, Clark's Nutcracker, Townsend's Solitaire, Green-tailed Towhee, Prairie Falcon, and Red-breasted Nuthatch.

Sixteen miles up Bridger Canyon Road, the **Bridger Bowl** ski area provides good birding for migrating raptors with spectacular views of the Crazy, Absaroka, and Gallatin mountains. From the parking lot, follow the access road up to Deer Park, then take the strenuous, zig-zagging trail from the uppermost lift to the top of the ridge. Once on the ridge, walk about half a mile to the north. Large numbers of Golden Eagles and many other raptors soar along this ridge on their journey south. Viewing is best from mid-September to early November, with peak numbers of Golden Eagles reported in mid-October.

From Bridger Bowl, drive three miles to the fork in the road at Brackett Creek. Turn left and continue two miles to **Battle Ridge Campground**. Here, patient birders may see Blue Grouse, Williamson's Sapsucker, Three-toed Woodpecker, and, with luck, the rare Great Gray Owl. The campground at **Fairy Lake** is more remote than Battle Ridge and is frequented by Red Crossbill. To reach Fairy Lake, drive north from Battle Ridge one mile and turn left at the Fairy Lake sign. This road bounces uphill for seven miles to the campground; spring runoff or drenching summer storms can make the climb treacherous even for four-wheel drive vehicles. From the campground, a steep two-mile hike leads to 9,670-foot **Sacagewea Peak**, the highest peak in the Bridgers. Summer hikers can see American Pipit and Rosy Finch.

Back on the outskirts of Bozeman, the **Story Hills** rise just northeast of town. This is private property, but travel is allowed on the main road. Please respect the landowner's rights and stay on the road. Habitats include riparian, sage/grassland, and a scattering of conifers. The hills provide good viewing for Red-tailed Hawk, American Kestrel, Lazuli Bunting, Brewer's Sparrow, Vesper Sparrow, White-crowned Sparrow, Northern Oriole, Red Crossbill, and Western Meadowlark.

Lindley Park and the adjacent **Sunset Hills Cemetery** offer surprisingly good birding within city limits on the east end of Main Street. Both Black-capped and Mountain Chickadees are seen here, as are Black-billed Magpie, Common Nighthawk, Lincoln's Sparrow, Cassin's Finch, Red Crossbill, and Pine Siskin. Birding is also good here in winter, notably for Bohemian Waxwing, Cedar Waxwing, and Common Redpoll. These same winter species are seen at bird feeders throughout Bozeman, as are Rosy Finches (most typically the Gray-crowned race, and occasionally Black and Hepburn's races). The cemetery, which includes John Bozeman's grave, closes at dark.

Head south from Main Street on South Church to **Gallagator Linear Park**, which is an abandoned railroad grade that now serves as a greenbelt from South Church to Kagy Boulevard. A walk through the park should yield an array of songbirds. Look for Calliope Hummingbird here in the summer,

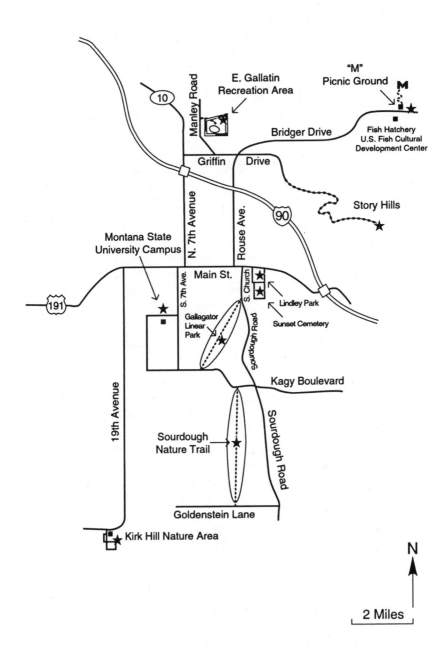

especially in June or July.

The **Sourdough Nature Trail**, south of Bozeman, is an excellent birding area. From Main Street, head south on South Church (Sourdough Road) for six miles to Goldenstein Lane. Go right on Goldenstein for one mile and park where the road crosses Sourdough Creek. Hike north on the trail from Goldenstein Lane through lush vegetation along Sourdough Creek. Watch for Northern Waterthrush and the more common MacGillivray's Warbler and Savannah Sparrow in spring and early summer. The trail offers especially good birding for warblers in spring.

Birdwatching on the campus of **Montana State University** is inconsistent but can be good, especially during fall, winter, and spring. Waterfowl sometimes gather on the small pond on South 11th across from the Arts and Architecture building, and the trees around the Danforth Chapel (east of Wilson Hall) often harbor songbirds.

The **Kirk Hill Nature Area**, ten miles south of Bozeman at the right-angle turn in 19th Avenue, is well worth a visit. A series of trails wends up into the foothills, providing exciting birding. Look for Warbling Vireo, Lincoln's Sparrow, and even Ruffed Grouse in summer, and Great Gray Owl and Three-toed Woodpecker in winter. If pressed for time, take the 200-yard hike up the trail to the footbridge and return on the loop back to the parking lot.

Hyalite Canyon is a popular recreation area for local residents. Birding can be good here, but traffic may be heavy, especially in summer. Try one of the six Forest Service campgrounds if you're staying in the Bozeman area. For best birding results, get started early in the morning before the traffic builds up.

West of Bozeman, the **River Road** parallels the Gallatin River, providing good birding for many riparian species. Drive west on Main Street (Highway 84) eight miles to Four Corners and turn south on U.S. 191 to Gallatin Gateway, home of Stacy's Bar where the sound of country western music fills the air. Turn west onto the main road through Gallatin Gateway and cross the Gallatin River. Go straight onto the fair-weather River Road, which runs north for about ten miles to Sheds Bridge 1.5 miles west of Four Corners. In summer, watch for Red-naped Sapsucker, Northern Oriole, Gray Catbird, and Sandhill Crane. Save this drive for a sunny day—even a little rain quickly turns this road to gumbo.

Northwest of Bozeman, between Belgrade and Manhattan, the **Central Park Ponds** attract good numbers of waterfowl year-round thanks to the warm-springs source. Travel south on Heeb Road just off Frontage Road or Highway 2 to reach the ponds. Tundra Swan sometimes stop here during migration. An open field on the west side of **Heeb Road** provides serves as a fall staging area for Sandhill Crane and provides excellent views of the cranes from Late August to mid-September.

Madison Buffalo Jump State Monument, seven miles south of Logan off I-90, combines good birding with a fascinating look at Native American history. Plains Indians relied on the buffalo for food, clothing, bone tools, and even shelter, building their tipis from the tanned hides. Before the advent of the horse and rifle, one of the most effective hunting techniques was to drive bison herds over cliffs or "buffalo jumps." The tactic worked best on cliffs that were disguised by the lay of the land, such as this abrupt bluff overlooking the Madison River. By the time a stampeding herd recognized the danger ahead, the sheer panic and force of the animals behind would force hundreds of buffalo over the edge to their deaths. The entire Indian encampment then set to work butchering and curing the meat and preparing hides. Today, Madison Buffalo Jump is filled with echoes from the past, and the present song of many birds. The bluffs and cottonwood stands are home to Rock Wren, Mourning Dove, Horned Lark, Black-billed Magpie, and Cliff Swallow. Golden Eagle hunt ground squirrels on the plains, and waterfowl fly above the Madison en route between Ennis Lake and the Three Forks wetlands. Be alert for rattlesnakes, especially in spring and summer.

North of Three Forks, the **Missouri River Headwaters State Park** offers camping, picnicking, and excellent birding in a mix of habitats, including lush riparian vegetation, grasslands, mountain mahogany and juniper, and numerous cliffs and outcrops. Take the Three Forks exit off of I-90 and drive two miles east on Highway 2. Turn north on Highway 286 and watch for the park signs.

The Gallatin, Madison, and Jefferson rivers join here to form the Missouri River, also funneling many migrant birds through the area in spring, with numbers peaking in April and May. Birders can choose from three distinct areas at Headwaters State Park. The first is **Fort Rock**. Stop at the parking lot on the east side of the park road and take the short but rewarding hike along the rimrock of Fort Rock or stroll along the gravel road through grasslands to the Madison River. Another trail leads through riparian vegetation along the Jefferson River. Likely species here include Double-crested Cormorant, Eastern Kingbird, Red-naped Sapsucker, Rufous-sided Towhee, Yellow Warbler, Northern Oriole, and American Goldfinch.

The **picnic area** a half mile north along the road has more trees, and Western Wood-Pewee and Red-naped Sapsucker are usually present in summer. Finally, the third area is down by the **boat ramp** on the Missouri River one-quarter mile past the picnic area, where large cliffs and willows across the river provide habitat for Red-tailed Hawk, Prairie Falcon, White-throated Swift, Violet-green Swallow, Rock Wren, and on occasion Turkey Vulture and Canyon Wren.

The **Three Forks Ponds**, visible south of I-90 on the outskirts of Three Forks, are also worth a stop. Turn south toward town immediately after getting off I-90. Various waterfowl are found here, as are Osprey during summer and the occasional Common Loon during migration (April through May, and October through November).

Nineteen miles west of Three Forks on Highway 2, visit **Lewis and Clark Caverns State Park** to see spectacular limestone formations in the largest known caverns in the state. The 2,735-acre park is open from May 1 to September 30. Take the guided tour through the caverns, and save some time

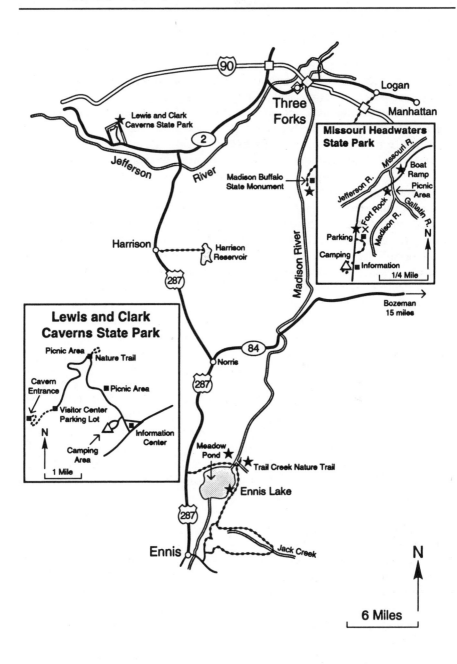

to birdwatch along the scenic park drive from the information center at the entrance to the visitor center near the caves. Birding is especially good at the picnic area and adjacent nature trail, and at the visitor center. Look for Hairy Woodpecker, Black-capped Chickadee, Rock Wren, House Wren, Warbling Vireo, Orange-crowned Warbler, MacGillivray's Warbler, Western Tanager, Lazuli Bunting, Green-tailed Towhee, Rufous-sided Towhee, and Chipping Sparrow.

From the caverns, head south on U.S. Highway 287 to **Harrison Reservoir**, just east of the town of Harrison. Birding is good here in the spring and fall if enough water is in the reservoir to attract migrating shorebirds and waterfowl, and attendant raptors. In the summer, the boating pressure tends to keep the birds away or well-concealed.

Forty-six miles south of Three Forks on U.S. 287, the town of Ennis spreads on the flats beside the Madison River. To the northeast of town, **Ennis Lake** acts as a magnet for large numbers of birds. The northwest shore of the lake is popular among the windsurfing crowd, so birdwatchers are better off driving south through Ennis and across the Madison River. Take the first left south of the bridge and head toward the east shore of Ennis Lake. The road passes through the hamlet of Jeffers, where a turn to the east leads to a fourteen-mile loop drive on the **Cedar Creek alluvial fan** and possible sightings of Long-billed Curlew and Horned Lark. This side trip continues on to Jack Creek, home to American Dipper, before turning west again and back to the main road to Ennis Lake. Birds seen along either route include Yellow Warbler, Warbling Vireo, Black-billed Magpie, and Mountain Bluebird. The southeast end of the lake is usually crowded with birds, including Western Grebe, Clark's Grebe, American White Pelican, Double-crested Cormorant, Bald Eagle, Sora, Franklin's Gull, Yellow-headed Blackbird, and the occasional Trumpeter Swan. This is also a spring and fall staging area for migrating Trumpeter Swan, Tundra Swan, Common Loon, and various species of gulls and waterfowl. Drive one mile along the narrow dirt road above the Madison where it flows out of Ennis Lake to Trail Creek. The 100-yard **Trail Creek Nature Trail** offers good birding, with likely sightings of Gray Catbird, MacGillivray's Warbler, and Yellow Warbler. Many of these same species are found at the **Meadow Pond Area** on the north end of Ennis Lake.

Helpful Information:
Elevation: Bozeman, 4,795 ft.
Habitat(s): Riparian, lake, wetland, grassland, coniferous forest, cliffs, urban parks.
Best Birding Season(s): Spring, summer, winter.
Best Birding Month(s): April through July.
Montana Highway Map Location: 5-F, 5-G.
Hazards: Mosquitoes, horseflies.
Nearest Food, Gas, Lodging: Bozeman, Three Forks, Ennis.
Camping: Hyalite Canyon, Gallatin Canyon, Battle Ridge, Fairy Lake (all

USFS); KOA at Bozeman Hotsprings; Missouri Headwaters SP; Lewis and Clark Caverns SP; Ennis.
Land Ownership: Private, city, state, USFS.
Additional Information: MDFWP,1400 S. 19th Street, Bozeman, MT 59715 ph: (406) 994-4042.
Recommended Length of Stay: 2 to 3 days.

43 WEST YELLOWSTONE AND VICINITY

General Information: *The town of West Yellowstone is well-known to millions of tourists as a busy souvenir stop at the west entrance to Yellowstone National Park. But the area is rich in history and offers excellent birding opportunities as well.*

West Yellowstone, Montana, borders the west side of Yellowstone National Park. Nearby Targhee Pass is named after Bannock Indian Chief Targhee. Chief Joseph led his band of Nez Perce Indians through this pass in 1877 on his famous 2,000-mile journey from central Idaho to the Bear Paw Mountains in northcentral Montana, trying to evade U.S. troops. Famous scout and trapper Jim Bridger led Captain Reynolds through what is today called Reynolds Pass, also known as Low Pass due to its low elevation (6,836') on the continental divide.

Birding Information: Common Raven frequent the town of **West Yellowstone** year-round, but large numbers are especially apparent during winter. **Baker's Hole Campground**, on the Gallatin National Forest just north of town, is an excellent place to watch birds and camp, particularly in summer. Common Yellowthroat, Yellow Warbler, Osprey, and Great Blue Heron are often observed from the campground.

Targhee Pass, on the Idaho/Montana line just west of West Yellowstone, was named after the Bannock Indian Chief Targhee. The forested pass on U.S. Highway 20 is a good place to see Steller's Jay and Pine Grosbeak year-round and an occasional Great Gray Owl, particularly in spring and fall.

From late October through early November, large numbers of Trumpeter Swan and Tundra Swan congregate on the **Madison Arm of Hebgen Lake**. American White Pelican and a wide variety of waterfowl can be found on the **Grayling Arm** of Hebgen Lake in summer. Common Loon appear in large numbers on the main body of Hebgen Lake in April and September.

In 1959 a large earthquake shook the area, setting off a landslide that blocked the Madison River below Hebgen Lake, creating **Earthquake Lake**. The Earthquake Lake Visitor Center offers excellent interpretive displays of this cataclysmic event. The region around West Yellowstone and Hebgen Lake remains the most seismically active area in the entire Rocky Mountains. Barrow's Goldeneye, Osprey, and Bald Eagle can be found at

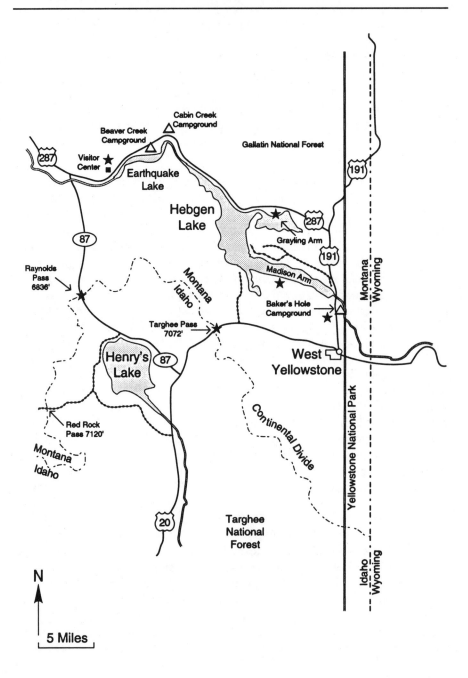

N

5 Miles

Earthquake Lake in summer, and Golden Eagle have been observed near the visitor center.

West from Earthquake Lake on U.S. 287, Highway 87 runs south for eighteen miles over Raynolds Pass to Henrys Lake in Idaho and a junction with U.S. 20. Famous scout and trapper Jim Bridger once led Captain Raynolds through this 6,836-foot pass that now bears the captain's name. **Raynolds Pass** is an excellent place to see large numbers of migrating raptors, especially during April and September.

Helpful Information:

Elevation: West Yellowstone, 6,667 ft.

Habitat(s): Riparian, lake, coniferous forest, sagebrush flats.

Best Birding Season(s): Summer and fall.

Best Birding Month(s): May, June, October.

Montana Highway Map Location: 5-H.

Hazards: Grizzly bears, mosquitoes.

Nearest Food, Gas, Lodging: West Yellowstone.

Camping: Baker's Hole, Cabin Creek, Beaver Creek.

Land Ownership: USFS, private.

Additional Information: Gallatin National Forest, P.O. Box 130, Federal Building, Bozeman, MT 59771 ph: (406) 587-6701.

Recommended Length of Stay: 4 to 8 hours.

44 RED ROCK LAKES NWR AND THE CENTENNIAL VALLEY

General Information: *Red Rock Lakes, creek, and river are named after the red-colored rock outcrops near the town of Dell along Interstate 15. In 1935, Red Rock Lakes Migratory Bird Refuge was established, later renamed Red Rock Lakes National Wildlife Refuge. The Centennial Valley (and mountain range) was named in honor of the 100th anniversary of this country and coinciding with settlement by white men in this valley. The Centennial Valley was once used by Bannock Indians as a travel corridor between the Bighole Valley and the Yellowstone country. The National Geographic Society locates the true headwaters of the Missouri River in the extreme east end of the Centennial Valley on the upper reaches of Hellroaring Creek in the Sawtell Range (on the Montana side). The Centennial Mountain Range lies on the Continental Divide, and is one of the few mountain ranges in North America that runs in an east/west direction.*

Red Rock Lakes National Wildlife Refuge is located in the scenic and isolated Centennial Valley of southwestern Montana, about forty-five miles west of West Yellowstone, and ninety miles southeast of Dillon. The 42,000-acre refuge contains a vast array of habitat, including high-elevation sage brush-grasslands, wet meadows and wetlands at 6,600 feet, cool aspen-coniferous forests and coniferous forests of the subalpine zone, and harsh alpine habitats on the high peaks of the Centennial Mountains. These diverse habitats give Red Rocks its unique character and provide food and cover for a correspondingly diverse range of wildlife.

Birding Information: Birding at Red Rock Lakes is spectacular. More than 50,000 ducks and geese may stage here during migration, and shorebirds are also found during this period. The Trumpeter Swan was rescued from near-extinction here, and more than 100 Trumpeters live and breed on the refuge and in the Centennial Valley, making this one of the most important Trumpeter Swan nesting areas in North America. A variety of gulls and terns can be seen wheeling above the lakes, as can American White Pelicans, and the surrounding uplands harbor a rich diversity of raptors and passerines.

Only a small percentage of birds found in the Centennial Valley are year-round residents. Most summer birds leave the valley to winter elsewhere. Spring migration is very slow here, and many migrants pass over Red Rock Lakes without stopping due to the lingering snowpack. Fall migration, however, is much more dramatic. From August to mid-November tremendous numbers of birds stage at Red Rock Lakes, including Tundra and Trumpeter Swans, Bald Eagles, and waterfowl in the tens of thousands.

The birding season here is extremely short. The refuge may be inaccessible until mid-May at the earliest, and birdlife is abundant until Red Rock Lakes freeze over, usually by early November.

Travel in the Centennial Valley is a challenge at best, a nightmare at worst.

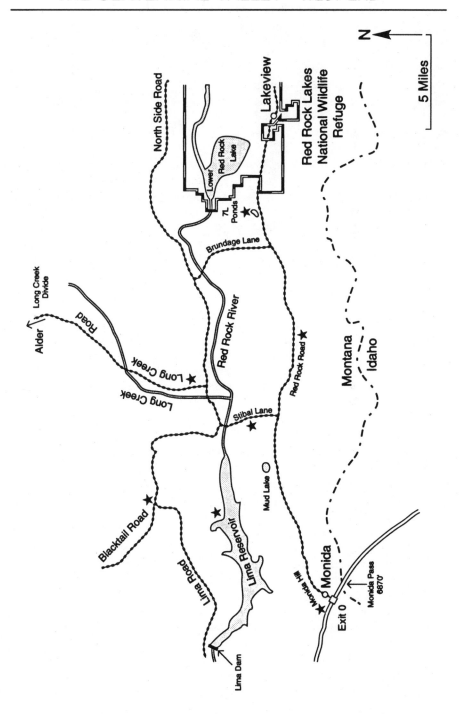

Red Rock Lakes National Wildlife Refuge.

The main road through the refuge runs from Henry's Lake in the east to Monida in the west. Monida (a contraction of the names Montana and Idaho) is as close to a ghost town as a place can get while still harboring a few live residents, but road conditions from Monida are more reliable, especially in the spring. Red Rock Pass, on the east side, is usually closed or snow-covered until mid-May.

Even during summer, area roads may be difficult to travel. The main road is dirt with some gravel, and road conditions deteriorate rapidly under heavy rain. All secondary roads have fair-weather surfaces and are impassible when wet. When rain threatens, head for the main road from Lakeview to Monida, or expect to wait it out until the roads dry. Flat tires are a way of life in the Centennial Valley, especially right after the roads are graded. Check the tread and air pressure in your tires before traveling to Red Rock lakes, and drive with care, especially on unsettled gravel. Remember to gas up before entering the valley, either in Lima on I-15 or at the truck stop at Henry's Lake Junction. Information kiosks are found at both the east and west entrances to the refuge on Red Rock Road, at refuge headquarters in Lakeview, and also at the northeast corner of the refuge on the Elk Lake Road.

Most visitors to the Red Rocks **Centennial Valley** approach the refuge from the **west**, hurrying over the twenty-eight miles of gravel road between Monida on I-15 and the refuge boundary. But this stretch of road holds ample opportunities for birding at a slower pace, with several worthwhile detours along the way. Two miles east of Monida on Red Rock Road, the ridges of **Monida Hill** provide updrafts for Swainson's and Ferruginous Hawks. Monida Hill also offers excellent views of the expansive Centennial Valley to the east and Lima Reservoir to the north. Trumpeter Swans are occasionally seen on **Mud Lake**, eight miles east from Monida, and more regularly on Lima Reservoir, but access to the reservoir is difficult due to extremely poor roads. Relatively unvisited and undisturbed by humans, Lima Reservoir attracts thousands of Canada Geese, which molt here in summer.

The first major road heading north from Red Rock Road is **Stibal Lane**, about eleven miles from Monida. At the junction of these two roads, watch for Swainson's Hawk, Red-tailed Hawk, and American Crow. Drive north along Stibal Lane scanning the grasslands for Sandhill Crane, Killdeer, Long-billed Curlew, Wilson's Phalarope, Horned Lark, and Cliff Swallow. Where the road crosses the Red Rock River, stop to look for a variety of birdlife including Cinnamon Teal, Willet, Yellow-headed Blackbird, and more rarely Peregrine Falcon and Marbled Godwit. The road forks after crossing the river. Head northwest on the **Blacktail Road/Lima Road** for good opportunities to see Ferruginous Hawk, Swainson's Hawk, Rock Wren, and Golden Eagle. Or turn northeast to connect with the **North Side Road**, which eventually ends up at Elk Lake at the east end of the valley. This drive yields birds commonly found throughout the Centennial Valley. Three miles east of Stibal Lane on the North Side Road, the **Long Creek Road** to the north boasts good birding for Sandhill Crane, Long-billed Curlew, Horned Lark, Sage Thrasher, Yellow Warbler, Wilson's Warbler, Vesper Sparrow, Brewer's Sparrow, Lincoln's Sparrow, and a variety of raptors. The Long Creek Road is rough when dry and impassible when wet.

For the less adventurous, heading east on the main **Red Rock Road** toward Red Rock Lakes still provides outstanding birdwatching. Mountain Bluebirds are abundant along the road and a search of the valley almost always rewards the birder with sightings of Red-tailed Hawk, American Kestrel, Swainson's Hawk, Ferruginous Hawk, Sandhill Crane, Brewer's Blackbird, Brewer's Sparrow, Savannah Sparrow, and Brown-headed Cowbird.

CAUTION: About nineteen miles east from Monida, Brundage Lane beckons to travelers, enticing unsuspecting birders north toward the heart of the valley. Do NOT attempt to drive down Brundage Lane unless you enjoy digging your vehicle out of mud. Better birding lies ahead on the main road.

Continuing east on the Red Rock Road, stop about twenty miles from Monida opposite the **7L Ponds** north of the road to look for Trumpeter Swan, Sandhill Crane, Green-tailed Towhee, Clark's Nutcracker, Brewer's Sparrow, Warbling Vireo, and Yellow-rumped Warbler. The next couple of miles heading east between these ponds and the refuge boundary are good for Cooper's Hawk and Northern Goshawk.

The **east** entrance to the Centennial Valley and Red Rock Lakes is popular among summer visitors traveling to and from Yellowstone National Park.

Red Rock Lakes National Wildlife Refuge.

From West Yellowstone, drive twelve miles west on U.S. Highway 20, over Targhee Pass to Henry's Lake Junction (U.S. 20 and Highway 87) in Idaho. From the junction, take one of two routes around Henry's Lake.

The first option is to head north 5.2 miles on Highway 87 around the north side of **Henry's Lake**. This dirt road is heavily traveled by anglers and summer home residents, so the dust can be annoying at times. Birds found along this road include Western Grebe, American White Pelican, Bald Eagle, Red-tailed Hawk, Swainson's Hawk, and Forster's Tern. The second option is to drive four miles south of Henry's Lake Junction to another dirt road immediately west of the bridge over the Henry's Fork. This road is less traveled and goes around the south end of Henry's Lake through woodlands (Douglas fir, aspen) and open meadows. Swainson's Hawk, Red-naped Sapsucker, Williamson's Sapsucker, Red-breasted Nuthatch, and Cassin's Finch can be found here. Birding is good along this road to the junction west of Henry's Lake. Both of these dirt roads converge at a junction near Duck Creek just west of Henry's Lake. From this junction, drive west 3.5 miles through aspen and conifers to 7,120-foot **Red Rock Pass**.

On or near the pass be on the lookout for Ruffed Grouse, Red-naped Sapsucker, Williamson's Sapsucker, Red-breasted Nuthatch, and Lazuli Bunting. As the road descends to **Alaska Basin**, keep watch for the elusive Northern Goshawk and Hermit Thrush. In the broad sagebrush grassland/ wet-meadow flat of Alaska Basin, look for Golden Eagle, Sandhill Crane, Long-billed Curlew, American Crow, Mountain Bluebird, Sage Thrasher,

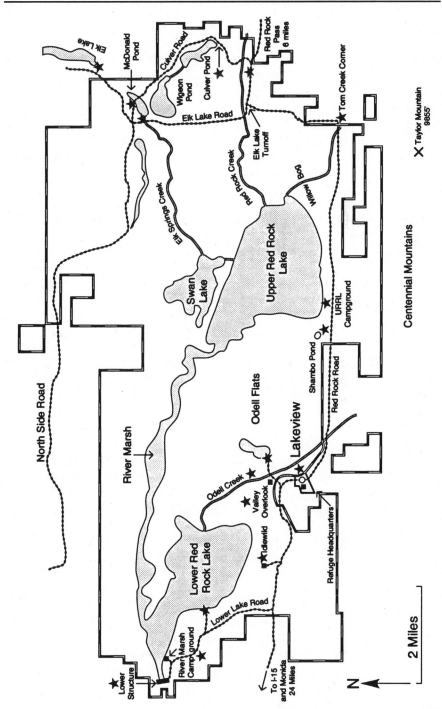

Brewer's Sparrow, Vesper Sparrow, and, for the lucky, Peregrine Falcon. In the willows along Red Rock Creek look for Yellow Warbler, Wilson Warbler, Common Yellowthroat, and Song Sparrow. The vista south offers excellent views of avalanche chutes in the Centennial Mountains.

Upper Red Rock Lake Campground is the best birding area on the refuge, and in the Centennial Valley. It is centrally located along the Red Rock Road, and offers a pleasant place to camp, with fabulous vistas and good drinking water. The great diversity of birds found here reflects the diversity of vegetation. A walk from the campground past the drinking water supply and down to the lakeshore is always worthwhile. The area within a one-mile radius of the campground provides excellent birding. Species likely to be encountered include Eared Grebe, Western Grebe, American White Pelican, Great Blue Heron, Black-crowned Night-Heron, Trumpeter Swan, Canada Goose, Northern Pintail, Blue-winged Teal, Gadwall, American Wigeon, and on occasion Clark's Grebe and Peregrine Falcon. Around the campground look for Red-naped Sapsucker, Western Wood-Pewee, Willow Flycatcher, Dusky Flycatcher, Tree Swallow, Swainson's Thrush, Cedar Waxwing, Warbling Vireo, Yellow Warbler, MacGillivray's Warbler, Wilson's Warbler, Black-headed Grosbeak, Western Tanager, Chipping Sparrow, and, with luck, Great Horned Owl and Calliope Hummingbird. Birders should also try an early morning or evening walk along the Red Rock Road.

Shambo Pond, noted for its nesting Trumpeter Swans, is just a half mile west of the Upper Lake campground on the Red Rock Road. One mile west from Shambo Pond, an overlook above **Odell Flats** is always productive for Sandhill Crane and on rare occasions Whooping Crane. Large numbers of Mountain Bluebirds are seen along the Red Rock Road in the 3.5 miles from Shambo Pond to Lakeview. Stop where the road crosses **Odell Creek**, about 2.5 miles west of the Upper Lake campground (or 1.5 miles east of Lakeview), for a good chance of seeing Yellow Warbler, Wilson's Warbler, Warbling Vireo, Pine Siskin, and Spotted Sandpiper.

Lakeview is an extremely small town, with more buildings than people. Refuge information can be obtained in Lakeview either at the headquarters during regular weekly working hours or at the information kiosk next to the headquarters building. Birding in town is fair, but not as good as other areas in the Centennial Valley. Yellow Warbler, Pine Siskin, and Lincoln Sparrow are easily detected in the willows west of the headquarters area. Great Gray Owls are seen periodically in the Douglas fir foothills of the Centennials, south and slightly west of the headquarters area. Also look for Lazuli Bunting in town.

Head west out of Lakeview and stop a half mile north of town at **Valley Overlook**, otherwise known as Odell Creek Corner, for an interesting view and to get oriented. Drive west another 1.5 miles to **Idlewild** (an isolated aspen stand), where Lincoln's Sparrow, Tree Swallow, and Red-naped Sapsucker are usually found. Look for Lazuli Bunting south of the road in the Idlewild area.

At the west end of the refuge (roughly three miles from Lakeview), the fair-weather Lower Lake Road ends up at **Lower Red Rock Lake** and a dam known as the **Lower Structure**. Drive 1.5 miles north on Lower Lake Road, then a half mile east to a turnout on the shore of Lower Red Rock Lake. Birding here is excellent. Species likely to be encountered include Eared Grebe, Western Grebe, Double-crested Cormorant, Great Blue Heron, White-faced Ibis, Trumpeter Swan, Northern Harrier, Franklin's Gull, Forster's Tern, Black Tern, Marsh Wren, Savannah Sparrow, and, with a little luck, Clark's Grebe and Peregrine Falcon. Return to the Lower Lake Road and drive north for a little more than a mile to the Lower Structure. Along the way, watch for Horned Lark, Vesper Sparrow, and Savannah Sparrow. The rare Whooping Crane is seen periodically in this area. Immediately before the Lower Structure look for Wilson's Phalaropes, American Avocet, Willet, and Killdeer in the shallow ponds. A variety of other shorebirds frequent this area during late summer/fall migration. Red-necked Phalaropes can be found here on occasion from late July through early September. Many species of waterfowl, similar to those found on the Lower Lake, frequent the vicinity of the Lower Structure and the **River Marsh Campground**, one-quarter mile to the east. Camping here is marginal due to mosquitoes and poor access roads.

Birding is equally exciting on the east end of the refuge. From Upper Red Rock Lake Campground, drive east two miles to the **Willow Bog** area on the north side of the road. Look for Swainson's Hawk and the well-camouflaged Long-eared Owl. Moose also frequent the bog. Views of Upper Red Rock Lake in the distance usually include Trumpeter Swans and American White Pelicans. Continue east 1.5 miles on the Red Rock Road to **Tom Creek Corner** (a ninety-degree turn to the north). Mountain Bluebirds and Tree Swallows are abundant along this stretch of road. From Tom Creek Corner, look for Sandhill Crane and Long-billed Curlew in the grasslands to the south, and Swainson's Hawk, Red-tailed Hawk, Common Snipe, Rock Wren, Savannah Sparrow, and Sandhill Crane along the road for the next two miles north to the Elk Lake Turnoff. Stop at the Elk Lake turnoff for wonderful views of the Centennial Range and the Centennial Valley to the south and west.

The first three miles from the Elk Lake turnoff along the **Elk Lake Road** usually yield Trumpeter Swan, Swainson's Hawk, Sora, Sandhill Crane, Common Snipe, Yellow Warbler, Common Yellowthroat, Marsh Wren, Savannah Sparrow, and Lincoln's Sparrow. Roughly four miles from the turnoff on Red Rock Road, **Elk Lake** lies just outside the refuge boundary. Look for Great Blue Heron, Trumpeter Swan, Bald Eagle, Red-tailed Hawk, Swainson's Hawk, Black-billed Magpie, American Crow, and Rock Wren here. A undeveloped Forest Service campground is found at the south end of Elk Lake, and there is an out-of-the-way resort offering drinks, meals, and lodging about one mile up the road on the northwest side of the lake.

Culver Road, which is closed during the nesting season, runs roughly five miles from the north end of Elk Lake Road to join the Red Rock Road near the east entrance of the refuge. The road meanders around Culver, Wigeon, and MacDonald ponds, providing good birding for Bald Eagle, Sandhill Crane, Ruby-crowned Kinglet, Trumpeter Swan, and numerous other species of waterfowl.

Helpful Information:

Elevation: Upper Red Rock Lake, 6,609 ft; Taylor Mtn, 9,855 ft.
Habitat(s): Sagebrush-grassland, wet meadows, marsh, willow, aspen, coniferous forests, alpine.
Best Birding Season(s): Spring, summer.
Best Birding Month(s): May-August, late October-early November.
Montana Highway Map Location: 4-H.
Hazards: Mosquitoes, fair-weather roads, flat tires, moose, dust, sudden storms.
Nearest Food, Gas, Lodging: Lima, West Yellowstone, junction of Idaho Highways 87 and 20.
Camping: Upper Red Rock Lake; Elk Lake; River Marsh.
Land Ownership: Refuge: USFWS; adjacent lands: BLM, USFS, private.
Additional Information: Red Rock Lakes National Wildlife Refuge, Monida Star Route, Box 15, Lima, MT 59739 ph: (406) 276-3536.
Recommended Length of Stay: 2 to 5 days.

45 DILLON AND THE BIG HOLE VALLEY

General Information: *Dillon was named for Sydney Dillon, president of the Union Pacific Railroad, who was instrumental in establishing the railroad line from Ogden, Utah, to Butte, Montana. The name "Beaverhead" aptly describes a local rock formation and landmark that Sacajawea pointed out to Lewis and Clark. Sacajawea was also known as "Bird Woman." The term Big Hole was the early trapper's name for the large basin surrounded by mountains in the upper reaches of the Big Hole River. It was also the site of the historic 1877 Battle of the Big Hole, involving Chief Joseph and Col. Gibbon.*

Bannack is a ghost town rich in mining history. It was the first territorial capital of Montana, and receives its name from the Bannock Indians who previously occupied the area. At the site of present-day Clark Canyon Reservoir, the confluence of the Beaverhead and Red Rock rivers, Lewis and Clark abandoned their canoes and traveled cross country over 7,373-foot Lemhi Pass—and over the Continental Divide—in August of 1805.

Birding Information: Dillon is the largest town in Beaverhead County, which is Montana's largest county. On the outskirts of town, try **Poindexter Slough** and the **Sewage Treatment Ponds** for an array of birds. Poindexter Slough is a fishing access site off Frontage Road south of Dillon. Park where the road crosses the railroad tracks and look to the west side of the road. This small backwater features willow thickets, bulrushes, cattails, and wet meadows. Look for Sandhill Crane, Sora, Gray Catbird, Yellow Warbler, Red-winged and Yellow-headed Blackbirds. At the Sewage Treatment Ponds about one mile north of Dillon on Highway 41 watch for Tundra and Trumpeter Swans, gulls, and other waterfowl in spring and fall. Summer visitors include American Avocet, Eared Grebe, Wilson's Phalarope, and a variety of waterfowl.

About ten miles south of Dillon on I-15, **Rattlesnake Cliffs** offer reliable viewing of Prairie Falcon. Nearby **Barretts Park** (operated by the Bureau of Reclamation) is a nice place to picnic, RV camp, and watch birds, including White-throated Swift, Tree Swallow, Cliff Swallow, Violet-green Swallow, Barn Swallow, House Wren, and Northern Oriole.

Clark Canyon Reservoir, about twenty miles south of Dillon on I-15, is an excellent place to watch birds. The spillway area and nature trail below the dam include cattail, bulrush, and willow habitats, which provide excellent cover for Cinnamon Teal, American Kestrel, Sora, American Coot, Cliff Swallow, Marsh Wren, Common Yellowthroat, Song Sparrow, and Yellow-headed Blackbird. The birding is particularly good at the south end of Clark Canyon Reservoir. Take the Red Rock Exit from I-15 just south of the reservoir and drive north on the **Old Armstead Road**. Look in the cottonwoods and along the Red Rock River for Great Blue Heron, which also may be seen fishing anywhere along the shoreline of the reservoir. The

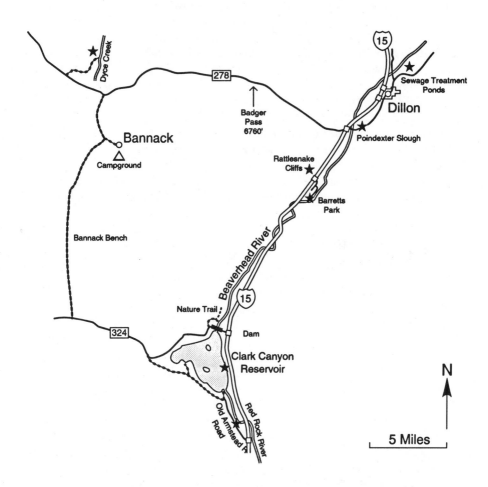

reservoir also harbors American White Pelican, Franklin Gull, California Gull, and a variety of waterfowl in summer. Adjacent wet meadows are home to Savannah Sparrow and Sandhill Crane. During spring and fall, Common Loon and Bald Eagle gather on the reservoir. The road continues around the southwest side of the reservoir through dry uplands surrounded by rock escarpments. This is an excellent place to view Ferruginous Hawk. From here the road loops back to the dam and I-15.

About seven miles north of Dillon on Highway 41, the **Anderson Lane** area is worth exploring. Head west on the dirt road toward a bridge over the Beaverhead River. Habitat here ranges from ponds and small marshes to

Ghostly buildings now stand empty in the once thriving town of Bannack.

roadside ditches. A wide variety of waterfowl, shorebirds, passerines, and raptors are seen here. Savannah Sparrow, Turkey Vulture, and Wilson's Phalarope are often found along the road. Twelve miles north of Dillon on Highway 41 stop at the **Beaverhead Rock State Monument** to look for Yellow Warbler, Rock Wren, Prairie Falcon, and Golden Eagle. The fields between Dillon and Twin Bridges are a major staging area for Sandhill Crane in the fall, with numbers peaking from early to mid-September.

The **Burma Road** provides interesting birding along the lower Big Hole River, though this route is best avoided in wet weather. Take Highway 41 south from Twin Bridges for six miles (or twenty-one miles north of Dillon) and turn west. The road passes through lush riparian habitat and flats of old-growth big sagebrush with rocky outcrops. Watch for Turkey Vulture, Red-tailed Hawk, Golden Eagle, American Kestrel, Prairie Falcon, Great Horned Owl, Common Nighthawk, Downy Woodpecker, Northern Flicker, Violet-green Swallow, Northern Rough-winged Swallow, Cliff Swallow, Rock Wren, Gray Catbird, Sage Thrasher, Warbling Vireo, Yellow Warbler, MacGillivray's Warbler, and Lazuli Bunting. Stop at **Notch Bottom** and **Glen** fishing access sites to look for Northern Oriole in the tall cottonwoods along the river. Drive slowly between the Glen fishing access and the junction with Highway 91 to enjoy the birding along the Big Hole River.

Head south on **Highway 91** through Thief Junction to Dillon to see Horned Lark and Golden Eagle, which are fairly common in this stretch. Also watch for Red-tailed Hawk, Ferruginous Hawk, and Swainson's Hawk. Or

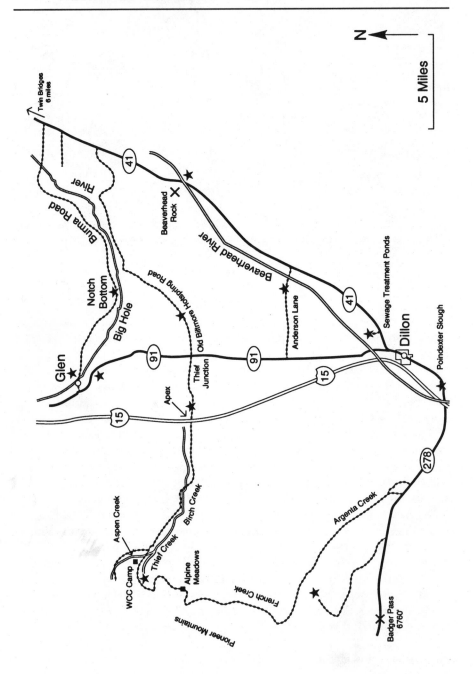

N

5 Miles

turn east at Thief Junction on the graveled **Old Biltmore Hotsprings road**, which eventually ends up on Highway 41 between Dillon and Twin Bridges. There's a good chance of seeing Golden Eagle, Prairie Falcon, Horned Lark, American Crow, Black-billed Magpie, Red-tailed Hawk, and McCown's Longspur along the way.

Also from Thief Junction, a gravel road leads west three miles to the **Apex interchange** on I-15. McCown's Longspur and Horned Lark are common along here and Cliff Swallow can be found at the underpass at Apex. The **Birch Creek Road** continues west from Apex into the Pioneer Mountains, and Long-billed Curlew are frequently sighted within the first two miles. After passing the National Forest boundary, look for the reclusive Lewis' Woodpecker. Turn left at the confluence of Thief Creek and Birch Creek, about seven miles from Apex. Stop at the first bridge to look for American Dipper. Birding the willow bottoms here or at the Aspen picnic area half a mile up the Birch Creek road can be quite good.

Further up **Thief Creek**, isolated stands of spruce and fir shelter Red-breasted Nuthatch, Ruby-crowned Kinglet, and Red Crossbill. Also watch for the less commonly seen Three-toed Woodpecker, Pine Grosbeak, Northern Goshawk, Spruce Grouse, and Blue Grouse. The alpine meadows atop the Thief Creek and French Creek divide are a good place to see White-crowned Sparrow, not to mention the pleasant view and colorful wildflowers. Either turn around here, or return by way of French Creek and the old mining district of Argenta, eventually ending up on Highway 278 nine miles west of Dillon.

Displaying Sage Grouse are always a wonderful sight. There are two Sage Grouse dancing grounds, or leks, west of Dillon just off Highway 278. One lek is located near **Ermont**, roughly twenty-two miles from Dillon. The road enters Ermont with the A-frame of the old Ermont Mine on the left. Take the next right and head one mile east. Stop along this ridge and listen for the booming sounds of strutting Sage Grouse. The other Sage Grouse lek is located near **Dyce Creek**, approximately thirty-one miles west of Dillon. This lek also rests on a small ridge or knob not far from the fair-weather road. For best results, arrive on the leks well before sunrise and remain in your vehicle. Walking out on the lek will only displace the grouse. Early to mid-April is usually the best time to observe the strutting grouse, though a four-wheel-drive vehicle may be needed at this time of year. For more information on these leks, contact the Montana Department of Fish, Wildlife and Parks office in Bozeman.

Bannack, the first territorial capital of Montana, is worth visiting for birding and a slice of Montana history. En route from Dillon to Bannack, Highway 278 crosses 6,760-foot **Badger Pass** where Green-tailed Towhee and Brewer's Sparrow are easily seen. The gravel road from Highway 278 to Bannack is an excellent area to see Sage Thrasher. Even within the well-preserved ghost town of Bannack, now a state park, the birding is quite good. Look for Rock Wren, Lazuli Bunting, Northern Oriole, Mountain Bluebird, and Black-headed Grosbeak. Camping at Bannack is also fun, with birding right in the campground along Grasshopper Creek.

Traveling west and north into the **Big Hole valley**, Sandhill Crane and Savannah Sparrow are common in the roadside irrigated meadows. The Big Hole is noted for being the land of 10,000 haystacks, and many of the ranchers use a unique contraption of wooden posts and poles known as a "beaverslide" to stack their hay. Rough-legged Hawk are easy to spot in the winter, and Great Gray Owl winter in forested foothills. During the fall Great Gray Owl can sometimes be seen in the timber along **Forest Service Road 945** to Twin Lakes (take Highway 278 about seven miles south from Wisdom and turn west at the Forest Access sign on the gravel road). East of Wisdom, The **Steel Creek** ranger cabin and campground area offers good birding for an array of sagebrush and forest species. Drive a half mile north of Wisdom on Highway 43 and go east six miles on the Steel Creek Road. Near the cabin look for Northern Harrier, Golden Eagle, Red-tailed Hawk, American Kestrel, Killdeer, Black-billed Magpie, and Common Raven. Several trails lead into the pine- covered foothills of the Pioneer Mountains from the cabin and from the campground a half mile east on the road. In the forest watch for Red-breasted Nuthatch, Gray Jay, Clark's Nutcracker, and Dark-eyed Junco.

Big Hole National Battlefield, west of Wisdom on Highway 43, has a small but excellent exhibit at the visitor center on early Native American life, and summer birdwatching is interesting. A side road ends at a parking lot on the North Fork of the Big Hole River. Take the trail to Nez Perce Camp to see American Crow, Warbling Vireo, Yellow Warbler, Northern Water-thrush, MacGillivray's Warbler, and Common Yellowthroat. Also hike to the Siege Area, Monument, and Howitzer Capture Site if time allows. The trail climbs out of the riparian zone and along the lower coniferous treeline. Other birds likely to be encountered include Western Wood-Pewee, Clark's Nut-cracker, Red-winged Blackbird, Cassin's Finch, and Pine Siskin.

West on Highway 43, look for Boreal Owl on **Chief Joseph Pass** and along the bumpy Forest Service road to **Hogan cabin**, about 1.5 miles west of the May Creek campground.

The **Wise River-Polaris Scenic Byway** is a pleasant road that works its way through the Pioneer Mountains from the town of Wise River on Highway 43 to Highway 278 about twenty-five miles west of Dillon. Plan on a fair amount of time to travel this National Forest Scenic Byway. Every year the Forest Service paves more of this road, but it is tastefully designed. There are ample opportunities for camping, hiking, fishing, and rockhounding along this route. Bird species likely to be encountered include Western Tanager, Red Crossbill, Ruby-crowned Kinglet, Golden-crowned Kinglet, Clark's Nutcracker, and Pine Grosbeak. The side road to **Maverick Ski Area** (about eleven miles north of Highway 278) is quite good birding for the species mentioned above plus Red-naped Sapsucker, Hairy Woodpecker, and the occasional Pileated Woodpecker, which are more typically found west of the Continental Divide in Montana. Stop at the Polar Bar, Montana's smallest saloon, for refreshments and some genuine Montana atmosphere.

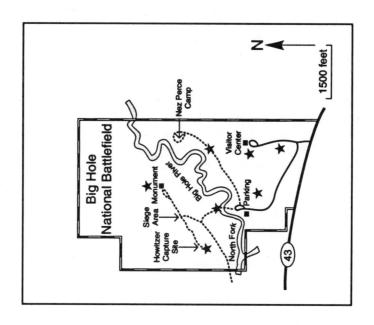

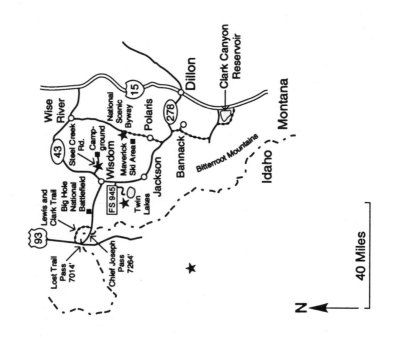

Helpful Information:

Elevation: Dillon, 5,096 ft; Clark Canyon Reservoir, 5,560 ft;
Birch Cr./French Cr. divide, 8,892 ft.

Habitat(s): Riparian, lake, sagebrush, irrigated pasture, coniferous forest.

Best Birding Season(s): Late spring through early summer.

Best Birding Month(s): May, June.

Montana Highway Map Location: 2-G, 3-G, 4-G, H-3.

Hazards: Mosquitoes, fair-weather roads, extreme winter cold.

Nearest Food, Gas, Lodging: Dillon, Jackson, Wisdom, Wise River.

Camping: Clark Canyon Reservoir, Barrett's Park, Bannack State Park,
Wise River Scenic Byway, Lower Miner Lakes, Twin Lakes.

Land Ownership: Private, USFS, BLM, state, Bur. of Rec., NPS.

Additional Information: Beaverhead National Forest, 610 N. Montana
Street, Dillon, MT 59725 ph: (406) 683-3900. Purchase Interagency Visitor
Map of SW Montana, available at most local government agency offices.
Also ask in local bookstores for the sixteen-page booklet *Finding Birds in
Beaverhead County* by Dan Block.

Recommended Length of Stay: 2 to 3 days.

NOTES

NOTES

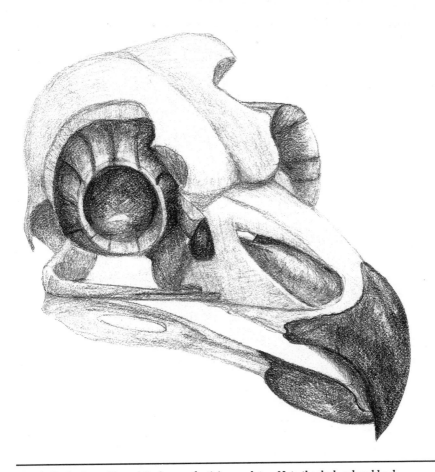

The skull of a Great Horned Owl, an unforgiving predator. Note the dark colored beak.

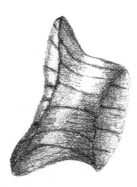

The sclerotic ring from the eye of a Great Horned Owl. These thin overlying bony plates protect and strengthen the eyeball especially during collision with prey or other objects.

CHAPTER 4
CHECKLIST, SEASONAL OCCURRENCE, AND ABUNDANCE OF MONTANA BIRDS

Approximately 388 species of birds have been recorded in Montana to date. Of these, 295 species have been reliably documented as occurring in Montana, and the remaining ninety-three species are considered unusuals or accidentals. The following checklist of Montana birds includes a bar graph for each species indicating seasonal occurrence and abundance on a monthly basis. Symbols also show which species are known to breed in Montana and their general distribution within the state. The sequence in which species are presented in this chapter follows the checklist order established by the American Ornithologists' Union. A key to the symbols used in this checklist is found at the bottom of each page.

SAMPLE:

✓	SPECIES	Breeding Evidence	Distrib.	Monthly Occurrence and Abundance J F M A M J J A S O N D
▢	Red-tailed Hawk	■	S	• • ▬▬▬ • •

■ =direct evidence of breeding (nest or dependent young observed)
S =statewide distribution; E =found primarily in the eastern 2/3 of Montana; W =found primarily in the western 1/3 of Montana
• • • • • =very rare to rare; ▬▬▬▬ =uncommon to relatively common; ▬▬▬▬▬▬ =common to abundant

Finally, a simple checklist is provided for previously reported unusual or accidental species. Few records exist for these birds and information on their occurrence in Montana is quite limited. These birds are either out of their normal range or are found in very limited habitat types. Sightings of unusuals or accidentals are rare indeed.

The information presented here is based on the best knowledge available, but our understanding of birds and their distribution is constantly growing. Use this checklist as an aid for planning your birding trips and for studying particular species, but remember that bird populations and ranges are always changing. Today's "facts" may be challenged by tomorrow's observations in the field. The author welcomes birders' comments for future revisions of this checklist.

✓	SPECIES	Breeding Evidence	Distrib.	Monthly Occurrence and Abundance (J F M A M J J A S O N D)
☐	Common Loon	■	W E	uncommon/common Apr–Nov; rare Dec
☐	Pied-billed Grebe	■	S	rare Jan–Mar; uncommon/common Apr–Oct; rare Nov–Dec
☐	Horned Grebe	■	S	rare Apr–Nov
☐	Red-necked Grebe	■	W E	uncommon/common Apr–Sep; rare Sep–Nov
☐	Eared Grebe	■	S	common Apr–Oct; rare Oct–Nov
☐	Western Grebe	■	S	common Apr–Oct; rare Oct–Nov
☐	Clark's Grebe	■	S	rare Apr–Nov
☐	American White Pelican	■	W E	common Apr–Oct; rare Nov
☐	Double-crested Cormorant	■	S	common Apr–Oct
☐	American Bittern	■	S	rare Apr–Nov
☐	Great Blue Heron	■	S	rare Jan; common Feb–Oct; rare Nov–Dec
☐	Snowy Egret	■	S	rare Apr–Oct
☐	Cattle Egret		S	rare May–Aug
☐	Black-crowned Night-Heron	■	S	uncommon/common May–Sep
☐	White-faced Ibis	■	S	rare Apr–Oct
☐	Tundra Swan	■	S	rare Jan–Feb; uncommon Mar; uncommon Oct–Nov; rare Dec
☐	Trumpeter Swan	■	W	—
☐	Mute Swan	■	W	rare year-round
☐	Greater White-fronted Goose		S	rare May
☐	Snow Goose		S	uncommon Apr–May; uncommon Oct–Nov
☐	Ross' Goose		S	uncommon Apr; uncommon Oct–Nov
☐	Canada Goose	■	S	common year-round
☐	Wood Duck	■	S	rare Apr; rare May; common Jun–Sep; rare Oct–Dec
☐	Green-winged Teal	■	S	common Apr–Nov
☐	Mallard	■	S	common year-round
☐	Northern Pintail	■	S	rare Jan–Feb; common Mar–Oct; rare Nov–Dec
☐	Blue-winged Teal	■	S	common Apr–Nov; rare Dec
☐	Cinnamon Teal	■	S	common Apr–Oct; rare Dec

■ =direct evidence of breeding (nest or dependent young observed)
S =statewide distribution; E =found primarily in the eastern 2/3 of Montana; W =found primarily in the western 1/3 of Montana
• • • • • =very rare to rare; ▬▬▬ =uncommon to relatively common; ▬▬▬ =common to abundant

✓	SPECIES	Breeding Evidence	Distrib.	Monthly Occurrence and Abundance
				J F M A M J J A S O N D
▢	Northern Shoveler	■	S	
▢	Gadwall	■	S	
▢	Eurasian Wigeon		S	
▢	American Wigeon	■	S	
▢	Canvasback	■	S	
▢	Redhead	■	S	
▢	Ring-necked Duck	■	S	
▢	Greater Scaup		S	
▢	Lesser Scaup	■	S	
▢	Harlequin Duck	■	W	
▢	Oldsquaw		S	
▢	Surf Scoter		S	
▢	White-winged Scoter		S	
▢	Common Goldeneye	■	W E	
▢	Barrow's Goldeneye	■	W E	
▢	Bufflehead	■	S	
▢	Hooded Merganser	■	W E	
▢	Common Merganser	■	S	
▢	Red-breasted Merganser		S	
▢	Ruddy Duck	■	S	
▢	Turkey Vulture	■	S	
▢	Osprey	■	○	
▢	Bald Eagle	■	S	
▢	Northern Harrier	■	S	
▢	Sharp-shinned Hawk	■	S	
▢	Cooper's Hawk	■	S	
▢	Northern Goshawk	■	S	
▢	Broad-winged Hawk		S	

■ =direct evidence of breeding (nest or dependent young observed)
S =statewide distribution; E =found primarily in the eastern 2/3 of Montana; W =found primarily in the western 1/3 of Montana
• • • • • =very rare to rare; ▬▬▬▬ =uncommon to relatively common; ▬▬▬▬ =common to abundant

233

✓	SPECIES	Breeding Evidence	Distrib.	Monthly Occurrence and Abundance (J F M A M J J A S O N D)
☐	Swainson's Hawk	■	S	
☐	Red-tailed Hawk	■	S	
☐	Ferruginous Hawk	■	S	
☐	Rough-legged Hawk		S	
☐	Golden Eagle	■	S	
☐	American Kestrel	■	S	
☐	Merlin	■	S	
☐	Peregrine Falcon	■	W E	
☐	Gyrfalcon		S	
☐	Prairie Falcon	■	S	
☐	Gray Partridge	■	S	
☐	Chukar	■	S	
☐	Ring-necked Pheasant	■	S	
☐	Spruce Grouse	■	W	
☐	Blue Grouse	■	S	
☐	White-tailed Ptarmigan	■	W	
☐	Ruffed Grouse	■	S	
☐	Sage Grouse	■	E	
☐	Sharp-tailed Grouse	■	E	
☐	Wild Turkey	■	S	
☐	Virginia Rail	■	S	
☐	Sora	■	S	
☐	American Coot	■	S	
☐	Sandhill Crane	■	S	
☐	Whooping Crane		S	
☐	Black-bellied Plover		S	
☐	Lesser Golden Plover		S	
☐	Semipalmated Plover		S	

■ =direct evidence of breeding (nest or dependent young observed)
S =statewide distribution; E =found primarily in the eastern 2/3 of Montana; W =found primarily in the western 1/3 of Montana
• • • • • =very rare to rare; ▬▬▬ =uncommon to relatively common; ▬▬▬ =common to abundant

✓	SPECIES	Breeding Evidence	Distrib.	J	F	M	A	M	J	J	A	S	O	N	D
☐	Piping Plover	■	E					•	•	•	•	•	•		
☐	Killdeer	■	S			━	━	━	━	━	━	━	━	━	
☐	Mountain Plover	■	E				•	•	•	•	•	•	•		
☐	Black-necked Stilt	■	S					•	•	•	•	•	•		
☐	American Avocet	■	S				─	─	─	─	─	─			
☐	Greater Yellowlegs		S				─	─	•	─	─	─	•		
☐	Lesser Yellowlegs		S				─	─	─	─	─	•	•		
☐	Solitary Sandpiper		S				─	─		─	─				
☐	Willet	■	S				─	─	─	─	─	•			
☐	Spotted Sandpiper	■	S				─	─	─	─	─				
☐	Upland Sandpiper	■	S				─	─	─	─	─	•			
☐	Whimbrel		S					•				•			
☐	Long-billed Curlew	■	S				─	─	─	─	─	•			
☐	Marbled Godwit	■	S				─	─	─	─	─	•			
☐	Ruddy Turnstone		S				•	•			•	•			
☐	Sanderling		S					•	•			•	•		
☐	Semipalmated Sandpiper		S					─			─				
☐	Western Sandpiper		S					─	─	─	─	─	•		
☐	Least Sandpiper		S				─	─	─	─	─	•	•		
☐	Baird's Sandpiper		S					─	─	─	─	─	•		
☐	Pectoral Sandpiper		S				•	•			•	•	•		
☐	Dunlin		S					•				•	•		
☐	Stilt Sandpiper		S									•	•		
☐	Short-billed Dowitcher		S								•	•			
☐	Long-billed Dowitcher		S					─			─	─			
☐	Common Snipe	■	S		━	━	━	━	━	━	━	━	━	━	
☐	Wilson's Phalarope	■	S					─	─	─	─	─			
☐	Red-necked Phalarope		S					•	•		•	•	•		

■ =direct evidence of breeding (nest or dependent young observed)
S =statewide distribution; E =found primarily in the eastern 2/3 of Montana; W =found primarily in the western 1/3 of Montana
• • • • • =very rare to rare; ━━━━━ =uncommon to relatively common; ━━━━━ =common to abundant

✓	SPECIES	Breeding Evidence	Distrib.	J	F	M	A	M	J	J	A	S	O	N	D
☐	Franklin' Gull	■	S					━	━	━	━	━			
☐	Bonaparte's Gull		S					•		•	•	•	•	•	
☐	Ring-billed Gull	■	S				━	━	━	━	━	━	•	•	•
☐	California Gull	■	S				━	━	━	━	━	━	━		•
☐	Herring Gull		S				•	•			•	•		•	
☐	Caspian Tern	■	S					━	━	━	•	•	•		
☐	Common Tern	■	S					━	━	━	━	━			
☐	Forster's Tern	■	S					•	•	•	•	•	•		
☐	Least Tern	■	E					•	•	•	•	•			
☐	Black Tern	■	S					━	━	━	━	━			
☐	Rock Dove	■	S	━	━	━	━	━	━	━	━	━	━	━	━
☐	Mourning Dove	■	S					━	━	━	━	━	•		•
☐	Black-billed Cuckoo	■	E					━	━	━	━	•			
☐	Yellow-billed Cuckoo		E					•	•	•	•	•			
☐	Eastern Screech-Owl	■	E	•	•	•	•	•	•	•	•	•	•	•	•
☐	Western Screech-Owl	■	W	•	•	•	•	•	•	•	•	•	•	•	•
☐	Great Horned Owl	■	S	━	━	━	━	━	━	━	━	━	━	━	━
☐	Snowy Owl		S	•	•	•								•	•
☐	Northern Pygmy-Owl	■	S	•	•	•	•		•	•	•	•	•	•	•
☐	Burrowing Owl	■	S				━	━	━	━	━	━			
☐	Barred Owl	■	W	•	•	•	•	•	•	•	•	•	•	•	•
☐	Great Gray Owl	■	S	•	•	•	•	━	━	━	•	•	━	•	•
☐	Long-eared Owl	■	S	━	━	━	━	•	•	•	━	•	━		
☐	Short-eared Owl	■	S	━	━	━	━	•	•	•	•	•	━	━	
☐	Boreal Owl	■	S	━	━	━	•	•	•	•	•	━	•	•	•
☐	Northern Saw-whet Owl	■	S	━	━	━	━	•	•	•	•	•	•	━	━
☐	Common Nighthawk	■	S				•	•	━	━━	━━	━	•		
☐	Common Poorwill	■	E					━	━	━	━	━			

■ =direct evidence of breeding (nest or dependent young observed)
S =statewide distribution; E =found primarily in the eastern 2/3 of Montana; W =found primarily in the western 1/3 of Montana
• • • • • =very rare to rare; ━━━━ =uncommon to relatively common; ━━━━ =common to abundant

✓	SPECIES	Breeding Evidence	Distrib.	Monthly Occurrence and Abundance J F M A M J J A S O N D
▭	Black Swift	■	W	
▭	Chimney Swift	■	E	
▭	Vaux's Swift	■	W	
▭	White-throated Swift	■	S	
▭	Ruby-throated Hummingbird	■	E	
▭	Black-chinned Hummingbird	■	W	
▭	Calliope Hummingbird	■	S	
▭	Broad-tailed Hummingbird	■	S	
▭	Rufous Hummingbird	■	S	
▭	Belted Kingfisher	■	S	
▭	Lewis' Woodpecker	■	S	
▭	Red-headed Woodpecker	■	E	
▭	Red-naped Sapsucker	■	S	
▭	Williamson's Sapsucker	■	S	
▭	Downy Woodpecker	■	S	
▭	Hairy Woodpecker	■	S	
▭	Three-toed Woodpecker	■	S	
▭	Black-backed Woodpecker	■	S	
▭	Northern Flicker	■	S	
▭	Pileated Woodpecker	■	W	
▭	Olive-sided Flycatcher	■	S	
▭	Western Wood-Pewee	■	S	
▭	Willow Flycatcher	■	S	
▭	Least Flycatcher	■	S	
▭	Hammond's Flycatcher	■	S	
▭	Dusky Flycatcher	■	S	
▭	Cordilleran Flycatcher	■	S	
▭	Say's Phoebe	■	S	

■ =direct evidence of breeding (nest or dependent young observed)
S =statewide distribution; E =found primarily in the eastern 2/3 of Montana; W =found primarily in the western 1/3 of Montana
• • • • • =very rare to rare; ▬▬▬▬ =uncommon to relatively common; ▬▬▬▬ =common to abundant

✓	SPECIES	Breeding Evidence	Distrib.	Monthly Occurrence and Abundance J F M A M J J A S O N D
▢	Cassin's Kingbird	■	E	• • • • •
▢	Western Kingbird	■	S	▬▬▬▬▬
▢	Eastern Kingbird	■	S	▬▬▬▬
▢	Horned Lark	■	S	▬▬▬▬▬▬▬▬▬▬▬▬
▢	Tree Swallow	■	S	▬▬▬▬▬
▢	Violet-green Swallow	■	S	▬▬▬▬▬
▢	Northern Rough-winged Swallow	■	S	▬▬▬▬▬ •
▢	Bank Swallow	■	S	▬▬▬▬
▢	Cliff Swallow	■	S	▬▬▬▬
▢	Barn Swallow	■	S	▬▬▬▬▬
▢	Gray Jay	■	S	▬▬▬▬▬▬▬▬▬▬▬▬
▢	Steller's Jay	■	W	▬▬▬▬▬▬▬▬▬▬▬▬
▢	Blue Jay	■	S	• • • • • • • • • • •
▢	Pinyon Jay	■	S	▬▬▬▬▬▬▬▬▬▬▬▬
▢	Clark's Nutcracker	■	S	▬▬▬▬▬▬▬▬▬▬▬▬
▢	Black-billed Magpie	■	S	▬▬▬▬▬▬▬▬▬▬▬▬
▢	American Crow	■	S	▬▬▬▬▬▬▬▬▬▬▬▬
▢	Common Raven	■	S	▬▬▬▬▬▬▬▬▬▬▬▬
▢	Black-capped Chickadee	■	S	▬▬▬▬▬▬▬▬▬▬▬▬
▢	Mountain Chickadee	■	S	▬▬▬▬▬▬▬▬▬▬▬▬
▢	Boreal Chickadee	■	W	• • • • • • • • • • • •
▢	Chestnut-backed Chickadee	■	W	• • • • • • • • • • • •
▢	Red-breasted Nuthatch	■	S	▬▬▬▬▬▬▬▬▬▬▬▬
▢	White-breasted Nuthatch	■	S	▬▬▬▬▬▬▬▬▬▬▬▬
▢	Pygmy Nuthatch	■	S	• • • • • • • • • • • •
▢	Brown Creeper	■	S	▬▬▬▬▬▬▬▬▬▬▬▬
▢	Rock Wren	■	S	• ▬▬▬▬▬▬▬ •
▢	Canyon Wren	■	S	• • • • • •

■ =direct evidence of breeding (nest or dependent young observed)
S =statewide distribution; E =found primarily in the eastern 2/3 of Montana; W =found primarily in the western 1/3 of Montana
• • • • • =very rare to rare; ▬▬▬▬▬ =uncommon to relatively common; ▬▬▬▬▬ =common to abundant

✓	SPECIES	Breeding Evidence	Distrib.	Monthly Occurrence and Abundance
☐	House Wren	■	S	
☐	Winter Wren	■	W	
☐	Sedge Wren		E	
☐	Marsh Wren	■	S	
☐	American Dipper	■	S	
☐	Golden-crowned Kinglet	■	S	
☐	Ruby-crowned Kinglet	■	S	
☐	Eastern Bluebird	■	E	
☐	Western Bluebird	■	W	
☐	Mountain Bluebird	■	S	
☐	Townsend's Solitaire	■	S	
☐	Veery	■	S	
☐	Swainson's Thrush	■	S	
☐	Hermit Thrush	■	S	
☐	American Robin	■	S	
☐	Varied Thrush	■	W	
☐	Gray Catbird	■	S	
☐	Northern Mockingbird	■	S	
☐	Sage Thrasher	■	S	
☐	Brown Thrasher	■	S	
☐	American Pipit	■	S	
☐	Sprague's Pipit	■	S	
☐	Bohemian Waxwing	■	S	
☐	Cedar Waxwing	■	S	
☐	Northern Shrike		S	
☐	Loggerhead Shrike	■	S	
☐	European Starling	■	S	
☐	Solitary Vireo	■	S	

(Monthly columns: J F M A M J J A S O N D)

■ =direct evidence of breeding (nest or dependent young observed)
S =statewide distribution; E =found primarily in the eastern 2/3 of Montana; W =found primarily in the western 1/3 of Montana
• • • • • =very rare to rare; ———— =uncommon to relatively common; ▬▬▬ =common to abundant

✓	SPECIES	Breeding Evidence	Distrib.	Monthly Occurrence and Abundance
☐	Warbling Vireo	■	S	common to abundant May–Aug; uncommon to May, Aug–Sep
☐	Red-eyed Vireo	■	S	uncommon to relatively common Jun–Aug
☐	Tennessee Warbler	■	S	very rare to rare May–Aug
☐	Orange-crowned Warbler	■	S	uncommon to relatively common May–Sep
☐	Nashville Warbler	■	W E	very rare to rare May, Aug
☐	Yellow Warbler	■	S	common to abundant May–Jul; uncommon to Aug
☐	Yellow-rumped Warbler	■	S	common to abundant May–Sep; very rare Oct, Nov
☐	Townsend's Warbler	■	W	uncommon to relatively common May–Aug; very rare Sep
☐	Blackpoll Warbler		S	very rare to rare May, Jul, Aug
☐	Black-and-white Warbler	■	S	very rare to rare May, Jun, Aug, Sep
☐	American Redstart	■	S	uncommon to relatively common Jun–Aug
☐	Ovenbird	■	S	uncommon to relatively common Jun–Aug; very rare Aug
☐	Northern Waterthrush	■	S	uncommon to relatively common May–Aug
☐	MacGillivray's Warbler	■	S	uncommon to relatively common May–Aug
☐	Common Yellowthroat	■	S	uncommon to relatively common May–Aug
☐	Wilson's Warbler	■	S	uncommon to relatively common May–Sep
☐	Yellow-breasted Chat	■	S	uncommon to relatively common Jun–Aug
☐	Western Tanager	■	S	uncommon to relatively common May–Aug
☐	Rose-breasted Grosbeak		S	very rare Jun
☐	Black-headed Grosbeak	■	S	uncommon to relatively common May–Aug
☐	Lazuli Bunting	■	S	uncommon to relatively common May–Aug
☐	Indigo Bunting		S	very rare Jun, Jul
☐	Green-tailed Towhee	■	S	uncommon to relatively common May–Sep; very rare Oct, Dec
☐	Rufous-sided Towhee	■	S	uncommon to relatively common May–Sep; very rare Oct, Dec
☐	American Tree Sparrow		S	uncommon to relatively common Jan–Mar, Oct–Dec; very rare Apr, May, Sep
☐	Chipping Sparrow	■	S	common to abundant May–Aug; very rare Sep
☐	Clay-colored Sparrow	■	S	uncommon to relatively common May–Aug; very rare Sep
☐	Brewer's Sparrow	■	S	uncommon to relatively common May–Aug

■ =direct evidence of breeding (nest or dependent young observed)
S =statewide distribution; E =found primarily in the eastern 2/3 of Montana; W =found primarily in the western 1/3 of Montana
• • • • • =very rare to rare; —————— =uncommon to relatively common; ▬▬▬▬ =common to abundant

✓	SPECIES	Breeding Evidence	Distrib.	Monthly Occurrence and Abundance J F M A M J J A S O N D
▭	Field Sparrow	■	S	
▭	Vesper Sparrow	■	S	
▭	Lark Sparrow	■	S	
▭	Lark Bunting	■	S	
▭	Savannah Sparrow	■	S	
▭	Baird's Sparrow	■	S	
▭	Grasshopper Sparrow	■	S	
▭	Le Conte's Sparrow	■	S	
▭	Sharp-tailed Sparrow		S	
▭	Fox Sparrow	■	S	
▭	Song Sparrow	■	S	
▭	Lincoln's Sparrow	■	S	
▭	White-throated Sparrow		W E	
▭	White-crowned Sparrow	■	S	
▭	Harris' Sparrow		W E	
▭	Dark-eyed Junco	■	S	
▭	McCown's Longspur	■	S	
▭	Lapland Longspur		S	
▭	Chestnut-collared Longspur		S	
▭	Snow Bunting		S	
▭	Bobolink	■	S	
▭	Red-winged Blackbird	■	S	
▭	Western Meadowlark	■	S	
▭	Yellow-headed Blackbird	■	S	
▭	Rusty Blackbird		S	
▭	Brewer's Blackbird	■	S	
▭	Common Grackle	■	S	
▭	Brown-headed Cowbird	■	S	

■ =direct evidence of breeding (nest or dependent young observed)
S =statewide distribution; E =found primarily in the eastern 2/3 of Montana; W =found primarily in the western 1/3 of Montana
• • • • • =very rare to rare; ▬▬▬ =uncommon to relatively common; ▬▬▬▬ =common to abundant

Monthly Occurrence and Abundance

✓	SPECIES	Breeding Evidence	Distrib.	J	F	M	A	M	J	J	A	S	O	N	D
▢	Orchard Oriole	■	E					•	•	•	•				
▢	Northern Oriole	■	S					▬	▬	▬	▬				
▢	Rosy Finch	■	W E	▬	▬			•	•	•	•	•	▬	▬	▬
▢	Pine Grosbeak	■	S												
▢	Purple Finch		S	•										•	•
▢	Cassin's Finch	■	S		•	•	▬	▬	▬	▬	▬		•	•	•
▢	House Finch	■	S	▬	▬	▬	▬	▬	▬	▬	▬	▬	▬	▬	▬
▢	Red Crossbill	■	S	▬	▬	▬	▬	▬	▬	▬	▬	▬	▬	▬	▬
▢	White-winged Crossbill		S	•	•	•	•	•	•	•	•	•	•	•	•
▢	Common Redpoll		S	▬	▬							•	▬	▬	▬
▢	Hoary Redpoll		S	•	•	•								•	•
▢	Pine Siskin	■	S	•	•	•								•	•
▢	American Goldfinch	■	S	•	•	•	•	▬	▬	▬	▬		•	•	
▢	Evening Grosbeak	■	S	▬	▬	▬	▬	▬	▬	▬	▬	▬	▬	▬	▬
▢	House Sparrow	■	S	▬	▬	▬	▬	▬	▬	▬	▬	▬	▬	▬	▬

■ =direct evidence of breeding (nest or dependent young observed)
S =statewide distribution; E =found primarily in the eastern 2/3 of Montana; W =found primarily in the western 1/3 of Montana
• • • • • =very rare to rare; ▬▬▬▬ =uncommon to relatively common; ▬▬▬ =common to abundant

Unusuals or Accidentals ✓

- [ ] Red-throated Loon
- [ ] Pacific Loon
- [ ] Yellow-billed Loon
- [ ] Least Bittern
- [ ] Great Egret
- [ ] Little Blue Heron
- [ ] Green-backed Heron
- [ ] Yellow-crowned Night-Heron
- [ ] Wood Stork
- [ ] Brant
- [ ] American Black Duck
- [ ] Garganey
- [ ] Black Scoter
- [ ] Red-shouldered Hawk
- [ ] Willow Ptarmigan
- [ ] Greater Prairie-Chicken (Historical Record)
- [ ] Northern Bobwhite
- [ ] Yellow Rail
- [ ] Common Moorhen
- [ ] Snowy Plover
- [ ] Hudsonian Godwit
- [ ] Black Turnstone
- [ ] Red Knot
- [ ] White-rumped Sandpiper
- [ ] Curlew Sandpiper
- [ ] Buff-breasted Sandpiper
- [ ] American Woodcock
- [ ] Red Phalarope
- [ ] Pomarine Jaeger
- [ ] Parasitic Jaeger
- [ ] Long-tailed Jaeger

- [ ] Laughing Gull
- [ ] Mew Gull
- [ ] Thayer's Gull
- [ ] Iceland Gull
- [ ] Glaucous Gull
- [ ] Glaucous-winged Gull
- [ ] Great Black-backed Gull
- [ ] Black-legged Kittiwake
- [ ] Sabine's Gull
- [ ] Ivory Gull
- [ ] Marbled Murrelet
- [ ] Ancient Murrelet
- [ ] Band-tailed Pigeon
- [ ] White-winged Dove
- [ ] Barn Owl
- [ ] Flammulated Owl
- [ ] Northern Hawk Owl
- [ ] Whip-poor-will
- [ ] Anna's Hummingbird
- [ ] Red-bellied Woodpecker
- [ ] Yellow-bellied Sapsucker
- [ ] White-headed Woodpecker
- [ ] Eastern Wood-Pewee
- [ ] Alder Flycatcher
- [ ] Eastern Phoebe
- [ ] Ash-throated Flycatcher
- [ ] Great Crested Flycatcher
- [ ] Scissor-tailed Flycatcher
- [ ] Purple Martin
- [ ] Blue-gray Gnatcatcher
- [ ] Gray-cheeked Thrush

✓

- Wood Thrush
- Philadelphia Vireo
- Northern Parula
- Chestnut-sided Warbler
- Magnolia Warbler
- Cape May Warbler
- Black-throated Blue Warbler
- Black-throated Gray Warbler
- Black-throated Green Warbler
- Blackburnian Warbler
- Yellow-throated Warbler
- Pine Warbler
- Prairie Warbler
- Palm Warbler
- Bay-breasted Warbler
- Kentucky Warbler

- Connecticut Warbler
- Mourning Warbler
- Canada Warbler
- Painted Redstart
- Summer Tanager
- Scarlet Tanager
- Northern Cardinal
- Blue Grosbeak
- Dickcissel ■
- Black-throated Sparrow
- Sage Sparrow ■
- Swamp Sparrow
- Golden-crowned Sparrow
- Smith's Longspur
- Brambling

■ =direct evidence of breeding (nest or dependent young observed)

NOTES

Common Raven. The ecological equivalent of a raptor.

CHAPTER 5
MONTANA BIRD SPECIALTIES

Toss the word "Montana" into a conversation among a dozen birders, and you'll quickly hear the names of a dozen different birds, each proclaimed to be an exemplar of birding in the state: Trumpeter Swan, Harlequin Duck, Bald Eagle, Spruce Grouse, Great Gray Owl, Boreal Owl, Lewis' Woodpecker, Clark's Nutcracker, Common Raven, Bohemian Waxwing, Townsend's Warbler, and Rosy Finch. In fact, more than 100 birds could be classified as "Montana Specialties"—species that are unique to the state or representative of Montana habitats, and that are much sought after by North American birders.

This chapter presents information on the seasonal distribution of 137 Montana bird specialties. Included for each species are maps showing general bird distribution across the state, habitat preferences, your chances of seeing or hearing the bird, and a list of key sites (described in Chapter 3) where the bird is known to occur. The solid shading on the maps indicates either year-round or seasonal range of the species and the diagonal shading represents areas where birds are likely to be found during migration. Diagnostic features are given for some species, such as voice, plumage, courting and feeding habits, or flight pattern. A list of abbreviations used in this chapter appears at the bottom of each page.

Common Loon

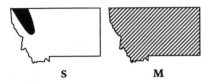

S   M

Habits: Mountain lakes; sometimes large marshes, large slow-flowing rivers; also reservoirs during migration. Produces wonderful calls including tremolo, yodel, wail.

Chances: Moderate

Key Sites: Glacier NP, Fortine, Seeley Lake, Yellowstone NP

Red-necked Grebe

S   M

Habits: Lakes, ponds, reservoirs with margins of reeds of sedges; stock ponds and reservoirs during migration. This large grebe shows white patches in flight.

Chances: Moderate

Key Sites: Blackfeet Indian Reservation, Georgetown Lake, Glacier NP, Ninepipe NWR

American White Pelican

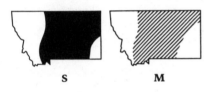

S   M

Habits: Large rivers and lakes; feeds communally and in unison;- characteristic high elevation soaring and gliding, sometimes far from nearest water, often in flocks.

Chances: Moderate

Key Sites: Bowdoin NWR, Canyon Ferry Reservoir, Fort Peck Reservoir, Yellowstone NP

Tundra Swan

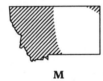

M

Habits: Lakes and reservoirs (sometimes large rivers) ranging from mountains to prairie. Typically feeds in shallow water. Call is an off-tone whistle.

Chances: Moderate

Key Sites: Benton Lake NWR, Freezout Lake, Red Rock Lakes NWR, Yellowstone NP

Trumpeter Swan

S   M

Habits: Summer: lakes, ponds, marshes, reservoirs with emergent vegetation; also large slow-flowing rivers during migration. Call is a deep "ho-hoh."

Chances: Moderate

Key Sites: Red Rock Lakes NWR, Yellowstone NP, Freezout Lake

General Distribution: S=Summer; W=Winter; Y=Year-round; M=During migration
NWR=National Wildlife Refuge; NP=National Park; NRA=National Recreation Area; NHS=National Historic Site
Mts.=Mountains; SP=State Park

Snow Goose

M

Habits: Reservoirs, marshes, sometimes cultivated fields. Usually found in large flocks. Call is a "kowk," somewhat off-tune, given in flight and on ground.

Chances: Moderate

Key Sites: Benton Lake NWR, Freezout Lake

Ross' Goose

M

Habits: Reservoirs, marshes, sometimes cultivated fields. Extremely small. Found in flocks; often alone. Call is a "luk-luk."

Chances: Difficult

Key Sites: Benton Lake NWR, Freezout Lake

Green-winged Teal

Y   S

Habits: Lakes, marshes, ponds, creeks, rivers. Characteristic teal flight, reeling from side to side. Call is a high-pitched whistle resembling bells.

Chances: Excellent

Key Sites: Freezout Lake, Lee Metcalf NWR, Ninepipe NWR, Red Rock Lakes NWR

Cinnamon Teal

S

Habits: Shallow lake margins, ponds, marshes. Characteristic teal flight, reeling from side to side. Call is rarely heard.

Chances: Moderate

Key Sites: Freezout Lake, Lee Metcalf NWR, Ninepipe NWR, Red Rock Lakes NWR

Ring-necked Duck

S   W

Habits: Marshes, lakes, rivers with dense emergent vegetation (particularly bulrush). Characteristic ring around the bill. Male mostly silent, hissing note during breeding season.

Chances: Moderate

Key Sites: Benton Lake NWR, Freezout Lake, Red Rock Lakes NWR

General Distribution: S=Summer; W=Winter; Y=Year-round; M=During migration
NWR=National Wildlife Refuge; NP=National Park; NRA=National Recreation Area; NHS=National Historic Site
Mts.=Mountains; SP=State Park

Lesser Scaup

S W + M

Habits: Lakes, ponds, reservoirs, marshes. Found throughout most of Montana. Quite numerous.

Chances: Excellent

Key Sites: Benton Lake NWR, Bowdoin NWR, Freezout Lake, Ninepipe NWR, Red Rock Lakes NWR

Harlequin Duck

S

Habits: Rapids, fast-moving water, cascading creeks and rivers often lined with boulders or cobble rocks. Very small size. Blends in perfectly with boulders, cobbles.

Chances: Difficult

Key Sites: Glacier NP, Kootenai Falls, Yellowstone NP

Barrow's Goldeneye

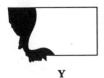

Y W + M

Habits: Summer: lakes, ponds, rivers usually bordered by trees or with trees nearby. Winter & Migration: most lakes, ponds, marshes, rivers. Female's orange bill turns black in summer.

Chances: Excellent

Key Sites: Glacier NP, Red Rock Lakes NWR, Yellowstone NP

Hooded Merganser

S W + M

Habits: Lakes, ponds, reservoirs, rivers. Most are observed during migration. Relatively small size. Head crests can be inflated or deflated.

Chances: Moderate

Key Sites: Glacier NP, Kalispell, Missoula, Metcalf NWR

Turkey Vulture

S

Habits: Various open terrain; unusual in alpine areas, high elevations, or in continuous forests. Extraordinary sense of smell and sight for seeking out carrion.

Chances: Moderate

Key Sites: Bighorn Canyon NRA, Billings,

General Distribution: S=Summer; W=Winter; Y=Year-round; M=During migration
NWR=National Wildlife Refuge; NP=National Park; NRA=National Recreation Area; NHS=National Historic Site
Mts.=Mountains; SP=State Park

Osprey

S   M

Habits: Primarily along rivers, lakes, and reservoirs; during migration almost anywhere. Feeds primarily on fish. Hunts fish from a perch or by hovering. Dives feet-first in the water.

Chances: Moderate

Key Sites: Lee Metcalf NWR, C.M. Russell NWR, Helena, Yellowstone NP

Bald Eagle

S   W

Habits: Summer: found near water or close to water. Winter & Migration: every conceivable habitat type. Feeds on fish and ducks in summer, and fish, ducks, carrion, gut piles in winter.

Chances: Moderate

Key Sites: Summer: Kootenai River, Missouri River, Yellowstone NP. Winter: Libby Dam, Canyon Ferry Reservoir

Northern Goshawk

Y + M

Habits: Forests (primarily mixed species), forest edges, ridges, clearings. Hunts at low levels, through forest understory.

Chances: Difficult

Key Sites: Red Rock Lakes NWR, Seeley Lake, Yellowstone NP

Swainson's Hawk

S

Habits: Open grasslands, sagebrush-grasslands, or irrigated grasslands with scattered trees. Migrates to the pampas of Argentina in winter.

Chances: Moderate

Key Sites: Red Rock Lakes NWR, Yellowstone NP, Big Hole.

Ferruginous Hawk

S   M

Habits: Often found in grasslands, also sage-brush-grasslands, plains, prairies, badlands. Preys on ground squirrels, prairie dogs, etc. The largest buteo in North America.

Chances: Moderate

Key Sites: Centennial Valley, C.M. Russell NWR, Dillon

General Distribution: S=Summer; W=Winter; Y=Year-round; M=During migration
NWR=National Wildlife Refuge; NP=National Park; NRA=National Recreation Area; NHS=National Historic Site
Mts.=Mountains; SP=State Park

Rough-legged Hawk

W

Habits: Open areas, primarily grasslands, cultivated fields, or sagebrush-grasslands. Feeds primarily on voles. Seldom found in areas with deep snows.

Chances: Excellent

Key Sites: Ninepipe NWR, Freezout Lake, Bozeman, Paradise Valley, Great Falls

Golden Eagle

Y

Habits: Variable terrain from plains to alpine areas, most often associated with open terrain and/or cliffs. Kills probably the greatest diversity of prey of any North American raptor.

Chances: Moderate

Key Sites: Decker, Dillon, Livingston

American Kestrel

 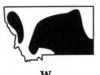

S + M   W

Habits: Open and partially open country with scattered trees, cultivated lands, even urban areas. Nests in cavities in trees, cliffs, and sometimes buildings. Feeds on mice, grasshoppers, small birds. Hunts by hovering.

Chances: Excellent

Key Sites: Ninepipe NWR, Missoula, Bozeman, Lee Metcalf NWR, Billings

Peregrine Falcon

S   W + M

Habits: Summer: open country with cliffs. Migration: open country with large concentrations of birds. Dives and captures prey in mid air.

Chances: Difficult

Key Sites: Summer: Red Rock Lakes NWR, Yellowstone NP. Migration: Benton Lake, Freezout Lake, Ninepipe NWR

Gyrfalcon

W

Habits: Prefers open country. Cyclic winter occurrence. Perches on ground, fence post, or telephone pole. Hunts ducks, pheasants, and grouse. Hunts prey on ground and in the air.

Chances: Difficult

Key Sites: Benton Lake, Ninepipe NWR, Fort Peck

General Distribution: S=Summer; W=Winter; Y=Year-round; M=During migration
NWR=National Wildlife Refuge; NP=National Park; NRA=National Recreation Area; NHS=National Historic Site
Mts.=Mountains; SP=State Park

Prairie Falcon

Y

Habits: Open dry country in mountains or plains. Captures both mammal and bird prey. Superb ground squirrel predator.

Chances: Moderate

Key Sites: Bighorn Canyon NRA, Ekalaka

Gray Partridge

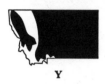

Y

Habits: Agricultural land, open grasslands. Usually found in flocks.

Chances: Moderate

Key Sites: Decker, Freezout Lake, Lewistown, Bison Range, Polson, Ninepipe NWR

Spruce Grouse

Y

Habits: Coniferous forests, primarily spruce, especially with shrub understory. Frequents trails and gravel roads. A small grouse.

Chances: Difficult

Key Sites: Glacier NP, Seeley Lake

Blue Grouse

Y

Habits: Coniferous forest, especially open ridges, edges, and disturbed areas. Male with unique courtship display in spring, inflates cervical air sac.

Chances: Moderate

Key Sites: Glacier NP, Yellowstone NP, Bison Range

White-tailed Ptarmigan

S + M

Habits: Summer: tree line to high alpine summits, primarily open country. Winter: exposed alpine ridges and conifers. Very small size with cryptic plumage.

Chances: Difficult

Key Sites: Glacier NP, Mission Mts.

General Distribution: S=Summer; W=Winter; Y=Year-round; M=During migration
NWR=National Wildlife Refuge; NP=National Park; NRA=National Recreation Area; NHS=National Historic Site
Mts.=Mountains; SP=State Park

Sage Grouse

Y

Habits: Plains and intermountain valleys with large stands of sagebrush. Males courtship display communally on leks in spring.

Chances: Moderate

Key Sites: Billings, Dillon, Winnett

Sharp-tailed Grouse

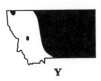

Y

Habits: Grasslands with creeks or coulees with shrubs for escape cover. Males courtship display communally on leks in spring.

Chances: Moderate

Key Sites: Benton Lake NWR, Bowdoin NWR, Billings

Wild Turkey

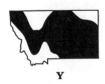

Y

Habits: Forest and open woodlands, either coniferous-deciduous or mixed, most often in mountains and foothills. Often found near ranches. Roosts in large numbers in communal roost at night.

Chances: Moderate

Key Sites: Ekalaka, Decker, Kalispell, Roundup

Sandhill Crane

S + M

Habits: Marshes, wet meadows, seeps. Unique wild guttural call. Congregate in large numbers at staging areas during migration.

Chances: Moderate

Key Sites: Centennial Valley, Dillon, Yellowstone NP

Piping Plover

S

Habits: Cobble or small pebble beaches most typically associated with alkali lakes and reservoirs, occasionally sand bars on rivers. Adults and young blend in perfectly with pebble substrate.

Chances: Difficult

Key Sites: Fort Peck, Medicine Lake NWR

General Distribution: S=Summer; W=Winter; Y=Year-round; M=During migration
NWR=National Wildlife Refuge; NP=National Park; NRA=National Recreation Area; NHS=National Historic Site
Mts.=Mountains; SP=State Park

Mountain Plover

S + M

Habits: Shortgrass prairie, heavily grazed grasslands, prairie dog towns on relatively flat terrain or benches. Often overlooked due to small size.

Chances: Difficult

Key Sites: C.M. Russell NWR (west side)

Black-necked Stilt

S + M

Habits: Shallow ponds; alkali lakes around marshes, lakes, ponds. Feeds on aquatic life by wading in shallow water.

Chances: Difficult

Key Sites: Benton Lake NWR, Freezout Lake

Upland Sandpiper

S

Habits: Open grassy uplands; pastures; hay fields. Characteristically found perching on fence posts.

Chances: Difficult

Key Sites: Benton Lake NWR, Billings, Decker

Long-billed Curlew

S

Habits: Grasslands on flat areas or benches. Especially shortgrass prairie or grazed pastures. Blends in remarkably well with grassland.

Chances: Moderate

Key Sites: Centennial Valley, Dillon, Ekalaka

Marbled Godwit

S + M

Habits: Summer: grasslands, wet meadows; Migration: mudflats, beaches. Conspicuous in beaches, well concealed in grasslands.

Chances: Moderate

Key Sites: Benton Lake NWR, Bowdoin NWR, Centennial Valley

General Distribution: S=Summer; W=Winter; Y=Year-round; M=During migration
NWR=National Wildlife Refuge; NP=National Park; NRA=National Recreation Area; NHS=National Historic Site
Mts.=Mountains; SP=State Park

Franklin's Gull

S + M

Habits: Marshes, prairie lakes; sometimes wet meadows, grasslands, plowed fields. Feeds in large flocks on insects and even earthworms.

Chances: Moderate

Key Sites: Benton Lake NWR, Bowdoin NWR, Freezout Lake, Red Rock Lakes NWR

Forster's Tern

S + M

Habits: Marshes, shorelines of prairie lakes. Searches shallow water, hovers, then plunges head first for small fish.

Chances: Moderate

Key Sites: Big Lake, Red Rock Lakes NWR, Canyon Ferry Reservoir

Least Tern

S

Habits: Sandbars/gravel bars on large rivers. Searches shallow water areas for tiny fish.

Chances: Difficult

Key Sites: Fort Peck, Fort Union NHS, Culbertson

Black Tern

S + M

Habits: Marshes, lakes, ponds especially bordered with bulrush or tall emergent vegetation. Feeds primarily on insects on water's surface or in the air.

Chances: Moderate

Key Sites: Blackfeet Indian Reservation, Bowdoin NWR, Red Rock Lakes NWR

Black-billed Cuckoo

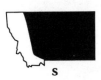

S

Habits: Riparian areas with thick shrub understory. Very secretive. Call a diagnostic "cu-cu-cu" or "cu-cu-cu-cu-cu."

Chances: Difficult

Key Sites: Billings, Fort Peck, Youngs Creek

General Distribution: S=Summer; W=Winter; Y=Year-round; M=During migration
NWR=National Wildlife Refuge; NP=National Park; NRA=National Recreation Area; NHS=National Historic Site
Mts.=Mountains; SP=State Park

Flammulated Owl

S

Habits: Open coniferous forests (dry sites with large ponderosa pine or Douglas-fir). There are more Flammulated Owls in Montana than the records show. Primarily insectivorous. May through June best. Call a whistled "hoot" every 2-3 seconds.

Chances: Difficult

Key Sites: Bitterroot Mts., Helena, Missoula

Eastern Screech-Owl

Y

Habits: Riparian, open deciduous woodlands. Secretive. Voice is a tremulous low whistle descending rapidly at end. Also horse-like whinny.

Chances: Difficult

Key Sites: Billings, Chester

Western Screech-Owl

Y

Habits: Riparian, open deciduous woodlands. Voice is a series of hollow, even whistles, accelerating at end reminiscent of bouncing bell.

Chances: Difficult

Key Sites: Missoula

Snowy Owl

W

Habits: Open country, grasslands, fields, meadows, pastures. Perches on fence posts, haystacks, even on ground. Cyclic winter occurrence.

Chances: Difficult

Key Sites: Bowdoin NWR, Freezout Lake, Ninepipe NWR

Northern Pygmy-Owl

Y

Habits: Coniferous or mixed forests especially near running water. In winter often seen at lower elevations and in towns and cities. Diurnal.

Chances: Difficult

Key Sites: Missoula, Yellowstone NP

General Distribution: S=Summer; W=Winter; Y=Year-round; M=During migration
NWR=National Wildlife Refuge; NP=National Park; NRA=National Recreation Area; NHS=National Historic Site
Mts.=Mountains; SP=State Park

Burrowing Owl

S + M

Habits: Open grasslands; shortgrass prairie; prairie dog towns. Also seeks out burrows made by badgers and ground squirrels. Lines nest and burrow entrance with manure. Diurnal.

Chances: Moderate

Key Sites: Big Lake, Chester, C.M. Russell NWR

Great Gray Owl

Y

Habits: Coniferous or mixed forests at mid to high elevations. Actively calling March—May. Crepuscular, nocturnal, and diurnal. May move to lower elevations in winter.

Chances: Difficult

Key Sites: Bozeman, Red Rock Lakes NWR, Yellowstone NP

Boreal Owl

Y

Habits: Coniferous or mixed forests at mid to high elevations often near meadows. Actively calling Jan.—April. Call resembles snipe winnowing, but sound doesn't fade. Nocturnal. Best found in winter.

Chances: Difficult

Key Sites: Cooke City, Lolo Pass, Lost Trail Pass, Yellowstone NP

Northern Saw-whet Owl

Y   W

Habits: Summer: In western Montana coniferous or coniferous-deciduous forests; in eastern Montana savannah ponderosa pine. Some move to lower elevations and out on plains in the winter. Calls Feb. through May. Call is a monotonous "too too" whistle note repeated hundreds of times.

Chances: Difficult

Key Sites: Yellowstone NP, Decker, Missoula, Glacier NP

Common Poorwill

S

Habits: Dry coniferous savannah forest, shrubby areas. Forages over grasslands for insects.

Chances: Moderate

Key Sites: C.M. Russell NWR, Billings

General Distribution: S=Summer; W=Winter; Y=Year-round; M=During migration
NWR=National Wildlife Refuge; NP=National Park; NRA=National Recreation Area; NHS=National Historic Site
Mts.=Mountains; SP=State Park

Black Swift

S

Habits: Cliffs near wet or moist areas; large waterfalls. Secures insects in the air. In good weather hunts high, inclement weather hunts low over water or near ground.

Chances: Difficult

Key Sites: Glacier NP

Chimney Swift

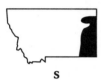

S

Habits: Towns, cities, riparian areas. Hunts insects high in air during good weather, closer to ground during inclement weather. Gregarious, hunts in flocks.

Chances: Moderate

Key Sites: Fort Peck, Glendive, Sidney

Vaux's Swift

S

Habits: Frequents areas near water; woodland openings, river valleys. Roosts in cavities of trees, sometimes in chimneys.

Chances: Moderate

Key Sites: Glacier NP, Kalispell, Missoula

White-throated Swift

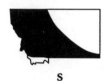

S

Habits: Hilly, mountainous country particularly cliffs and canyon walls. Forages during the day in a variety of habitats. Roosts/nests in colonies.

Chances: Moderate

Key Sites: Billings, Missouri Headwaters SP, Helena

Black-chinned Hummingbird

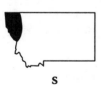

S

Habits: Riparian zone or deciduous thickets in or adjacent to coniferous forest.

Chances: Difficult

Key Sites: Bull River, Libby

General Distribution: S=Summer; W=Winter; Y=Year-round; M=During migration
NWR=National Wildlife Refuge; NP=National Park; NRA=National Recreation Area; NHS=National Historic Site
Mts.=Mountains; SP=State Park

Calliope Hummingbird

S

Habits: Open coniferous, deciduous, mixed forests in mountains or mountain valleys. Often perches mid-day on tops of dead aspen or willow to defend territory.

Chances: Moderate

Key Sites: Glacier NP, Missoula, Seeley Lake

Rufous Hummingbird

S

Habits: Variety of habitats from intermountain valleys to timberline. Seeks out fireweed flowers in disturbed areas.

Chances: Moderate

Key Sites: Beartooth Mts., Glacier NP, Yellowstone NP

Broad-tailed Hummingbird

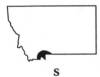

S

Habits: Douglas fir, lodgepole pine. Seeks out fireweed flowers in disturbed areas.

Chances: Moderate

Key Sites: Beartooth Mts., Red Rock Lakes NWR, Yellowstone NP

Lewis' Woodpecker

S

Habits: Prefers riparian (cottonwoods) and coniferous forests (particularly ponderosa pine). Seeks out standing decayed trees.

Chances: Moderate

Key Sites: Long Pines, Plains, Youngs Creek

Red-headed Woodpecker

S + M

Habits: Open woodlands, especially cottonwood but also conifers; open situations with scattered trees. Besides blood red head, bright conspicuous white wing patches highly visible in flight. Call is a loud "queer or quee-ah."

Chances: Moderate

Key Sites: C.M. Russell NWR, Fort Peck, Roundup, Lewistown

General Distribution: S=Summer; W=Winter; Y=Year-round; M=During migration
NWR=National Wildlife Refuge; NP=National Park; NRA=National Recreation Area; NHS=National Historic Site
Mts.=Mountains; SP=State Park

Red-naped Sapsucker

S

Habits: Deciduous or deciduous-coniferous woodlands, especially aspen, birch, alder. Drills a series of holes called a "well." Sugary sap attracts insects, buds, mammals, butterflies.

Chances: Excellent

Key Sites: Beartooth Mts., Blackfeet Indian Reservation, Libby

---

Williamson's Sapsucker

S

Habits: Open coniferous woodland (especially Douglas-fir), sometimes coniferous-deciduous mix. Drills linear "well" in lodgepole, larch to attract insects.

Chances: Moderate

Key Sites: Centennial Valley, Kalispell, Yellowstone NP

Three-toed Woodpecker

Y

Habits: Coniferous forests, especially disturbed sites (burned areas, avalanche chutes, wind sheers). Specialists at chipping bark, seeks trees with bark intact.

Chances: Moderate

Key Sites: Glacier NP, Missoula, Yellowstone NP

Black-backed Woodpecker

Y

Habits: Coniferous forests (most often spruce-fir) especially disturbed sites (burned areas, avalanche chutes, wind sheers). Specialists at chipping bark, seeks trees with bark intact.

Chances: Difficult

Key Sites: Glacier NP, Missoula, Yellowstone NP

Pileated Woodpecker

Y

Habits: Mature woodlands with standing dead trees, coniferous and/or deciduous trees. Drills characteristic large rectangular holes in trees.

Chances: Moderate

Key Sites: Glacier NP, Libby, Missoula

General Distribution: S=Summer; W=Winter; Y=Year-round; M=During migration
NWR=National Wildlife Refuge; NP=National Park; NRA=National Recreation Area; NHS=National Historic Site
Mts.=Mountains; SP=State Park

Olive-sided Flycatcher

S

Habits: Prefers dead conifers. Call from high in top of dead tree or live tree with dead top. Seeks out burned or insect-damaged areas.

Chances: Moderate

Key Sites: Bridger Mts., Glacier NP, Missoula, Yellowstone NP

Western Wood-Pewee

S

Habits: Open woodlands (deciduous coniferous, mixed) particularly aspen, cottonwood, pine. Perches in shade of canopy. Voice: "pe-ur."

Chances: Excellent

Key Sites: Billings, Missouri Headwaters SP, Livingston

Willow Flycatcher

S

Habits: Shrubs along streams (especially willow) and shrubs near open areas. Voice: "fitz-bew." Sings from elevated perch.

Chances: Moderate

Key Sites: Big Hole, Bull River, Dillon

Least Flycatcher

S

Habits: Open deciduous or mixed woodland, riparian. Sings and hunts from elevated perch. Voice: "che bec."

Chances: Excellent

Key Sites: Bull River, Missouri Headwaters SP, Great Falls

Hammond's Flycatcher

S

Habits: Mature coniferous or mixed forest in mountains. Prefers closed canopy, dark moist shaded areas. Voice hoarser more emphatic than Dusky Flycatcher: "seweep sup seep."

Chances: Moderate

Key Sites: Beartooth Mts., Bigfork, Missoula

General Distribution: S=Summer; W=Winter; Y=Year-round; M=During migration
NWR=National Wildlife Refuge; NP=National Park; NRA=National Recreation Area; NHS=National Historic Site
Mts.=Mountains; SP=State Park

Dusky Flycatcher

S

Habits: Open deciduous or open mixed woodland. Best separated from Hammond's Flycatcher by habitat. Voice: "selip churp teep."

Chances: Moderate

Key Sites: Glacier NP, Red Rock Lakes NWR, Yellowstone NP

Say's Phoebe

S + M

Habits: Open dry areas with buildings, fences, shrubs for perches. Flicks tail up and down on perch before sallying out and snapping up insects.

Chances: Moderate

Key Sites: Decker, Great Falls, Miles City

Cassin's Kingbird

S

Habits: Dry savannah woodland, ponderosa pine-juniper, open riparian. Hunts from high perch overlooking open spaces.

Chances: Difficult

Key Sites: Ashland, Birney

Gray Jay

Y

Habits: Coniferous and coniferous-deciduous, forests, forest openings. Can mimic sounds of other birds, especially hawks. Caches food in the form of a bolus, most often in a tree.

Chances: Excellent

Key Sites: Bridger Mts., Snowy Mts., Yellowstone NP, Beartooth Mts.

Steller's Jay

Y

Habits: Coniferous forest, coniferous-deciduous forests (especially dark canopy such as spruce-fir). Expert mimic, often imitates hawks, sometimes even loons.

Chances: Moderate

Key Sites: Glacier NP, Lolo Pass, Seeley Lake

General Distribution: S=Summer; W=Winter; Y=Year-round; M=During migration
NWR=National Wildlife Refuge; NP=National Park; NRA=National Recreation Area; NHS=National Historic Site
Mts.=Mountains; SP=State Park

Pinyon Jay

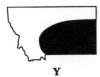

Y

Habits: Dry sites with ponderosa pine-juniper. In winter cottonwood-juniper. Mostly gregarious, often seen in large flocks. Very nomadic.

Chances: Moderate

Key Sites: Gardiner, Livingston, Whitehall

Clark's Nutcracker

Y

Habits: Open coniferous forests in mountains or foothills, forest edges. Principal distributor of whitebark pine.

Chances: Excellent

Key Sites: Glacier NP, Pine Butte Swamp, Yellowstone NP, Beartooth Mts.

Black-billed Magpie

Y

Habits: Open country with thickets or scattered trees, especially near active or abandoned farms/ranches. Builds large round dome-shaped stick nest in shrub or tree.

Chances: Excellent

Key Sites: Choteau, Dillon, Miles City

Common Raven

Y

Habits: Variety of habitats from foothills to alpine summits. Most prevalent in the mountains. Expert fliers often performing barrel-rolls, dives, tumbles, besides gliding and soaring.

Chances: Excellent

Key Sites: Beartooth Mts., Gardiner, West Yellowstone

Mountain Chickadee

Y

Habits: Coniferous forests up to timberline, occasionally deciduous woodlands and thickets. Forages often in tree crowns.

Chances: Excellent

Key Sites: Lewis & Clark Caverns SP, Seeley Lake, Red Lodge

General Distribution: S=Summer; W=Winter; Y=Year-round; M=During migration
NWR=National Wildlife Refuge; NP=National Park; NRA=National Recreation Area; NHS=National Historic Site
Mts.=Mountains; SP=State Park

Boreal Chickadee

Y

Habits: Coniferous humid forests at high elevations, especially spruce -fir. Voice: slow, high pitched "sickaday-day."

Chances: Difficult

Key Sites: Glacier NP, Whitefish Range

Chestnut-backed Chickadee

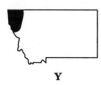

Y

Habits: Coniferous and coniferous-deciduous humid forests. Voice: rapid shrill "tsick-a-dee-dee."

Chances: Difficult

Key Sites: Fortine, Glacier NP

Pygmy Nuthatch

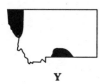

Y

Habits: Ponderosa pine, and ponderosa savannah. Characteristic soft staccato pipping call.

Chances: Difficult

Key Sites: Billings, Missoula, Kalispell

Winter Wren

Y + M

Habits: Moist coniferous forests with dense understory, often near water. Migration: also deciduous thicket. Forages in understory. Sings from low to high perches.

Chances: Moderate

Key Sites: Glacier NP, Fortine, Libby

Marsh Wren

S + M

Habits: Bulrush, cattail marshes with shallow or slow-flowing water. Secretive yet noisy. Voice: energetic, bubbly, staccato song.

Chances: Excellent

Key Sites: Benton Lake, Bowdoin NWR, Ninepipe NWR

General Distribution: S=Summer; W=Winter; Y=Year-round; M=During migration
NWR=National Wildlife Refuge; NP=National Park; NRA=National Recreation Area; NHS=National Historic Site
Mts.=Mountains; SP=State Park

American Dipper

Y

Habits: Rushing mountain stream from foothills to timberline. In winter lower elevations, sometimes slow-flowing water. Characteristic raising and lowering of body by lowering legs when standing on rock.

Chances: Excellent

Key Sites: Beartooth Mts., Glacier NP, Missoula

Eastern Bluebird

S

Habits: Deciduous riparian, open areas near mature trees, farm houses, nest boxes.

Chances: Difficult

Key Sites: Fort Peck, Fort Union NHS, Sidney

Western Bluebird

S + M

Habits: Open coniferous forests (ponderosa pine savannah), sometimes deciduous-coniferous forests adjacent to open areas. Forages in open country.

Chances: Moderate

Key Sites: Dixon, Paradise, Plains

Mountain Bluebird

S + M

Habits: Open country adjacent to coniferous, deciduous, coniferous-deciduous forests from lowlands to timberline. During migration found in open areas from lowlands to alpine. Hunts from a perch or by hovering.

Chances: Excellent

Key Sites: Long Pines, Pine Butte Swamp, Red Rock Lakes NWR

Townsend's Solitaire

S   W

Habits: Open coniferous forests, especially Douglas-fir. Frequents junipers in winter feeding on juniper berries. Voice: musical song; monotones single note whistle call.

Chances: Moderate

Key Sites: Bozeman, Livingston, Missoula

General Distribution: S=Summer; W=Winter; Y=Year-round; M=During migration
NWR=National Wildlife Refuge; NP=National Park; NRA=National Recreation Area; NHS=National Historic Site
Mts.=Mountains; SP=State Park

Swainson's Thrush

S + M

Habits: Deciduous shrubs, also coniferous woods, and willow and alder thickets. Voice: musical song, each phrase rising slightly higher.

Chances: Moderate

Key Sites: Bigfork, Bull River, Lewistown

Hermit Thrush

S + M

Habits: Coniferous forests, coniferous-deciduous forests. Inhabits forest floor, occasionally in understory. Wonderful ethereal, bell-like song with pauses between phrases.

Chances: Moderate

Key Sites: Glacier NP, Missoula, Yellowstone NP

Varied Thrush

S + M   W

Habits: Dark humid coniferous forests. Forages in lower understory, especially forest floor. Song is an eerie quavering off-tone whistle followed by a pause.

Chances: Moderate

Key Sites:

Sage Thrasher

S

Habits: Dry sagebrush plains, saltbrush, thickets on arid hillsides. Male sings from a high perch. Pleasant, energetic song reminiscent of Catbird or Mockingbird but without pauses.

Chances: Moderate

Key Sites: Bannack, Centennial Valley, Shields Valley

American Pipit

S + M

Habits: Summer: primarily alpine, sometimes timberline. Migration: open areas (beaches, fields, mudflats). Feeds on ground; frequently wagging tail, walks instead of hopping.

Chances: Moderate

Key Sites: Beartooth Mts., Glacier NP, Yellowstone NP

General Distribution: S=Summer; W=Winter; Y=Year-round; M=During migration
NWR=National Wildlife Refuge; NP=National Park; NRA=National Recreation Area; NHS=National Historic Site
Mts.=Mountains; SP=State Park

Sprague's Pipit

S + M

Habits: Grasslands, native shortgrass prairie. Difficult to see. Song diagnostic as bird circles in air. Song a series of descending "sewee, sewee, sewee, sewee, sewee," etc.)

Chances: Moderate

Key Sites: Blackfeet Indian Reservation, Harlowton, Pine Butte Swamp

---

Bohemian Waxwing

S   W

Habits: Summer: humid coniferous or coniferous-deciduous forests. Winter: towns and cities with fruit and berry trees and shrubs; junipers and juniper berries. Seen in large flocks.

Chances: Summer: Difficult. Winter: Excellent

Key Sites: Summer: Whitefish Range. Winter: Billings, Bozeman, Missoula, Yellowstone NP

Cedar Waxwing

Y

Habits: Open deciduous or deciduous-coniferous forests, riparian. Most often in small flocks. In summer often catches insects like a flycatcher. Often found with Bohemian Waxwings in winter.

Chances: Moderate

Key Sites: Fortine, Libby, Red Rock Lakes NWR

Northern Shrike

W

Habits: Open areas close to thickets, shelterbelts, shade trees; abandoned homesteads, corrals. Hunts from an elevated perch.

Chances: Moderate

Key Sites: Benton Lake NWR, Great Falls, Ninepipe NWR

Loggerhead Shrike

S + M

Habits: Open areas close to thickets, shelterbelts, shade trees; near abandoned homesteads and corrals. Hunts from an elevated perch. Impales prey on fence wires, thorns, and thistles.

Chances: Moderate

Key Sites: Billings, Great Falls, Miles City

General Distribution: S=Summer; W=Winter; Y=Year-round; M=During migration
NWR=National Wildlife Refuge; NP=National Park; NRA=National Recreation Area; NHS=National Historic Site
Mts.=Mountains; SP=State Park

Solitary Vireo

S + M

Habits: Open coniferous or coniferous-deciduous woodlands. Song is a series of sweet whistled phrases, interrupted by deliberate pauses.

Chances: Moderate

Key Sites: Bigfork, Libby, Missoula

Warbling Vireo

S

Habits: Open mature-deciduous, deciduous-coniferous woodlands, riparian. Song a musical warble, similar yet less energetic and quieter than a Purple Finch.

Chances: Excellent

Key Sites: Bozeman, Dillon, Lewistown, Missoula

Red-eyed Vireo

S + M

Habits: Open mature deciduous forest, riparian; shade trees in parks. Song has rising inflection, and sounds as if the bird were asking questions and answering them.

Chances: Moderate

Key Sites: Bigfork, Lewistown, Libby

Orange-crowned Warbler

S + M

Habits: Deciduous, deciduous-coniferous woodlands with abundant deciduous shrub understory. Blends in perfectly with leaf canopy. Song is a fading colorless trill.

Chances: Moderate

Key Sites: Bigfork, Blackfeet Indian Reservation, Lewis & Clark Caverns SP

Nashville Warbler

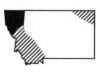

S + M

Habits: Open deciduous or coniferous woodlands with brushy undergrowth. Song is in two parts: "seebit, seebit, seebit, seebit, tititititi."

Chances: Moderate

Key Sites: Bull River, Libby, Missoula

General Distribution: S=Summer; W=Winter; Y=Year-round; M=During migration
NWR=National Wildlife Refuge; NP=National Park; NRA=National Recreation Area; NHS=National Historic Site
Mts.=Mountains; SP=State Park

Townsend's Warbler

S + M

Habits: Coniferous forests, particularly spruce-fir. sings from treetops, yet difficult to see. Song is either "dzeer, dzeer, dzeer, tseetsee" or "weazy, weazy, seesee."

Chances: Moderate

Key Sites: Bull River, Glacier NP, Whitefish Range

Black-and-white Warbler

S

Habits: Deciduous woodlands, riparian. Forages in lower to middle branches. Song is rolling "weetsy, weetsy, weetsy, weetsy, weetsy, weetsys."

Chances: Difficult

Key Sites: Culbertson, Fort Peck

Ovenbird

S

Habits: Deciduous closed-canopy woodlands (sometimes deciduous-coniferous woodlands). Found on the ground especially in the leaf litter. Song is a classical "teacher, teacher, teacher, teacher."

Chances: Moderate

Key Sites: Beartooth Mts., Blackfeet Indian Reservation, Snowy Mts.

Northern Waterthrush

S + M

Habits: Deciduous, shrubby thickets (particularly willow or alder) along streams, ponds, or near standing water. Conifers (dead & alive) are sometimes used. Very difficult to observe. Song is easily identified: a loud staccato ending in "chew, chew, chew."

Chances: Moderate

Key Sites: Big Hole Battlefield NHS, Blackfeet Indian Reservation, Glacier NP

Western Tanager

S

Habits: Open coniferous and mixed woodland (especially Douglas fir). Feeds and nests high in tree. Song resembles American Robin but hoarser and lower. Produces common "purty" call-note.

Chances: Excellent

Key Sites: Bigfork, Snowy Mts., Beartooth Mts.

General Distribution: S=Summer; W=Winter; Y=Year-round; M=During migration
NWR=National Wildlife Refuge; NP=National Park; NRA=National Recreation Area; NHS=National Historic Site
Mts.=Mountains; SP=State Park

Lazuli Bunting

S

Habits: Open brushy country. Sings from an elevated perch. Song is loud at different pitches, "swip, swip, swip, zu, zu, ee, see, see, sip, see, see."

Chances: Moderate

Key Sites: Big Timber, Miles City, Missoula

Green-tailed Towhee

S

Habits: Open foothills with either sagebrush, thickets or both. Blends in well with environments. Sings from elevated perch. Song is identified by "weet-churr-cheeee-churr," "mew" call note.

Chances: Moderate

Key Sites: Bannack, Lewis & Clark Caverns SP, Red Lodge

Lark Bunting

S + M

Habits: Plains, prairies (particularly grass-lands, sagebrush-grasslands). Male very conspicuous especially along fences. Song is a series of "chugs."

Chances: Moderate

Key Sites: Decker, Harlowton, Lewistown, Winnett

Savannah Sparrow

S

Habits: Moist grasslands, wet meadows, irrigated hay fields. Concealed most of time, will sing from elevated perch. Song is a lisping "tsip, tsip, tsip, tisp, tse-wheeeeee-you."

Chances: Moderate

Key Sites: Big Hole, Bozeman, Freezout Lake

Baird's Sparrow

S

Habits: Dry grasslands (tall grasses); weedy fields. Difficult to see. Sings from top of grasses, weeds, or small shrubs. Song is two or three "zips."

Chances: Difficult

Key Sites: Bowdoin NWR, Dupuyer, Medicine Lake NWR

General Distribution: S=Summer; W=Winter; Y=Year-round; M=During migration
NWR=National Wildlife Refuge; NP=National Park; NRA=National Recreation Area; NHS=National Historic Site
Mts.=Mountains; SP=State Park

Grasshopper Sparrow

S + M

Habits: Old fields, prairie, grasslands with clumps of grass/weeds, weedy fields. Dry sites. Sings early morning to late evening. Song an insect-like buzz.

Chances: Moderate

Key Sites: National Bison Range, Ekalaka, Missoula

Le Conte's Sparrow

S

Habits: Moist tall grass and sedge meadows (damp thickly matted), shrubs on edge of meadow. Very difficult to see. Song is a very short insect-like buzz "tse-bzzzz."

Chances: Difficult

Key Sites: Glacier NP

Sharp-tailed Sparrow

S

Habits: Wet areas with tall emergent vegetation, marshes. Very difficult to see. Very elusive. Song is a "te-sheeeeee," the latter part high pitched, bubbly, and ending abruptly.

Chances: Difficult

Key Sites: Medicine Lake NWR

Lincoln's Sparrow

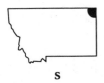

S + M

Habits: Wet areas; moist meadows with alder, willow, or conifers; wet brush areas.

Chances: Moderate

Key Sites: Livingston, Swan Lake, Red Rock Lakes NWR

McCown's Longspur

S

Habits: Shortgrass prairie (sparse vegetation), sometimes heavily grazed or barren land. Song is a pleasing assemblage of warbles/twitters given during display flight as bird descends with wings and tail spread.

Chances: Moderate

Key Sites: Blackfeet Indian Reservation, Chester, Roundup

General Distribution: S=Summer; W=Winter; Y=Year-round; M=During migration
NWR=National Wildlife Refuge; NP=National Park; NRA=National Recreation Area; NHS=National Historic Site
Mts.=Mountains; SP=State Park

Lapland Longspur

W

Habits: Open areas (weedy fields, grain stubble, plowed fields). Often found with Horned Larks and/or Snow Buntings.

Chances: Moderate

Key Sites: Benton Lake NWR, Chester, Choteau

Chestnut-collared Longspur

S

Habits: Shortgrass prairie. Short song given during display flight as bird descends to ground often short flight. Musical song similar to Western Meadowlark's. Call-note is a "til-lip."

Chances: Moderate

Key Sites: Chester, Harlowton, Roundup

Snow Bunting

W

Habits: Open areas (weedy fields, grain stubble, roadsides, grassy fields). Large conspicuous flocks often accompanied by Horned Larks and /or Lapland Longspurs.

Chances: Moderate

Key Sites: Benton Lake NWR, Bowdoin NWR, Fort Peck

Bobolink

Habits: Irrigated fields (tall grass, clover, alfalfa) open areas. Males conspicuous during breeding. Song is a unique assemblage of banjo-like notes made in flight or while perched.

Chances: Moderate

Key Sites: Billings, Winnett

Western Meadowlark

S + M   W

Habits: Grasslands, sagebrush-grasslands. Savannah; cultivated fields & pastures. In flight conspicuous white patch on either side of tail. Wonderful musical flute-like song. The official state bird of Montana and heralder of spring.

Chances: Excellent

Key Sites: Billings, Freezout Lake, Great Falls, Fort Peck

General Distribution: S=Summer; W=Winter; Y=Year-round; M=During migration
NWR=National Wildlife Refuge; NP=National Park; NRA=National Recreation Area; NHS=National Historic Site
Mts.=Mountains; SP=State Park

Orchard Oriole

S

Habits: Riparian, shade trees somewhat scattered as found in parks, rest areas, orchards. Sings from elevated perch. Song is a fast moving outburst of notes, including piping whistles and guttural sounds.

Chances: Difficult

Key Sites: Fort Peck, Glendive, Sidney

Rosy Finch

S   W

Habits: Open areas; Summer: alpine areas above timberline. Winter: low elevations (foothills, cities, towns, fields). In winter found in large flocks. Characteristic undulating flight.

Chances: Moderate

Key Sites: Winter: Billings, Bozeman, Missoula. Summer: Beartooth Mts., Glacier NP, Yellowstone NP

Pine Grosbeak

Y

Habits: Coniferous forests in mountains often cool and shady. Somewhat nomadic. Travels in small flocks. Call is a series of 2-3 musical warbles.

Chances: Moderate

Key Sites: Beartooth Mts., Glacier NP, Seeley Lake

Cassin's Finch

S

Habits: Open coniferous forests in mountains and foothills. Song similar to a Purple Finch. Unique call "kee-up" or "chidiup."

Chances: Moderate

Key Sites: Beartooth Mts., Missoula, Seeley Lake

Red Crossbill

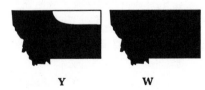

Y   W

Habits: Coniferous forests. Very nomadic. Found in flocks. Song short with whistles and warbles. Call "jip-jip" often made in flight.

Chances: Moderate

Key Sites: Bigfork, Decker, Ekalaka, Snowy Mts.

General Distribution: S=Summer; W=Winter; Y=Year-round; M=During migration
NWR=National Wildlife Refuge; NP=National Park; NRA=National Recreation Area; NHS=National Historic Site
Mts.=Mountains; SP=State Park

White-winged Crossbill

Y   W + M

Habits: Coniferous forests (especially spruce-fir, humid and cool sites in summer). Song is very musical with trills and warbles. Found usually in flocks. Call is a "cheet, cheet" made in flight.

Chances: Difficult

Key Sites: Summer: Glacier NP, Whitefish Range

Common Redpoll

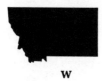

W

Habits: Open deciduous woodlands, weedy fields, shelterbelts, thickets. Found in flocks. Flight call is a "zit-zit."

Chances: Moderate-Difficult

Key Sites: Fort Peck, Kalispell, Malta

General Distribution: S=Summer; W=Winter; Y=Year-round; M=During migration
NWR=National Wildlife Refuge; NP=National Park; NRA=National Recreation Area; NHS=National Historic Site
Mts.=Mountains; SP=State Park

ABOUT THE AUTHOR AND ILLUSTRATOR

Terry McEneaney is very knowledgeable about Montana and its varied birdlife. He received his degree in wildlife biology from the University of Montana, and has spent the past twenty-five years birding all geographical regions of the state. His field work with state and federal wildlife agencies has given him the opportunity to live in more than a dozen towns in Montana. As a skilled mountaineer, he has explored some of the most impressive peaks and remote areas of the Big Sky state. He is author of two previous books, *Birds of Yellowstone*, and *The Uncommon Loon*, and has written numerous scientific and popular articles on birds. Terry takes great pride in having been a field biologist for his entire career. He is currently the staff ornithologist for Yellowstone National Park, and former biologist at Red Rock Lakes National Wildlife Refuge.

Karen L. McEneaney studied art in Massachusetts. Upon receiving a degree in art education, she taught school in Australia and Massachusetts before moving to Montana in 1984. She is currently an art specialist at a private alternative school in Bozeman, Montana. Her specialty is landscape watercolors and various mediums of wildlife art. Karen's works have been exhibited in Montana, Massachusetts, and Alaska, and she has illustrated two other books, *Birds of Yellowstone* and *The Uncommon Loon*. She resides with her husband, Terry, in Yellowstone National Park.

APPENDIX I
REPORTING RARE BIRD INFORMATION

Ornithology is one of the few sciences in which amateurs can and do make significant contributions to scientific knowledge. If bird observations are to stand the test of time, they must be thoroughly documented. Birders are encouraged to submit written detailed information (see sample bird observation form) on bird distribution or interesting, rare, accidental, or unusual birds by contacting:

Montana Natural Heritage Program
1515 E. 6th Ave. Helena, Montana 59620

For casual reporting or finding out immediately about rare birds over the telephone, please dial:

Montana Rare Bird Alert Telephone Number (406) 721-2935

Rare Bird Report Form
(for species annotated TES, SI, n=)

Species: _____ Observer's Name: _____

Date Observed: _____ Address: _____

Reporter's Name: _____ _____

Date Written: _____ Telephone No: _____

Other Observers: _____

QLL: _____ Nearest Town/Landmark: _____

Specific Location: _____

Township: _____ Range: _____ Section: _____

Describe the Habitat: _____

Plumage (Circle):   Sex   M   Describe Weather: _____

Adult   Immature   F   _____

Subadult   Juvenal   Unk   _____

Quality and direction of light: _____

Distance from Bird: _____ Duration of Observation: _____

Previous Experience with Species? _____

Discuss How Similar Appearing Species were Eliminated: _____

_____

_____

Report was Written: During or right after observation <u>or</u>

From memory, ____ hrs/ ____ days later.

Describe the bird you observed. Record only filed marks and behaviors you actually saw. State size (compared to similar size common bird). Record **relevant** information such as color, body shape, bill, legs, voice, behavior, no. of individuals, sex. Use back of form if more space is needed. **Print or type clearly.**

Send to:
MBD Committee, Montana Natural Heritage Program,
1515 E. 6th Ave., Helena, MT 59620.

APPENDIX II
MONTANA BIRDING ORGANIZATIONS

The following is a list of Audubon organizations in Montana:

State Office

Montana Audubon Council P.O. Box 595 Helena, MT 59624
Telephone (406) 443-3949

Area Organizations

Bitterroot Audubon Society P.O. Box 326 Hamilton, MT 59840

Flathead Audubon Society P.O. Box 715 Bigfork, MT 59911

Five Valleys Audubon Society P.O. Box 8425 Missoula, MT 59807

Last Chance Audubon Society P.O. Box 924 Helena, MT 59624

Pintlar Audubon Society 701 Montana Ave. #4 Deer Lodge, MT 59722

Rosebud Audubon Society P.O. Box 361 Miles City, MT 59301

Sacajawea Audubon Society P.O. Box 1711 Bozeman, MT 59715

Upper Missouri Breaks Audubon Society P.O. Box 2362 Great Falls,
MT 59403

Yellowstone Valley Audubon Society P.O. Box 1075 Billings, MT 59102

Montana Rare Bird Alert Telephone Number

Statewide (406) 721-2935

APPENDIX III
AGENCY INDEX

MONTANA DEPARTMENT OF FISH, WILDLIFE, AND PARKS
Montana Department of Fish, Wildlife, and Parks
1420 East 6th Avenue
Helena, MT 59620
(406) 444-2535
MDFWP Region 1
490 North Meridian
Kalispell, MT 59901
(406) 752-5501
MDFWP Region 2
3201 Spurgin Road
Missoula, MT 59801
(406) 542-5500
MDFWP Region 3
1400 South 19th Street
Bozeman, MT 59715
(406) 994-4024
MDFWP Region 4
4600 Giant Springs Road
Great Falls, MT 59406
(406) 454-3441
MDFWP Region 5
2300 Lake Elmo Road
Billings, MT 59105
(406) 252-4654
MDFWP Region 6
Rural Route 1 -4210
Glasgow, MT 59230
(406) 228-4365
MDFWP Region 7
Rural Route 1, Box 2004
Miles City, MT 59301
(406) 232-4365
MDFWP Region 8
1400 8th Avenue Helena, MT
59620 (406) 444-2602

MONTANA DEPARTMENT OF STATE LANDS
Department of State Lands
1625 11th Avenue
Helena, MT 59620
(406) 444-2074

UNIVERSITIES
MT State University Department of Biology
Bozeman, MT 59717
(406) 994-4549
University of MT Division of Biological Sciences
Missoula, MT 59812
(406) 243-5521

U.S FOREST SERVICE
U.S. Government Department of Agriculture U.S. Forest Service
Northern Region (Statewide Information) 200 Broadway
P.O. Box 7669 Missoula, MT
59907 (406) 329-3511

WESTERN MONTANA
BEAVERHEAD NATIONAL FOREST
Beaverhead National Forest
610 N. Montana St.
Dillon, MT 59725
(406) 683-3900
Dillon Ranger District
610 N. Montana St.
Dillon, MT 59725
(406) 683-3900
Wise River Ranger District
Box 100
Wise River, MT 59762
(406) 832-3178

Wisdom Ranger District
Box 238
Wisdom, MT 59761
(406) 689-3243
Sheridan Ranger District
Box 428
Sheridan, MT 59749
(406) 842-5432
Madison Ranger District
5 Forest Service Road
Ennis, MT 59729
(406) 682-4253

BITTERROOT NATIONAL FOREST
Bitterroot National Forest
316 North 3rd St.
Hamilton, MT 59840
(406) 363-3131
Stevensville Ranger District
88 Main St.
Stevensville, MT 59870
(406) 777-5461
Darby Ranger District
712 Highway 93 South P.O. Box 388
Darby, MT 59829
(406) 821-3913
West Fork Ranger District
6735 West Fork Road
Darby, MT 59829
(406) 821-3269
Sula Ranger District
7338 Highway 93 South
Sula, MT 59871
(406) 821-3678

DEERLODGE NATIONAL FOREST
Deerlodge National Forest
Federal Building
P.O. Box 400
Butte, MT 59703
(406) 496-3400

Deer Lodge Ranger District
91 Frontage Road
Deer Lodge, MT 59722
(406) 846-1770
Jefferson Ranger District
405 E. Legion
P.O. Box F Whitehall, MT 59729
(406) 287-3223
Philipsburg Ranger District
P.O. Box H
Philipsburg, MT 59858
(406) 859-3211
Butte Ranger District
1820 Meadowlark
Butte, MT 59701
(406) 494-2147

FLATHEAD NATIONAL FOREST
Flathead National Forest
1935 Third Avenue East
Kalispell, MT 59901
(406) 755-5401
Swan Lake Ranger District
P.O. Box 370
Bigfork, MT 59911
(406) 837-5081
Spotted Bear Ranger District
P.O. Box 310
Hungry Horse, MT 59919
(406) 752-7345(su)
(406) 387-5243(w)
Hungry Horse Ranger District
P.O. Box 340
Hungry Horse, MT 59919
(406) 752-5243
Glacier View Ranger District
P.O. Box W
Columbia Falls, MT 59912
(406) 892-4372
Tally Lake Ranger District
1335 Highway 93 South
Whitefish, MT 59937
(406) 862-2508

KOOTENAI NATIONAL FOREST

Kootenai National Forest
506 U.S. Highway 2 West
Libby, MT 59923
(406) 293-6211

Rexford Ranger District
1299 Highway 93 North
Eureka, MT 59917
(406) 296-2536

Fortine Ranger District
P.O. Box 116
Fortine, MT 59918
(406) 882-4451

Three Rivers Ranger District
1437 North Highway 2
Troy, MT 59935
(406) 295-4693

Libby Ranger District
1263 Highway 37
Libby, MT 59923
(406) 293-7741

Cabinet Ranger District
2693 Highway 200
Trout Creek, MT 59874
(406) 827-3534

Fisher River Ranger District
12557 Highway 37
Libby, MT 59923
(406) 293-7773

LOLO NATIONAL FOREST

Lolo National Forest
Building 24 Fort Missoula
Missoula, MT 59801
(406) 329-3750

Missoula Ranger District
Building 24-A Fort Missoula
Missoula, MT 59801
(406) 329-3814

Ninemile Ranger District
Box 616 Ninemile Road
Huson, MT 59846
(406) 626-5201

Plains/Thompson Falls Rgr. Dist.
P.O. Box 429 408 Clayton
Plains, MT 59859
(406) 826-3821(P)
(406) 827-3589(TF)

Seeley Lake Ranger District
P.O. Box 717,
18 Mile Marker Highway 83
North Seeley Lake, MT 59868
(406) 677-2233

Superior Ranger District
Superior, MT 59872 (406) 822-4233

CENTRAL MONTANA

GALLATIN NATIONAL FOREST

Gallatin National Forest
P.O. Box 130 Federal Building
Bozeman, MT 59771
(406) 587-6701

Big Timber Ranger District
P.O. Box A
Big Timber, MT 59011
(406) 932-5155

Livingston Ranger District
Route 62, Box 3197
Livingston, MT 59047
(406) 222-1892

Gardiner Ranger District
P.O. Box 5
Gardiner, MT 59030
(406) 848-7375

Bozeman Ranger District
601 Nikles
Bozeman, MT 59715
(406) 587-6920

Hebgen Lake Ranger District
P.O. Box 520
West Yellowstone, MT
59758 (406) 626-7369

HELENA NATIONAL FOREST

Helena National Forest
301 South Park Drawer 10014
Helena, MT 59626
(406) 449-5201
Townsend Ranger District
415 S. Front Box 29
Townsend, MT 59644
(406) 266-3425
Helena Ranger District
2001 Poplar Street
Helena, MT 59601
(406) 449-5490
Lincoln Ranger District
Box 219
Lincoln, MT 59639
(406) 362-4265

LEWIS AND CLARK NATIONAL FOREST

Lewis and Clark National Forest
1101 15th Street North Box 871
Great Falls, MT 59403
(406) 791-7700
Rocky Mountain Ranger District
1102 Main Avenue NW Box 340
Choteau, MT 59422 (406) 466-5341
Judith Ranger District
109 Central Avenue Box 484
Stanford, MT 59479
(406) 566-2292
Musselshell Ranger District
809 2 NW Box F
Harlowton, MT 59036
(406) 632-4391
Kings Hill Ranger District
204 West Folsom Box A
White Sulphur Springs, MT 59645
(406) 547-3361

EASTERN MONTANA

CUSTER NATIONAL FOREST

Custer National Forest
2602 First Avenue North P.O.
Box 2556
Billings, MT 59103
(406) 657-6361
Beartooth Ranger District
Rte. 2 Box 3420
Red Lodge, MT 59068
(406) 446-2102
Ashland Ranger District
Box 168
Ashland, MT 59003
(406) 784-2344
U.S. Government - Department of Interior Bureau of Land Management
Bureau of Land Management
Montana State Office
222 North 32nd Street P.O. Box 36800
Billings, MT 59107
(406) 255-2913

WESTERN MONTANA

BUREAU OF LAND MANAGEMENT

Butte District Office
106 North Parkmont P.O. Box 3388
Butte, MT 59702
(406) 494-5059
Dillon Resource Area
Ibey Building 1005 Selway Drive
Dillon, MT 59725
(406) 683-2337
Garnet Resource Area
3255 Fort Missoula Road
Missoula, MT 59801
(406) 239-3914
Headwaters Resource Area
106 Parkmont P.O. Box 3388
Butte, MT 59702
(406) 494-5059

CENTRAL MONTANA
BUREAU OF LAND MANAGEMENT
Lewistown District Office
Airport Road
Lewistown, MT 59457
(406) 538-7461
Valley Resource Area
Route 1-4775
Glasgow, MT 59230
(406) 228-4316
Havre Resource Area
West Second Street Drawer 911
Havre, MT 59501
(406) 265-9051
Phillips Resource Area
501 South Second St. East P.O. Box B
Malta, MT 59538
(406) 654-1240
Judith Resource Area
Airport Road
Lewistown, MT 59457
(406) 538-7461
Great Falls Resource Area
812 14th St. N. P.O. Box 2865
Great Falls, MT 59403
(406) 727-0503

EASTERN MONTANA
BUREAU OF LAND MANAGEMENT
Miles City District Office
Garryowen Road, P.O. Box 940
Miles City, MT 59301
(406) 232-4331
Powder River Resource Area
Miles City Plaza
Miles City, MT 59301
(406) 232-7000
Big Dry Resource Area
Miles City Plaza
Miles City, MT 59301
(406) 232-7000

Billings Resource Area
810 East Main Street
Billings, MT 59105
(406) 657-6262

U.S. GOVERNMENT DEPARTMENT OF INTERIOR
U.S. Fish and Wildlife Refuges
1. Benton Lake NWR P.O. Box 450 Black Eagle, MT 59414 (406) 727-7400
2. Bowdoin NWR P.O. Box J Malta, MT 59538 (406) 654-8706
3. Charles M. Russell NWR P.O. Box 110 Lewistown, MT 59457 (406) 538-8706
4. Lee Metcalf NWR P.O. Box 257 Stevensville, MT 59870 (406) 777-5552
5. Medicine Lake NWR HC 51, Box 2 Medicine Lake, MT 59247
6. Red Rock Lakes NWR Box 15, Monida Star Route Lima, MT 59739 (406) 276-3536
7. National Bison Range 132 Bison Range Road Moiese, MT 59824 (406) 644-2211

NATIONAL PARK SERVICE
Glacier National Park
West Glacier, MT 59936
(406) 888-5441
Yellowstone National Park
P.O. Box 168
Yellowstone National Park WY 82190
(307) 344-7381

BUREAU OF INDIAN AFFAIRS
Billings Area Office
316 North 26th Street
Billings, MT 59107
(406) 657-6145

APPENDIX IV
AMERICAN BIRDING ASSOCIATION
CODE OF ETHICS

We, the Membership of the American Birding Association, believe that all birders have an obligation at all times to protect wildlife, the natural environment, and the rights of others. We therefore pledge ourselves to provide leadership in meeting this obligation by adhering to the following general guidelines of good birding behavior.

I. Birders must always act in ways that do not endanger the welfare of birds or other wildlife.

In keeping with this principle, we will

- Observe and photograph birds without knowingly disturbing them in any significant way.
- Avoid chasing or repeatedly flushing birds.
- Only sparingly use recordings and similar methods of attracting birds and not use these methods in heavily birded areas.
- Keep an appropriate distance from nests and nesting colonies so as not to disturb them or expose them to danger.
- Refrain from handling birds or eggs unless engaged in recognized research activities.

II. Birders must always act in ways that do not harm the natural environment.

In keeping with this principle, we will

- Stay on existing roads, trails, and pathways whenever possible to avoid trampling or otherwise disturbing fragile habitat.
- Leave all habitat as we found it.

III. Birders must always respect the rights of others.

In keeping with this principle, we will

- Respect the privacy and property of others by observing "No Trespassing" signs and by asking permission to enter private or posted lands.
- Observe all laws and the rules and regulations which govern public use of birding areas.

- Practice common courtesy in our contacts with others. For example, we will limit our requests for information, and we will make them at reasonable hours of the day.
- Always behave in a manner that will enhance the image of the birding community in the eyes of the public.

IV.Birders in groups should assume special responsibilities.

As group members, we will

- Take special care to alleviate the problems and disturbances that are multiplied when more people are present.
- Act in consideration of the group's interest, as well as our own.
- Support by our actions the responsibility of the group leader(s) for the conduct of the group.

As group leaders, we will

- Assume responsibility for the conduct of the group.
- Learn and inform the group of any special rules, regulations, or conduct applicable to the area or habitat being visited.
- Limit groups to a size that does not threaten the environment or the peace and tranquility of others.
- Teach others birding ethics by our words and example.

GLOSSARY OF TERMS

Benthic—bottom-dwelling.

Coniferous—applied to trees: cone-bearing, mostly evergreens (referred to as conifers).

Continental Divide—the divide or high point that separates waters from flowing into either the Pacific Ocean or the Atlantic Ocean.

Crepuscular—active during the twilight hours.

Deciduous—shed periodically; applied to broad-leaved trees/shrubs that shed their leaves seasonally.

Diurnal—active during the day.

Fair-weather road—a road unsafe to travel during inclement weather: conditions deteriorate so rapidly vehicles often get stranded.

Gumbo—soil or road bed that turns into "molasses" type conditions when wet.

Lek—a dancing ground; courtship display area.

Migrant trap—a unique place where a diversity of birds congregate in unusually large numbers during migration.

Nocturnal—active at night.

Passerines—perching birds; the largest order of birds; comprises a large number of species (ranging in size from ravens to warblers and kinglets).

Raptor—a group of carnivorous birds also called birds of prey, which includes hawks, eagles, falcons, vultures, and owls; known for their rapacious means of acquiring prey.

Riparian—the habitat closely associated with water, such as vegetation bordering a stream or river.

SELECTED REFERENCES

American Ornithologists' Union. 1983. *The A.O.U. Checklist of N.A. Birds*. 6th Ed. A.O.U. Lawrence, Kansas.

Andrews, R. and R. Righter. 1992. *Colorado Birds*. Denver Museum of Natural History. Denver, Colorado.

Alt. D. and D. Hyndman. 1986. *Roadside Geology of Montana*. Mountain Press. Missoula, Montana.

Bailey, F. and V. 1918. *Wild Animals of Glacier National Park*. U.S. Government Printing Office. Wash., D.C.

Bent, A.C. 1915-1968. *Life Histories of North American Birds*. Dover Publications. New York. N.Y.

Bergeron, D. et.al. 1992. *P.D. Skaar's-Montana Bird Distribution*. Montana Heritage Program. Helena, Montana.

Block, D. 1990. *Finding Birds in Beaverhead County*. D. & G. Block. Dillon, Montana.

Bonham, D. and D. Cooper. 1986. *Birds of West-Central Montana*. Five Valleys Audubon Society. Missoula, Montana. R. Hutto, Editor.

Cannings, R., R. Cannings, and S. Cannings. 1987. *Birds of the Okanagan Valley, British Columbia*. Royal B.C. Museum. Victoria, B.C., Canada.

Davis, C.V. 1961. *A Distributional Study of the Birds of Montana*. Ph.D. dissertation. Oregon State Univ. Corvallis, Oregon.

Elrod, M. 1902. *A Biological Reconnaissance in the Vicinity of Flathead Lake*. U. of Montana. Missoula, Montana.

Fischer, C. & H. 1990. *Montana Wildlife Viewing Guide*. Falcon Press. Helena, Montana.

Godfrey, W.E. 1986. *The Birds of Canada*. Nat. Museum of Nat. Sci., Nat. Museums of Canada. Ottawa Canada.

Hand, R. 1953. *Bird Notes from Western Montana*. Condor: Vol. 55.

Helburn, N., M. Edie, and G. Lightfoot. 1962. *Montana in Maps*. Montana State University. Bozeman, Montana.

Last Chance Aud. Society. 1986. *Birding In The Helena Valley*. Last Chance Audubon Society. Helena, Montana.

Little, E. 1971. *Atlas of U.S. Trees*. USFS. Washington, D.C.

McEneaney, T. 1988. *Birds of Yellowstone*. Roberts Rinehart. Boulder, Colorado.

Olmsted, G. 1986. *Fielding's Lewis and Clark Trail*. W. Morrow & Co. Inc. New York, New York.

Peterson. R.T. 1990. *A Field Guide to Western Birds*. Houghton Mifflin Co. Boston, Mass.

Robbins, C.S.; B. Bruun; H.S. Zim. 1983. *A Field Guide to Bird Identification-Birds of North America*. Golden Press. New York, N.Y.

Saunders, A.A. 1921. *A Distributional List of the Birds of Montana*. Pacific Coast Avifauna, No. 14. Berkeley, California: Cooper Ornithological Society.

Scott, S.L. 1987. *Field Guide To The Birds of North America*. National Geographic Society. Wash., D.C.

Skaar, P.D. 1969. *Birds of the Bozeman Latilong*. Bozeman, Montana.

Skaar, P.D. et al. 1985. *Montana Bird Distribution*. Monograph No. 3. Montana Academy of Sciences. Vol. 44. MTDFW&P. Bozeman, MT..

Thompson, L. 1985. *Montana's Explorer's-The Pioneer Naturalists*. Geographic Series No. 9. Montana Magazine. Helena, Montana.

Tilly, F. 1991. *Hawk-watching's Little-Known Sites*. Birding. Aug. Issue. Am. Birding Association. Colo. Springs, Colorado.

Weydemeyer, W. Swan, D., and E. Rapraeger. 1940. *List of the Birds of W. Montana*. Condor: vol. 75, No. 4.

Weydemeyer, W. 1975. *Half-Century Record of the Breeding Birds of the Fortine Area, Montana: Nesting Data and Population Status*. Condor: Vol. 77, No. 3.

SITE & SPECIES INDEX

White Morph 139
White-breasted Nuthatch 25, 117, 152, 153, 159, 163, 175, 238
White-crowned Sparrow 24, 81, 82, 86, 104, 182, 203, 225, 241
White-faced Ibis 108, 111, 129, 219, 232
White-fronted Geese 39
White-tailed Ptarmigan 4, 23, 81, 234, 253
White-throated Sparrow 173, 241
White-throated Swift 54, 119, 164, 175, 176, 193, 195, 196, 206, 221, 237, 259
White-winged Crossbill 17, 24, 58, 64, 77, 84, 86, 88, 242, 275
White-winged Scoter 41, 69, 132, 139, 233
Whitefish Range 265, 268, 270, 275
Whitehall 264
Whooping Crane 140, 218, 219, 234
Wickham Gulch 159
Wigeons
  American 49, 62, 95, 106, 108, 111, 187, 218, 233
  Eurasian 39, 69, 106, 111, 233
Wild Canada Geese 69
Wild Turkey 69, 70, 147, 159, 175, 234, 254
Wildfowl Lane 39
Wildlife Exhibit 78
Wildlife Tour Route 133
Willet 96, 108, 111, 140, 147, 215, 219, 235
Williamson's Sapsucker 25, 60, 125, 195, 196, 203, 216, 237, 261
Willow Bog 219
Willow Flycatcher 44, 59, 60, 69, 71, 77, 88, 105, 119, 145, 171, 186, 218, 237, 262
Willow Park 196

Wilson's Phalarope 95, 108, 112, 147, 193, 215, 219, 221, 223, 235
Wilson's Warbler 47, 60, 77, 84, 86, 88, 182, 196, 215,218, 240
Winnett 254, 271, 273
Winter Wren 24, 35, 58, 60, 64, 81, 86, 239, 265
Wise River-Polaris Scenic Byway 226
Wolf Mountains 163
Wood Duck 36, 38, 39, 67, 69, 70, 71, 88, 123, 129, 152, 173, 184, 232
Woodpeckers
  Black-backed 4, 24, 237, 261
  Downy 36, 67, 113, 152, 159, 163, 167, 175, 201, 223, 237
  Hairy 67, 116, 125, 152, 159, 193, 195, 208, 226, 237
  Lewis' 1, 18, 24, 25, 35, 39, 47, 116, 159, 163, 225, 237, 260
  Pileated 24, 35, 36, 39, 44, 48, 58, 60, 67, 69, 78, 86, 226, 237, 261
  Red-headed 4, 24, 137, 152, 153, 237, 260
  Three-toed 4, 24, 25, 33, 86, 125, 195, 196, 203, 205, 225, 237, 261
Wood-Peewee, Western 84, 96, 101, 102, 116, 123, 133, 156, 162, 163, 167, 168, 177, 206, 218, 226, 237, 262
Wood Warbler 140
Woodland Park 69
Woodruff Park 152
Wrens
  Canyon 25, 119, 164, 168, 175, 176, 206, 238
  House 84, 86, 111, 113, 115, 123, 142, 145, 147, 163, 167, 173, 180, 208, 221, 239
  Marsh 39, 45, 66, 67, 69, 70, 71, 86, 108, 112, 129, 142, 147, 152, 219, 221, 239, 26

MAP INDEX

NOTES

NOTES

NOTES

NOTES